A Practical Guide to Managing Information Security

For a listing of recent titles in the *Artech House Technology Management and Professional Development Library*, turn to the back of this book.

A Practical Guide to Managing Information Security

Steve Purser

Artech House
Boston • London
www.artechhouse.com

Library of Congress Cataloging-in-Publication Data

Purser, Steve.
    A practical guide to managing information security/Steve Purser.
    p. cm.—(Artech House technology management library)
    ISBN 1-58053-702-2 (alk. paper)
    1. Computer security—Management. I. Title. II. Series.
    QA76.9.A25P88 2004
    658.4'78—dc22   2004041025

British Library Cataloguing in Publication Data

Purser, Steve
    A practical guide to managing information security. — (Artech House technology management library)
    1. Management information systems—Security measures 2. Computer security
    I. Title
    658.4'78

    ISBN 1-58053-702-2

Cover design by Igor Valdman

© 2004 ARTECH HOUSE, INC.
685 Canton Street
Norwood, MA 02062

Special permission to reproduce "CERT/CC Statistics 1988–2003," © 2003 by Carnegie Mellon University, is granted by the Software Engineering Institute.

®CERT and CERT Coordination Center are registered in the U.S. Patent and Trademark Office by Carnegie Mellon University.

International Standard Book Number: 1-58053-702-2
Library of Congress Catalog Card number: 2004041025

10 9 8 7 6 5 4 3 2 1

This book is dedicated to my wife, Katelijne, with sincere thanks for the continual help, support, and encouragement she has given me over the years.

Contents

Preface

Objectives

The principles underlying modern approaches to securing information and systems that process information are well documented and well understood by practitioners. Modern techniques and technologies for implementing these principles are also well documented, and it is hard to find an area of information security that has not been the subject of a book or at least an article. However, most of the existing literature seems to concentrate on particular areas of information security, and surprisingly few books cover the entire subject from a management perspective.

The main objective in writing this book was to help information-security managers bridge the gap between theory and practice in the area of information-security management. This book is therefore as much about management as it is about information security. Using a fictitious but realistic case study, the book describes a pragmatic approach to taking control and managing the entire information-security process within a large organization. With the exception of Chapters 2 and 3, which describe the tools available to information-security managers, the emphasis is on the decision-making process rather than on particular techniques or technologies. Every attempt has been made to illustrate the difficulties that are likely to be encountered when applying accepted theoretical ideas to operational environments and to show how these difficulties could be overcome. Important ideas are introduced at an early stage in the book and subsequently applied to a variety of different problems, such as developing the control framework, improving processes, and building the security architecture.

Intended readership

Although this book is primarily aimed at information-security managers, the content should prove interesting to most professionals working in the area of information security:

> ▸ Information-security managers will be able to adapt the methods used throughout the book to their own needs. They will also benefit from many of the examples, which are based on real-life experience.

- Security consultants will gain a better understanding of the way in which operational considerations affect the success or failure of security initiatives, which will enable them to align recommendations more closely with the needs of the organization.

- Internal auditors will be better placed to understand the difference between more theoretical treatments of information security and operational reality.

- Risk managers will benefit from the discussions on information-security risk and how it can be measured and subsequently managed. The way in which risk management techniques complement the control framework should be of particular interest.

- System administrators will be able to adjust their own security procedures and mechanisms to remove common weaknesses as exemplified by many of the examples used in the book.

- Business managers with a reasonable understanding of information technology (IT) will better understand opportunities for exercising more control over their functional areas. They will also learn when to challenge conventional wisdom in order to take advantage of business opportunities.

The book could also add value to academic courses on information security by illustrating the important relationship between management, process, and technology. In particular, students thinking of specializing in the area of information security will be able to use many of the ideas expressed in the text to examine other core course material from a different perspective.

Organization of the book

This book is organized into nine chapters and an appendix.

Chapter 1 provides an introduction to some of the key problems facing today's information-security managers. This chapter also introduces The Secure Bank, which will serve as a case study throughout the book. The remaining chapters show how the problems raised in this chapter can be overcome using tools and techniques commonly available in the marketplace.

Chapters 2 and 3 are dedicated to management techniques and technical tools, respectively. These chapters provide an overview of prevalent methods and tools and are pitched at quite a high level. Where tools are concerned, the discussion centers on classes of tools rather than particular solutions. In order to avoid an inappropriate level of detail, references to more detailed sources of information are provided when required.

Chapter 4 provides an overview of the approach to managing information security used throughout the rest of the book. This chapter concentrates on the more fundamental issues, such as how to obtain the buy-in of the management team and how to identify and involve stakeholders. This chapter sets the scene for the remaining chapters, each of which examines a particular aspect of the proactive approach in detail.

Chapter 5 explains how to develop a corporate strategy for securing information. This includes guidelines on how to prepare for the strategy and presents examples of the sort of issues that should be considered for inclusion.

Chapter 6 is concerned with security policy and standards. After presenting guidelines for the creation of a structured documentation set, the discussion concentrates on policy development and implementation. Security standards are introduced as a mechanism for translating policy requirements in specific operational environments. This culminates in the notion of the control framework and the ways that it relates to policy and risk analysis.

Chapter 7 illustrates ways to design and implement a stable information-security process. Key requirements for stable processes are presented. This is followed by a discussion on the reasons processes often fail in this area. Finally, a number of process improvement techniques are presented and illustrated.

Chapter 8 builds on the contents of Chapter 3 and presents a simple but effective method for designing and implementing the security architecture. Chapter 8 draws on many of the ideas of the preceding chapters and emphasizes the constant interplay between procedural and technical mechanisms.

Chapter 9 presents a number of techniques for increasing user awareness of security issues and encouraging active participation in the information-security process. This chapter shows how to prepare and execute a plan for educating staff at all levels of the organization and involving them in the information-security approach.

Finally, the appendix presents a very simple but highly effective approach to performing fast risk analyses.

Intended usage

This book is designed to be read from cover to cover, rather than as a reference text, although nothing precludes the use of the text as a source of reference. This is consistent with the goal of the book, which is to transmit a number of fundamental ideas and to support these ideas using examples. At the end of the day, it is the ideas that count and not the examples, although the latter can always be used as a source of inspiration.

Perhaps the most important message in the whole book is that the management approach is what makes the difference between good security and bad security. A successful approach to information security will be tailored to the requirements of the organization, will reflect cultural values, and will be sufficiently flexible to cope with change. This book provides guidelines for achieving this goal, but there is no recipe for success in this area. The extent to which individual managers succeed will depend on their abilities to take these ideas and adapt them to the local environment.

Acknowledgments

I would like to thank Tim Pitts of Artech House for providing me with the idea of writing this book in the first place and Tiina Ruonamaa for her support throughout the production of the manuscript. I would also like to thank the reviewer for his excellent comments and suggestions, which have considerably improved the structure of the book. Thanks also to Shaun O'Byrne for reviewing early versions.

Most of all, I would like to thank my wife, Katelijne, for her constant support and encouragement, without which this book would not have been possible. It is to her that I dedicate this book.

CHAPTER

1

Contents

The need for a proactive approach

1.1 Introduction

This book is about managing information security. It is *therefore* about managing risk in IT environments. The word "therefore" has been printed in italics, because although the association between information security and risk management may appear to be evident, experience shows that this is not necessarily so. Indeed, in the last few years, an enormous amount of attention has been given to technologies, methodologies, and techniques that, if sensibly deployed, can be used to reduce operational risk in IT environments. However, comparatively little attention has been given to the management aspects of this process. This is unfortunate as many nonspecialists now regard information security to be almost a black art, enshrouded in specialized jargon and requiring a lengthy initiation period. Ironically, the very techniques that we have developed to control risks in today's complex IT environments may now be preventing further progress by providing an inappropriate point of focus and clouding the discussion between business lines and IT professionals.

A clue to the rate at which risk is growing in IT environments is provided by a glance at the statistics provided by the Computer Emergency Response Team (CERT). The total number of security incidents recorded by the CERT rose from 2,412 in 1995 to 82,094 in 2002 (see Figure 1.1). This represents an increase of 3,403% [1].

A rapid comparison of data published in the 2002 Computer Security Institute (CSI)/Federal Bureau of Investigations Computer Crime and Security Survey with data from the corresponding 2001 survey also shows a trend towards increasing risk. A direct comparison shows that 90% of respondents detected security breaches in 2002 (85% in the 2001 report) and 80% of respondents acknowledged financial loss due to

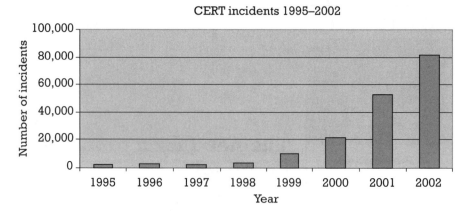

Figure 1.1 CERT incident statistics between 1995 and 2002. © 2003 by Carnegie Mellon University. Reproduced with permission of the Software Engineering Institute.

computer breaches (64% in the 2001 report). Where financial loss could be quantified, this led to a total loss of $455,848,000 in 2002 as compared to $377,828,700 in 2001 [2, 3]. For comparison, where malicious code attacks are concerned, Computer Economics, Inc., has estimated the economic impact due to malicious code attacks in 2001 to be $13.2 billion [4].

Interestingly, data published in the Symantec Internet Security Threat Report of February 2003 indicates a small drop (6%) in the overall cyber attack volume since the previous 6-month period, but shows that documented vulnerabilities in 2002 was 81.5% higher than in 2001. The report concludes that "the evidence clearly shows that the risk of cyber attacks and malicious code infections remains high for all Internet-connected organizations. In addition, the potential introduction of entirely new, and potentially more destructive, forms of malicious code and cyber attack tools represents a substantial future risk"[5].

Finally, the HoneyNet project [6, 7] and similar initiatives [8] have not only directly confirmed that the amount of hacking activity on the Internet is extremely high, but have also resulted in a better understanding of the methods used to attack systems. Of particular interest is the data published by the HoneyNet project on relative frequencies of different types of attack [7].

In interpreting statistical data, it is worth bearing in mind that many organizations do not report security incidents to the outside world for fear of negative publicity [9, 10]. According to the 2002 CSI/FBI Computer Crime and Security Survey, only 34% of enterprises that suffered serious attacks reported these incidents to law enforcement agencies in 2002, compared with 36% in 2001 and 25% in 2000 [3].

The aim of this book is to refocus attention on risk management and management tools in general as the primary means of controlling IT-related risk within the modern enterprise. This is in recognition of the fact that the notion of risk is specific to the organization and any approach to managing risk needs to take account of this. To some extent, the aim is also to point out where certain approaches can be misleading or lead to undesirable results. For instance, any approach to securing information that is based purely on following best practice will be difficult to reconcile with a conscious decision to accept more risk in this area. Indeed, it is pertinent to ask whether the term *best practice* without any qualification is meaningful given that different organizations have different attitudes to risk—what might be an optimal solution for one may not make any sense at all for another. Consider for example the issue of data confidentiality. Whereas a bank might invest considerable sums of money to keep the names of its customers confidential, this approach does not make a lot of sense for a company distributing marketing information and dealing largely with public information.

There are many situations in which the decision to accept more security-related risk may make a lot of sense, such as reducing the security functionality of a customer-facing application in order to reduce the time to market. This is an example in which the organization would weigh the business risk of losing out in a highly competitive market against the risk of suffering a security exposure and the associated consequences. It is therefore quite acceptable to take risks as long as this is done in the right way and involves the right people.

In other words, an optimal security framework does not necessarily mean the highest level of security that can be obtained for the money spent. *Optimal* means the most appropriate use of security given the business requirements, the legal and regulatory requirements, and the desired risk profile of the organization.

1.2   The reality of the modern enterprise

In most modern organizations things need to happen fast, often much faster than we are comfortable with. This is a reality that is here to stay, rather than a reflection of the current economic environment (which is not particularly optimistic at the time of writing). Things need to happen fast because we as consumers impose higher standards on producers and become rapidly impatient when our demands are not met. As a result, new markets can and do mature very rapidly, leading to intense competition. In such an environment, time to market is often a critical success factor, a fact that has led to a permanent change in the way we do business and has also had an impact on the way we perceive risk in general. This is just as true for service-oriented industries as it is for producers of consumable goods—one of the keys to success is the ability to deliver rapidly. In many ways the notion of the *Internet year* has become a reality.

It is clear that this notion of speed still needs to be incorporated into the methods we currently use to protect information, both in terms of our understanding of the problem and in terms of the effectiveness of the tools and techniques we use to solve it. With regard to the problem we are trying to solve, it is important to understand the value of information as a function of time. That is to say information that is valuable today is not necessarily so tomorrow, a fact that will certainly affect how we choose to protect it. Similarly, certain types of information will procure a competitive advantage for the foreseeable future and hence will need to be protected by techniques capable of withstanding the test of time. Note that this has to be understood in advance, as a change of philosophy might not be possible at a later date. Any information transmitted in encrypted form and captured by some form of sniffing technique 5 years ago might well be in danger if the lengths of the cryptographic keys were not chosen very conservatively. Whereas this is not important for a merger that has since happened, it may well be important for customer details or information relating to strategic weaknesses. Where techniques and tools are concerned, many products and methodologies are currently not being adopted due to the long gestation time before practical results are realized. Here in particular, there is a need to streamline current risk analysis techniques so as to make them compatible with timeframes of the order of the Internet year. This is not a trivial task.

In parallel, enterprises are being forced to cut their cost base in order to satisfy shareholders, although it might be argued that this is particularly true in times of economic recession. Inevitably, there comes a point at which reducing cost impacts either the quality of the deliverable or the rate at which it can be delivered. Consequently, some form of compromise is inherent in this operational model. More mature enterprises will develop operational models that allow them to make the necessary compromise according to a structured process, whereas less mature enterprises run the risk of suffering the impact in a more or less haphazard way. When economic conditions suddenly change, enterprises experience the impact both directly (in terms of the impact on their own operational model) and indirectly (in terms of the impact on the operational model to their suppliers and customers). In the domain of information security, the direct impact is often easy to understand. In difficult times, this will almost certainly result in decreased budgets, projects put on hold, and perhaps reduced headcount. The indirect impact of difficult economic conditions is more subtle, but in general it is not unreasonable to anticipate a reduced effort in most phases of the software life cycle and consequently an increase in bugs and vulnerabilities.

The net result of these trends is that information-security managers have to secure more complex environments, faster, using fewer resources. The solution to this problem is the subject of most of this book and involves remodeling the entire approach to information security to ensure that both short-term and long-term requirements are fully understood and that appropriate attention is given to each. This results in a process that is able to respond quickly to new business demands while still supporting a continual effort to create a stable framework for the future.

1.3 Evolution of organizational structures

Largely as a result of the economic factors discussed earlier, it is a fact that organizational structures change frequently in modern organizations. This presents several problems to the information-security practitioner, none of which are easy to resolve.

The first and most fundamental problem is related to knowledge and skill sets. Business managers play an important role in the information-security process, as they alone can put IT-related risk into a broader context and hence decide how to handle such risk. In addition, business managers are responsible for key activities in the security domain, such as acting as authorizers for new or modified access rights to applications and data—a routine, but critical, activity. It is clear that considerable knowledge and experience is necessary to carry out these responsibilities correctly.

Changes in organizational structure also often has a direct impact on the IT infrastructure in that these changes have to be modified in company databases so that automated processes and workflow solutions will continue to function as they should. This typically takes time, and a migration strategy is required to ensure that information is modified coherently. A very pertinent example of why this is important is related to changes in access rights. The reallocation of staff members to other duties within the organization usually involves a change of job function. As a general rule, access rights are seldom accumulated as a result of such a change. The standard approach to handling job rotations is to remove all nonstandard access and to grant a new set of access rights once these have been approved by the new business manager(s). In reality, changes have to happen fast and new managers may be slow to approve the new set of access rights. This can lead to a situation in which resources can no longer work with escalating problems. On a smaller scale, individual job rotations may be complicated by "friendly agreements" between the manager of the old department and the manager of the new department, resulting in a modification of the transfer date or an overlap of functions.

Finally, when staff members move to occupy new positions, they may be required to learn new procedures and systems quickly. Depending on the procedures and systems concerned, this may introduce considerable risk. A simple click of a button by an inexperienced employee could result in an e-mail containing confidential information being sent to a mailing list on the Internet.

A coherent response to these issues involves a combination of technical and procedural measures, accompanied by a strong user-awareness program.

1.4   Evolution of technical infrastructure

In order to cut costs successfully, while still maintaining revenue, we need to operate more efficiently. One of the tools at our disposal for achieving this is an increase in automation, and this has been one of the central themes underlying corporate growth in the last 20 years. The drive towards increased efficiency has been facilitated by a drastic increase in computing power, together with an almost universal deployment of easy-to-use graphical user interfaces (GUIs). This has transformed the workplace by permitting the automation of many mundane tasks.

More recently, the focus of this effort has been enlarged to include more complex activities such as management and engineering processes. As a result, a range of specialized software has been developed to provide support for these activities. Examples of this development include packages geared toward supporting essential management activities such as planning and financial control as well as computer-aided design (CAD) software. The IT industry itself has been one of the biggest beneficiaries of these developments and makes heavy use of software tools to support the planning and design of new applications.

Currently, there is a drive towards so-called *zero administration* software as exemplified by *plug and play* technologies. In some areas, current technology can offer solutions, which come close to this goal. However, it will never be possible to totally automate administration tasks relating to security because solutions that are fully automated cannot possibly detect and react to a change in context in the same way that the human brain does. In general, the less the system is administered, the less of a chance there is of spotting and reacting to unusual conditions. One of the hallmarks of a good system administrator is the ability to recognize what is normal behavior and what signs are indicative of problems. Staff dedicated to security administration tasks, such as firewall administration, tend to expend a lot of time and effort to develop this ability. In summary, the biggest threat to any system is the ingenuity of the human mind, and in order to respond adequately to this threat, human intervention is a critical part of any security response.

The net result of all of this is that modern businesses are highly dependent upon IT. This has resulted in a level of demand that necessitated several fundamental changes in the IT industry itself, each associated with a new and different paradigm for adding value to business processes. The way technology has evolved during this period is characterized by a series of technology cycles. A typical cycle involves the introduction of new concepts, an evaluation period, a period of large-scale deployment, and a maintenance period during which the technology coexists with other technologies.

Experience has shown that the evolution of security infrastructure capable of securing new technologies follows a similar cycle, but that there is a considerable delay between the introduction of new technology and the availability of this infrastructure. This is largely because added functionality is still a more powerful selling argument than strong security, and organizations will purchase software that they believe will procure a competitive advantage even when the associated security model is immature. As a result, technologies tend to become secure towards the end of the technology life cycle, just as new (insecure) technology is being introduced.

In the short term, this cyclic evolution model therefore results in a period of higher risk where new technology is introduced, but tools for securing it are very limited. More often than not, achieving an acceptable level of security during this period involves the creative use of compensating controls and an increased emphasis on procedural mechanisms. In the long term, the gradual adoption of software based on different technical models results in a significant increase in complexity and a consequent reliance on highly specific skill sets. This increased complexity has a number of serious consequences both in terms of technical issues and in terms of awareness and understanding.

At the technical level, complexity is a major concern when designing security architectures for heterogeneous environments. In particular, it becomes very difficult to ensure a coherent security framework across multiple platforms due to the difficulties associated with identifying and correcting weak points in such architectures. As an awareness issue, complexity is a barrier to understanding and can seriously impact the ability of organizations to take correct decisions when faced with new threats.

1.5 Limitations of policy-driven decision making

The rapid evolution of technology has not been without impact in the information-security domain, and there has been an immense amount of progress in the last few years in the area of tools and technologies designed to support information-security processes:

▸ Whereas the field of cryptography was still a highly specialized area in the commercial marketplace as little as 10 years ago, most staff currently working in the IT domain have some exposure to cryptography. Many have been directly involved with cryptographic techniques in one way or another.

▸ During the same period, network security technology has developed from simple, home-built firewalls to sophisticated gateways constructed from commercially available software. Such gateways typically combine different types of firewall systems with intrusion detection and monitoring systems and can be managed from a single workstation over a secure connection.

▸ A variety of host-based security tools are currently available, such as vulnerability scanners, host-based intrusion detection systems, file and disk encryption systems, and content scanners.

▸ Security software capable of providing services in a cross-platform environment is starting to be commercially available.

Unfortunately, many of the processes that these tools are designed to support have not evolved sufficiently to take full advantage of this new technology and currently present an obstacle to further improvement. For many, if not most, organizations, the process side of information security continues to be essentially axiomatic. Decisions are made mainly on the basis of policy requirements, and exposure to risk is often evaluated by making reference to static control frameworks. This approach works quite well for strategic decisions but does not offer much assistance where day-to-day decisions need to be made. In particular, in order to get maximum benefit from modern tools, it is important to understand and react to threat scenarios that may change rapidly and that are often difficult to relate back to fundamental concepts. To some extent, therefore, the technical tools at our disposal are revealing the changes that need to be made in order to provide a realistic control framework for commercial organizations.

Approaches such as British Standard (BS) 7799 [International Standards Organization (ISO)/International Electrotechnical Commission (IEC) 17799] have recognized the limitations of a purely policy-driven approach to information security and have responded by broadening the approach to include formalized risk-assessment techniques. In the case of BS 7799 itself, the inventory of important controls is interpreted using a risk-management framework—this is achieved by separating the standard into two distinct parts:

1. ISO/IEC 17799:2000 (Part 1) is also known as the *Code of Practice* and is essentially a catalogue of security controls.

2. BS 7799-2:2002 (Part 2) provides requirements for implementing an information-security management system (ISMS).

Of these, the second part of the standard is concerned with using risk-assessment techniques to select appropriate controls. This is an important development, as it makes the standard very flexible in terms of how it is to be implemented. However, critics have argued that this flexibility is also a weak point, as it limits the level of detail and makes the standard vague in certain areas [11]. A more serious drawback is the degree of effort required to implement the standard. This leads to increased cost and, more importantly, renders the approach more cumbersome. It remains to be seen whether this and similar standards will provide the ability to cope with rapidly changing business scenarios.

In a more general context, the financial sector has recognized the inadequacy of current approaches to controlling operational risk, and, in an attempt to respond to this problem, the Basel Committee on Banking Supervision issued the New Capital Accord (commonly known as Basel II) in 2001. The Basel Committee is recommending that financial institutions implement the conclusions of Basel II by 2006. This is an important development in the area of risk management, as it requires financial institutions to include operational risk in the calculation of capital adequacy requirements. This is both a good thing and a bad thing. It is a good thing because the Basel Committee has recognized the importance of operational risk as a contributor to the total risk profile of financial organizations (before Basel II, the emphasis was on controlling financial risk). It is a bad thing because it is essentially asking for quantitative risk management, and at the current time we have neither methodologies nor tools capable of yielding sensible results in the information-security domain.

In order to provide an optimal response to information-security risks, the security process must put less emphasis on the control framework itself and more emphasis on how this framework can sensibly be used to respond to business requirements. This involves taking this progression a step further and using risk analysis as the primary tool for decision making. This does not mean that security policy and control frameworks are not important; rather, they need to be challenged more often in the light of current contextual information.

1.6 Education and awareness

The increased complexity that has accompanied the rapid technological evolution of the past 2 decades has resulted in a high degree of specialization among technical staff and has rendered several aspects of IT relatively inaccessible to the nonspecialist. This is certainly true of information security, where it is not uncommon for both IT staff and business staff to confuse quite fundamental concepts (e.g., authentication and authorization).

To a certain extent, a lack of awareness of details is manageable in that it can be dealt with when the need arises. More problematic is a lack of awareness of the underlying risks and how to deal with them, and this type of problem can occur in a variety of contexts, as illustrated by the following examples:

▸ Executive management may not understand the extent to which the organization as a whole is exposed to risk.

▸ Information-security managers may be more focused on technology issues than on the risks these technologies are trying to reduce.

▸ End users may not have sufficient understanding of the risks associated with their day-to-day responsibilities to enable them to react correctly when faced with a problem.

Due to the trends discussed in the first part of this chapter, most organizations have witnessed a significant change in their risk profile during the last two decades. An indicator that companies are accepting and responding to the increased importance of operational risk management in general is the tendency towards the creation of a global risk management function within the enterprise, which effectively covers all aspects of IT risk, including those risks specifically related to IT security. This tendency has been noted by the Gartner group and has been adopted as a strategic-planning assumption for the period leading up to 2005 [12].

1.6.1 Management awareness

Although this move towards more effective operational risk management is certainly taking place, the trend is still in its infancy, and, where information security is concerned, both statistical data and methods for analyzing such data are relatively immature [10]. In the absence of reliable data and suitable tools, executive management may have a poor appreciation of the amount of risk that they are currently accepting. This may lead to inappropriate decisions and further exposure, where this is the case. Furthermore, organizations that rely heavily on a policy-driven approach to information security may actually be achieving a high level of compliance with policy while still accepting considerable risk. The extent to which organizations are susceptible to this sort of problem depends on how successfully they are able to translate high-level policy requirements into an approach capable of dealing with risk arising out of low-level issues. This can result in interesting paradoxes, such as organizations trying to enforce a risk-averse culture in a competitive environment where it is essential from a business perspective to take more risk in order to survive.

1.6.2   The technology trap

Closely related to problems of awareness are issues relating to how technology is perceived and how it is used to satisfy business requirements. In continually striving for more powerful and more efficient tools, there has been a tendency in the past to put too much emphasis on the technology aspects of securing information. One unfortunate side effect of this technology-focused approach is that it gives the illusion that this situation of constantly increasing risk is perfectly manageable and depends largely on how new tools are selected and deployed. In reality, in the future real security will probably depend more on our ability to reexamine old ideas and to change existing processes to enable them to cope with a greater spectrum of risk in a shorter time frame. This will almost certainly involve organizations accepting more risk in return for better business opportunities and will require a framework for decision making that permits sensible compromise.

The fact that the information-security domain is still dominated by technology issues is easily demonstrated by a cursory examination of the current literature and conference proceedings. Where security is concerned, any decision to adopt technologies purely on the basis of best practice should be avoided wherever possible. We have already made the point that best practice can be a rather nebulous concept at the best of times and what constitutes best practice for one organization may make little sense for another. Only by understanding the risks that the organization must face, the relative importance of those risks, and how any particular technology helps to reduce those risks, can we hope to exercise real control.

1.6.3   Awareness of end users

Finally, it is clear that end users must have a reasonable understanding of the threats to which their environment is exposed and how the security mechanisms and procedures at their disposition mitigate these risks. Developing this level of understanding presents a considerable challenge to staff who may have little exposure to technology apart from a basic understanding of the workstation. This is particularly true as new threats become increasingly buried in a mire of technical details and real security can often depend on an intricate balance of technical and procedural protection mechanisms.

The technique of social engineering seeks to take advantage of these difficulties by exploiting weaknesses associated with the end user. Techniques used vary considerably, but often involve the impersonation of someone having authority in order to gain access to restricted information. A typical scenario might involve calling elderly people and claiming to be from the credit card company. Certain elderly people, less aware of the technology involved and perhaps more trusting in nature, may be tempted to reveal their personal identification number (PIN) code if a plausible pretext were given by the caller. In a more familiar context, less experienced users might provide their password to an inside caller claiming to be a system administrator, especially if the caller could simulate a problem on their workstation.

Similarly, many attacks originating on the Internet rely on end users being unaware of the dangers associated with the technology they are using. When faced with the choice of launching a program within the browser to receive an additional service or a more pleasing format, most users will not take the time to reflect on the consequences of their decision on the security of their environment.

1.7 Operational issues

The recognition and resolution of operational issues is what makes the difference between a sound theoretical approach and an approach that is both based on sound principles and capable of succeeding in the real world. Where operational issues are concerned, the main challenges in today's environments are concerned with mastering the problems of *complexity* and *scalability.*

1.7.1 Complexity

Complexity is a major issue because it is necessary to understand a system in order to secure it. In fact, achieving real security usually requires in-depth knowledge, as an attacker will always seek to exploit the weakest aspect of any system, and serious vulnerabilities may hide in obscure functionality or configuration options.

One illustration of the complexity inherent in modern IT environments is provided by the problems organizations tend to experience when attempting to treat information as an asset. Most people recognize the importance of information in the workplace, but few are able to put a value on the information that they use on a day-to-day basis. Admittedly, this is not an easy thing to do and most people would not think of doing it anyway, but as we are in the business of protecting information it is probably best to have some idea of how much it is worth to us. One of the reasons that it is difficult to put a value on information is linked to the fact that people are not used to thinking of it as an asset in real terms. Nevertheless, it is clear that information is an asset and certain information can make the difference between a successful enterprise and an unsuccessful one.

Another more fundamental reason underlying these difficulties is the limited level of control that organizations really exercise over their data. Indeed, one of the principles underlying certain types of distributed architecture is that of location independence, which aims to render the location of data invisible (and irrelevant) to users [13]. Highly distributed architectures, based on principles such as these, can make it very difficult to retain a view of what data is being held by the organization and where it is stored. As a result, the documented description of the data repository and associated data classification (if it exists) may bear little resemblance to reality, and trying to estimate the associated value becomes a highly complex activity. For many enterprises, such an effort would take an unimaginably long time and the significance of the data itself would probably change as the study was proceeding. It is therefore often necessary to take a more pragmatic approach to this problem by looking at relative rather than absolute values together with the consequences of loss or alteration and considering the value of certain information as a function of time.

This complexity of modern IT infrastructures also represents a serious obstacle to achieving a coherent security framework across the organization. Indeed, achieving coherence across the enterprise is complicated by a number of issues:

  ▸ It is difficult to compare security services across platforms due to differences in concepts and terminology. The same comment applies to security data.

  ▸ The lack of cross-platform tools limits the extent to which organizations can obtain a global view of security-related data.

  ▸ Interfaces between different technologies are often difficult to analyze and may harbor unknown vulnerabilities.

In today's environments, it is important to look at solutions from an architectural viewpoint in addition to analyzing the particular system concerned. By taking an end-to-end view, it may be possible to offset vulnerabilities on a specific system by using compensating controls elsewhere in the architecture. Assessing issues from an architectural viewpoint will automatically require an analysis of scalability and integration, and it is precisely these aspects that are not usually considered when analyzing single systems.

The problem associated with interfaces is particularly important, as we can expect to experience problems where two different security subsystems, based on different design principles, are expected to work together smoothly. In this particular case, an already complex problem is often rendered more complex by communications issues. More often than not, such analyses involve experts from different backgrounds, using platform-specific concepts and nomenclature. It is easy to understand how errors creep into the process under such conditions.

1.7.2 Scalability

Scalability issues have grown hand in hand with complexity and have therefore also become increasingly important over the last few years. This change has been accentuated by the move towards distributed architectures and the rapid growth of interconnectivity in the last decade. In the days when the mainframe dominated the corporate IT environment, securing information was largely synonymous with securing the mainframe—a relatively simple model by today's standards, where system administrators may be responsible for securing hundreds of machines. The challenge to today's organizations is to define mechanisms and procedures for enforcing security that are capable of coping with this situation.

Common sense tells us that it is unlikely that procedures developed for the mainframe environment will be appropriate for modern, distributed architectures. This can easily be appreciated by considering the analysis of audit trail data. In a security context, audit trail data is reviewed in order to ascertain whether any unusual activity is going on or indeed whether a security breach has occurred. In the days of the mainframe, the log files were centralized on a single machine and could probably be counted on one hand. In today's environment, security administrators may be faced with the daunting task of analyzing data contained in hundreds of log files scattered throughout the enterprise. In particular, analyzing incidents is likely to involve examining log records on a cross-platform basis. Not only is the sheer volume of data a major problem under such circumstances, but there are technical constraints to be dealt with, such as ordering event information in an environment where there is no concept of network time (i.e., clocks are not synchronized). The key to solving this particular issue is to prioritize log information and use suitably designed filtering techniques to reduce the important information to a reasonable level.

Similar comments apply to documentation. Auditors in particular tend to place a lot of emphasis on good documentation, which is understandable as they are often trying to assess the underlying control process and therefore require an unambiguous source of reference. However, as auditors often perform their work on a system-by-system basis, recommendations to improve documentation can result in a documentation set that is unwieldy and impossible to maintain. Ironically, unwieldy documentation sets are also a symptom of many structured development methodologies, particularly when many projects are running in parallel. The problem here is the sheer volume of documentation that is produced compared to the limited number of resources capable of commenting on it and eventually approving it. This is an unrealistic scenario and tends to lead to documentation that is either not read at all or is read at a pace that does not allow sufficient time for digestion of the content and sensible comment.

A third and final example of the importance of operational issues is taken from the area of logical access control. The term access control refers to the process and mechanisms by which access to IT systems, functionality, and data is managed. Access control therefore includes the request for creation, modification, and suppression of accounts and associated access rights, the approval of such requests, their implementation, and verification. Although it is one of the simplest activities to understand at the surface level, access control is fraught with issues arising out of the complexity of modern systems and the scale to which they are often deployed. Technical issues are mainly related to the lack of compatibility, both in terms of concepts and notation, between different operating systems, middleware, database software, and applications. Procedural issues include the lack of scalability of administration procedures due to the requirement to define and maintain highly granular access rights and cumbersome workflow processes, which introduce unacceptable delays to the end user. Finally, organizational issues reflect some of the points discussed earlier in this chapter, notably the fact that approving and monitoring access requires a certain body of knowledge (and appreciation of risk), which is increasingly difficult to come by in environments that involve frequent changes of staff and management structures.

1.8   New challenges

Living in an age where the sharing of information among geographically distributed organizational units is a necessary part of doing day-to-day business has changed the way in which we perceive different facets of information security. In other words, the relative importance of different aspects of the control framework we adopt is constantly changing. Trust and privacy are two examples of issues that have grown dramatically in importance as a result of the increased deployment of networked applications.

1.8.1   Trust

The importance of understanding and managing the concept of trust has grown enormously since the days when IT infrastructures were based on the original mainframe model and internetworking was in its infancy. At this time, end users were given access to resources according to a very simple model, which involved authentication to "the system" using an identifier and a password. Once the user had been authenticated, the system would enforce logical access control by maintaining and enforcing a simple set of rules defining which users could access which resources. While the way in which we control access has not changed significantly in the intervening period, the way in which we authenticate users has undergone a radical transformation and is currently one of the most technically complex areas of information security. The drivers for this change are as follows:

▸ Today's information systems make extensive use of computer networks, and simple authentication schemes are not reliable in such an environment.

▸ More and more, we are required to exchange information with people we do not know, have never met, and may never meet.

In order to do electronic business in today's world, we require authentication models that can solve these problems while making no assumptions about the security offered by the underlying network. In other words, we require authentication models that work over networks assumed to be hostile. In this new environment, the very people we wish to do business with may be situated at vast distances, making any kind of face-to-face contact impossible. As a result, what started as a simple problem of authentication has now become a complex problem of trust. How can we be sure that the people using our systems are the people we think they are, and indeed how clear is our image of who we think they are?

At present, we have only partial answers to these questions. By deploying specially designed authentication protocols, based on a cryptographic approach, we can effectively solve the problem of authentication. However, the way in which we associate *security credentials* (the things end users possess in order to authenticate themselves) with end users involves creating and implementing trust models, and this area is still a subject of much discussion [14, 15].

Despite its tormented beginnings [16, 17], public key infrastructure (PKI) is still one of the most promising approaches in this area and has become the de facto standard for implementing trust on the Internet. In the PKI world, the user credentials take the form of a certificate, which can be thought of as an electronic passport. PKI implements a trust hierarchy in which certain trusted third parties, known as certification authorities, vouch for the certificates of users who subscribe to their services by signing them electronically.

The idea of a hierarchical model of trust is quite appealing until we try to identify the entity at the apex of the hierarchy. By definition, this certificate authority will be the basis of all trust relationships, and so everyone must trust it. Unfortunately, it is quite obvious that no such entity exists, and in real life there will always exist a multitude of trust hierarchies. This has nothing to do with PKI, but it is an inherent characteristic of how we extend trust to others. A partial response to this problem is to encourage interoperability between providers of trust services. This should increase the number of trust-enabled services by allowing existing end users to profit from an extended trust model. Note, however, that this assumes that the end users will be sufficiently aware of the underlying issues to judge whether the basis for trust is appropriate or not.

Just as it is difficult to decide to what extent to trust a little-known third party, *relying parties* (users that rely on certificates to perform some task) may experience problems in deciding the level of trust that can be associated with any given certificate. A certificate, like a passport, will enable us to associate an identity (and often a few associated details) with the bearer, but it will not tell us whether the bearer is an honest and trustworthy person. Neither a passport nor a certificate indicate how much trust we should extend to the bearer and what they are likely to do with any trust that we extend to them. This problem was illustrated by the Exploder ActiveX control, published by Fred McLain in 1996 in an attempt to demonstrate the potential security problems associated with ActiveX technology [18]. This control performed a shutdown of Windows 95 computers but could have conceivably performed far more malicious actions. The important point is that Fred McLain signed this control with his VeriSign personal software publisher's certificate before posting to the Web site. Although McLain's software publisher's certificate was subsequently revoked, the point had been made.

Finally, we mention in passing that PKI is costly, difficult to implement, and even more difficult to maintain, and this is proving a barrier to more widespread deployment. This poses problems for the future because if companies think that that this type of technology does not bring a net benefit, all things considered, then they will not implement it.

1.8.2 Privacy

The issue of privacy has become more problematic in recent years due to the ease with which electronic information can be stored and distributed. This ease of manipulation, together with the realization that a knowledge of consumer habits can boost profits, has resulted in a proliferation of marketing databases containing information about individuals. Unfortunately, controlling how this information is used and with whom it is exchanged is extremely difficult, which has led to a number of concerns regarding the capture and protection of such data. In the Web arena, these concerns have materialized in the form of an intense debate over what constitutes a good privacy policy and how it should be enforced in practice. This turns out to be particularly complex when companies are taken over or file for bankruptcy, as the information concerned may be considered as an asset (which could therefore be acquired by a third party).

This is not only true in a global context, but also in a more local context. Technology of increasing sophistication now allows extensive and relatively transparent monitoring of electronic communications within the organization. Possibilities include the interception of e-mails, the monitoring Internet access on an individual basis, and the recording of telephone calls. It seems that there is even a demand for software to monitor activity on a home computer and a corresponding market for tools that detect the presence of such software[1].

It is quite clear that monitoring of this nature needs to be controlled, although opinions differ widely on how and to what extent this should be done. There are, however, already concrete proposals for dealing with privacy in the workplace. These include the International Labor Organization's

---

1. Examples of monitoring tools that can be installed at home include Spector, eBlaster, SpyAOL, and Realtime-Spy. Examples of tools that detect installed monitors include Nitrous Anti-Spy, Spy Cop Home Edition, and Anti-Keylogger Pro.

"Conditions of Work Digest" [19] and, more recently, the "Top Ten Guide-lines to Workplace Privacy" released by the Privacy Council and Littler Mendelson in October, 2001, in the United States [20].

While it is true that attitudes towards privacy differ considerably between different countries, it is also clear that the privacy issue itself is becoming increasingly important. This fact is born out by the considerable activity in this field in the months preceding the attack of September 11, 2001, on the World Trade Center in New York. This debate became headline news in Europe as a result of the controversy surrounding the ECHELON interception system (in fact, the final report on the ECHELON system was published by the European Parliament only days before the World Trade Center incident [21]). The ECHELON system was designed to intercept private and business communications and to operate worldwide. Section 8 of the final report of the European Parliament Temporary Committee is dedicated to privacy issues and notes that: "Any act involving the interception of communications, and even the recording of data by intelligence services for that purpose, represents a serious violation of an individual's privacy." With respect to the issue of industrial espionage, the report notes that "The US intelligence services do not merely gather general economic intelligence, but also intercept communications between firms, particularly where contracts are being awarded, and they justify this on the grounds of combating attempted bribery." As a result of these and other related concerns, the report concludes that both organizations and individuals should consider using strong cryptography to protect transmissions.

Since the attack on the World Trade Center, the privacy debate has become considerably more complex, as we now need to achieve a suitable balance between consumer privacy and the right of governments to access data to aid the fight against terrorism.

1.9 Introducing The (not so) Secure Bank

To illustrate the points made in the different chapters of this book, we will follow the progress of The Secure Bank from its rather disorganized beginnings (at least as far as information security is concerned) to a situation of considerable maturity. In the case of The Secure Bank, this process will take somewhere between 2 and 3 years.

The Secure Bank offers commercial and private banking services to a range of customers. The bank has been in existence for well over a century and has grown fast. At the time we start our exercise, it employs 2,000 people in its headquarters and 600 people in its branch offices located throughout the world.

Like most other medium-sized financial institutions, The Secure Bank has already implemented a number of external network connections to facilitate its daily business. These connections can be organized into four major groups:

1. The connection to the Internet;

2. Leased-line connections to branch offices;

3. Various transmission control protocol/Internet protocol (TCP/IP) connections to third parties over a commercial network;

4. Dial-up access for technical support staff over the public switched telephone network (PSTN).

This situation is illustrated in Figure 1.2.

The Secure Bank has been around for quite some time and has therefore witnessed several different generations of technology. The bank has always prided itself on its innovative approach to satisfying client demands, and it is looking into the possibility of offering banking services to its customers over the Internet. However, a series of recent audits have revealed a number of serious deficiencies relating to information security, and the executive management team has decided to respond by bringing in a new manager to solve the outstanding issues while allowing the bank to launch its new service within the next year.

The Secure Bank has to contend with a number of issues if it is to realize its objectives. The most important problems are as follows:

▸ In the last few years, executive management has been extremely passive in the area of information security due to an apparent lack of incidents and a tolerant audit department. The latest wave of audits has, however, upset the audit committee, and management has been formally requested to show considerable progress within the next year.

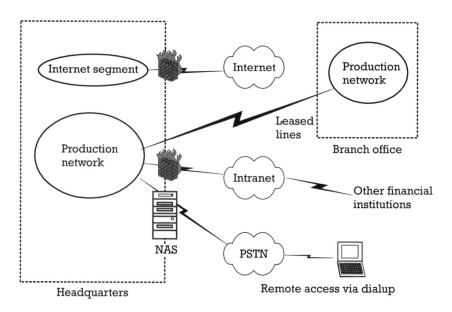

Figure 1.2 The Secure Bank—IT infrastructure.

- The bank currently carries out little risk analysis in the area of information security. Where security decisions are made, this is done on the basis of policy requirements.

- The security policy was written several years ago and is largely theoretical. As a result, few staff members have read it. No attempt has been made to interpret policy requirements by producing lower level documents, such as security standards.

- Responsibilities are poorly defined, and where descriptions of such responsibilities do exist, they do not match what happens in reality.

- The dialogue between the security department and the end users is poor. The main point of contact is a yearly presentation to the different departments. The presentation has not been updated for some time and does not provide a realistic vision of current threats and how to deal with them.

- Administration procedures are based on those originally defined for mainframe administration. These procedures do not scale well, and many of them are simply ignored. Until now, there has been little automation of these procedures.

- The bank has introduced new technology at several times in the past, but the security department has not been able to respond rapidly enough to requirements for securing the resulting applications. As a result, the internal infrastructure is extremely complex, and there is little standardization at the product level. In addition, many applications are insufficiently secured.

- The low priority of information security has resulted in low budgets and, as a result, the introduction of new tools has been very limited. Where tools have been acquired, this has been to satisfy specific requirements. This has led to a collection of point solutions, and economies of scale have not been realized.

As we progress through the book, we will use the example of The Secure Bank to show how the ideas under discussion can be applied in practice.

1.10 Summary

This chapter has briefly presented the important trends that have led to an increase in risk in IT environments and has shown how these trends have resulted in serious issues, which any coherent approach to information security must resolve.

Available statistics show that risk is increasing in IT environments at a time when increased competition is forcing organizations to produce faster and at lower cost. In an attempt to increase efficiency and productivity, enterprises tend to reorganize more frequently and are continually developing their IT infrastructure. As a result, most organizations have undergone significant changes in the last few years and are now highly reliant on their IT infrastructures and the skill sets needed to support them.

More than ever before, modern organizations need to make decisions fast, taking account of a complex mixture of risks and opportunities. Approaches to securing information using risk-management tools as the primary aid to decision making will be better placed to handle this complexity than those using a policy-driven approach. However, any approach based on risk management will only be effective if the different actors within the organization are able to develop an awareness of the risks to which the organization as a whole is exposed and how this affects them in their day-to-day duties.

Finally, measures undertaken to reduce risk must take into account issues relating to complexity and scalability if they are to stand the test of time.

References

[1] "CERT/CC Statistics 1988-2003," August 2003, http://www.cert.org/stats/cert_stats.html.

[2] "2001 CSI/FBI Computer Crime and Security Survey," *Computer Security Issues and Trends*, Vol. 7, No. 1, 2001, pp. 1–18.

[3] "2002 CSI/FBI Computer Crime and Security Survey," *Computer Security Issues and Trends*, Vol. 8, No. 1, 2001, pp. 1–22.

[4] "2001 Impact of Malicious Code Attacks," August 2003, http://www.cybersecure.ca/q2.asp.

[5] "Symantec Internet Security Threat Report: Attack Trends for Q3 and Q4 2002," August 2003, http://enterprisesecurity.symantec.com/content.cfm?articleid=1539&EID=0.

[6] The Honeynet Project, *Know Your Enemy: Revealing the Security Tools, Tactics and Motivations of the Black-hat Community*, Reading, MA: Addison Wesley, 2001.

[7] The Honeynet Project, "Know Your Enemy: Statistics," August 2003, http://project.honeynet.org/papers/stats.

[8] Hayday, G., "Exposed Server—Magnet for Hack Attacks," August 2003, http://zdnet.com.com/2100-1105-982554.html.

[9] "2002 CSI/FBI Computer Crime and Security Survey," *Computer Security Issues and Trends*, Vol. 8, No. 1, 2001, pp. 20–21.

[10] Mannion, C., and A. Dang Van Mien, "The Myth of Quantitative Risk Analysis," *Strategy, Trends and Tactics*, Stamford, CT: Gartner Group, 2002.

[11] Walsh, L. M., "Standard Practice: ISO 17799 Aims to Provide Best Practices for Security, but Leaves Many Yearning for More," August 2003, http://infosecuritymag.techtarget.com/2002/mar/iso17799.shtml.

[12] Witty, R. J., "Elements of a Successful IT Risk Management Program," *Strategy, Trends and Tactics*, Stamford, CT: Gartner Group, 2002.

[13] Haahr, M., "Architecture for Location Independent CORBA Environments (ALICE)," August 2003, http://www.dsg.cs.tcd.ie/Research/alice.

[14] Young, A., N. K.Cicovic, and D. Chadwick, "Trust Models in ICE-TEL," August 2003, http://www.darmstadt.gmd.de/ice-tel/reports/trustmodel.html.

[15] Goodenough, D., "A Heretic's View on Certificates," August 2003, http://www. dga.co.uk/customer/publicdo.nsf/public/WP-HERESY.

[16] Ellison, C., and B. Schneier, "Ten Risks of PKI: What You're Not Being Told About Public Key Infrastructure," *Computer Security Journal,* Vol. 16, No. 1, 2000, pp. 1–7.

[17] Campbell, A., "PKI is Dead! Long Live PKI!" August 2003, http://www. itsecurity.com/papers/reflex2.htm.

[18] Garfinkel, S., and G. Spafford, *Web Security, Privacy and Commerce,* O'Reilly and Associates, 1997, pp. 76–77.

[19] International Labour Organization, "Conditions of Work Digest, Volumes I, II and III," 1996.

[20] Sigvartsen, A. L., "Guidelines to Workplace Privacy," August 2003, http://www. infosatellite.com/news/2001/10/a311001workplace_security.html.

[21] Schmid, Gerhard, "Final Report on the Existence of a Global System for the Interception of Private and Commercial Communications (ECHELON Interception System)(2001/2098(INI))," August 2003, http://www.fas.org/ irp/program/process/rapport_echelon_en.pdf.

CHAPTER

2

Contents

Management techniques

2.1 Knowledge and experience

Arguably, the most important resource at the disposition of any information-security manager is the team that he or she leads. This team will be equipped with skill sets and knowledge relevant to the local site and varying levels of experience of other approaches gained from previous employers. It is good practice to track these skill sets within the team and to ensure that training initiatives develop the appropriate skills, achieving a correct balance between the requirements of the organization and the requirements of the individual. This is one of the areas in which it is absolutely necessary to manage proactively, as it is extremely difficult to define and execute an ambitious strategy if the staff turnover rate is high. Conversely, a unified team in which each member understands and is capable of fulfilling his or her role provides a strong foundation on which to build a long-term approach.

It turns out to be very useful to distinguish between skills that can be found in the external market place and skills that can only be acquired within the organization. The former covers skills and knowledge related to common practices, methodologies, and tools, whereas the latter represents practices and tools developed specifically for the organization and, in particular, the way in which information security is managed locally. One extreme example of the importance of local knowledge is related to in-house applications, where vulnerabilities and how to deal with them may not be documented and may only be understood by a small group of experienced staff. In practice, keeping legacy applications secure in a rapidly evolving IT architecture is one of the more difficult aspects of securing IT infrastructures, and security architectures tend to be of limited value here due to the limited possibilities for integration with older technologies. Ensuring that knowledge of

in-house applications is correctly managed is therefore an important task.
Staff development plans should take into account the following factors:

- The short- and long-term ambitions of those concerned;
- The short- and long-term needs of the organization;
- Possibilities for combining formal training with on-the-job training;
- Developing and maintaining coherent skill sets;
- Aligning promotions and remuneration with achievement.

The last point presents many organizations with problems because
information-security professionals are generally regarded as highly skilled
individuals, and there is usually a competitive marketplace for such skills.
The challenge here is to ensure that highly qualified staff are both recognized as such and retained, and this usually requires forward thinking and
active management.

Finally, due consideration of staff development issues should be integrated into day-to-day management routine. In this context, an approach
should be defined regarding the use of external service providers and consultants. Such expertise tends to be taken on in order to satisfy a short-term
requirement for which local staff do not have the required skills. Problems
can occur, however, when service provider contracts are prolonged indefinitely, especially where the external staff is performing the highly skilled
work and internal staff is taking care of the more mundane tasks. In some
sectors, regulatory requirements may impose tight restrictions here, such as
the necessity for security administration to be carried out by local
employees.

As part of the approach to manage skill sets within the team, managers
need to take account of their own requirements. One of the most difficult
issues facing managers is judging the level of personal knowledge required
to manage the team efficiently. This is a difficult issue because information
security is a vast subject and touches upon all areas of technology. In addition, it is often necessary to understand the details of particular technologies
in order to take the right decisions. The important rule here is:

> Managers should seek to maintain a level of knowledge that allows them to
> understand problems to the level of detail required to make a decision.

This seems obvious. Any less knowledge will impact a manager's ability
to understand the issues and take the right decision, and more knowledge is
inefficient. However, the problem here is that managers rely on their teams
to analyze problems in detail and to present the appropriate level of detail
when a decision is required. Teams do not remain static and managers cannot count on retaining particular skill sets indefinitely, so they need to be
prepared to compensate for deficiencies. A good approach is therefore to
maintain a broad spectrum of knowledge, covering major technical areas,
such as operating systems, database technology, and networks, and to aim

to retain the ability to drill down to more detail where required. Admittedly, this is not easy, but it is not necessary to master all technologies to achieve this, as technological solutions can be grouped together. Hence, anyone who has worked with one operating system should not find it overly difficult to develop a basic understanding of another. Similarly, the learning required to understand how network protocols work in general is considerable, but once acquired it forms the basis for understanding most network security issues.

By following trends in the industry, it should be apparent where most activity will be required in the near future and thus where to adapt personal training requirements appropriately. Conferences and training courses provide an ideal opportunity for identifying trends and often offer support for specialist discussion groups. In addition, professional organizations such as the Information Systems Security Association (ISSA) [1], the Information Security Forum [2], and members of the Club de la Sécurité des Systèmes d'Information X (CLUSIX) [3] network offer a forum for exchanging information between professionals. Organizations such as these play an important role in bringing information-security professionals together and encouraging information sharing at the practical level. Some of these organizations also support virtual user groups by providing mailing lists or bulletin boards for discussion (e.g., the certified information systems security professional (CISSP) Forum [4] and the New England Information Security User Group [5]).

2.2   Information relating to security incidents and vulnerabilities

A number of resources on the Internet provide information on current activity in the form of incident and vulnerability reports. In this age of global connectivity, where attacks against IT infrastructure can be conducted anonymously from the other side of the world, it is hard to imagine how information-security departments would operate in the absence of such sources.

Useful information sources for information-security managers include:

▸ The Forum of Incident Response and Security Teams (FIRST);

▸ Organizations selling customized data related to incidents and vulnerabilities;

▸ Full disclosure Web sites;

▸ Software vendors' Web sites.

FIRST was founded in 1990 and now encompasses over 100 incident response and security teams. For a list of current members, see [6]. The first emergency response teams, the CERT Coordination Center (CERT/CC) and the Computer Incident Advisory Capability (CIAC), were established as a result of Morris' Internet worm exploit in 1988 [7]. The FIRST forum aims to support the prevention, detection, and recovery from computer security incidents by rapidly communicating alert and advisory information, by enabling the sharing of security-related information, and by facilitating research and operational activities in this area [8].

As examples of FIRST members, both the CERT/CC and the CIAC publish a range of information related to information security, including practical guidelines for improving site security [9, 10], presentations, articles, and statistics. Interestingly, both organizations publish material for a wide range of audiences, including home users [11–13]. The latter is also useful in a commercial context, as it can be used to make professional staff aware of the risks associated with working at home and explain what measures should be taken to reduce this risk to acceptable levels. However, the most useful service offered by these and similar institutions is the timely publication of known vulnerabilities, incidents, and fixes. This is one of the most reliable sources of such data, and regular checking of recently published vulnerabilities is highly recommended.

In addition to membership in the FIRST forum, several companies offer this type of service on a chargeable basis. Examples include the F-Secure Radar service [14], the SecurityTracker Vulnerability and Patch Notification Service [15], and the Security Alert service offered by UNiTEL [16]. The added value here is that this type of service typically includes surveying a large number of sites and filtering the information to suit the specific requirements of the organization. It is worth carrying out a cost/benefit analysis before entering into such an agreement.

Full-disclosure Web sites constitute a second type of resource for information relating to security incidents. Used correctly, these sites complement the information provided by the FIRST network by providing the details of how incidents work. Often, it is possible to download source code for an exploit for further analysis or testing. In the past, there has been a lot of debate surrounding the utility of such sites and whether publishing of exploits contributes to the problem rather than solving it. Given the number of these sites now in existence, this debate has become largely academic and the real issue is separating the useful sites from the dangerous ones. Organizations are encouraged to act defensively in this area by interacting with these sites using stand-alone workstations or suitably prepared test environments.

Web sites of commercial software suppliers should be closely monitored for information relating to vulnerabilities and security patches. Some vendors now provide an alert system to notify end users of newly available critical patches, which is an efficient way to stay up to date; examples of vendors offering this type of service include Microsoft [17] and Macromedia [18]. In this context, it is also interesting to note that several personal firewall and antivirus software solutions include an automatic update mechanism, which is carried out using a secure channel between the client and the server system at the vendor's site. This is unlikely to be appropriate for commercial systems, as this kind of connection is likely to be blocked by firewall or proxy server software, but this is a useful function for home users or for enterprise staff who work out of the office on a company laptop.

Finally, many organizations specializing in information security host Web sites rich in information content that are mostly free. It is not possible to give a list of such sites in a book such as this, but the Web site of the SysAdmin, Audit, Network, Security (SANS) institute [19] is cited as an example.

2.3 Risk analysis and risk management

Most people have an intuitive idea of risk, but relatively few are capable of providing a working definition. We will take a practical view of risk and avoid a more mathematical approach, as this will allow us to develop a model of risk analysis that can easily be applied to everyday situations.

For our purposes, a risk is composed of a threat, a probability, and an impact:

Risk = Threat + Probability + Impact

Of these three elements, the threat is most often an external factor, which cannot be controlled. For instance, a third party looking to deface Web sites in order to pass a political message is an external threat over which we cannot reasonably expect to exert any control. An example of a threat that can be influenced is that of a frustrated employee, where it might be possible to recognize the signs of frustration and manage the situation. The probability of success and the impact are partially determined by external factors and partially determined by internal ones. External factors influencing the probability and impact include the level of determination of the attacker and the attacker's motives. Internal factors include the extent to which vulnerabilities are correctly controlled and how quickly the organization is able to detect and respond to attacks.

Throughout this book, the threat will be described textually using a scenario approach and both probability and impact will be qualified as high, medium, or low. The advantage of using semiquantitative techniques such as these is that the focus remains on the threat itself and the mitigating actions and not on issues relating to quantification. In reality, this level of precision is usually detailed enough to permit sensible management decisions, which is the aim of the exercise [20].

Quantitative risk analysis methods on the other hand are extremely difficult to apply in this area, due to the absence of reliable data, and may actually be misleading [21]. That said, the Basel II agreement requires financial institutions to develop quantitative models of operational risk by 2006, which is a strong incentive for these institutions to improve the quality of operational risk data.

There are essentially three ways to respond to a risk once it has been identified. The simplest response is to simply *accept* it. This is appropriate when the cost of mitigation is greater than the expected loss, providing of course that there are no legal or regulatory restrictions requiring another course of action. The most common way of dealing with risks in the information-security domain is to *manage* them. This implies defining and implementing mechanisms for reducing the risk to an acceptable level. When managing risks in this way, the risk is rarely reduced to zero, and it is important to identify the *residual risk* and to ensure that this is accepted by the appropriate business manager. Finally, risks can sometimes be *transferred* to a third party, usually via some form of insurance, although this can be difficult in the area of information security. Some risks, such as risk to reputation, cannot be transferred to third parties. When risks are transferred to a third party, the residual risk manifests itself as a franchise. This is summarized in Figure 2.1.

Managing risks invariably involves introducing control mechanisms of one kind or another. Because the scope for controlling the threat is limited, the usual approach is to reduce the level of vulnerability, thereby reducing the risk. When introducing control measures, it is important to take into account that risk-mitigating actions may themselves introduce new risks. To take a security-related example, the installation of a firewall may be identified as one of the actions for mitigating the risk of system penetration via the company's extranet. However, the implementation of a firewall introduces new risks of possible performance degradation or unavailability due to firewall problems. The residual risk arising from any set of mitigation mechanisms therefore includes two components: the initial (reduced) risk and risk introduced by the new control mechanisms.

There are many formalized approaches towards risk management in the information-security domain. Global risk analysis methodologies include méthode d'analyse des risques informatiques optimisés par niveau (MARION) [22], Méthode d'evaluation de la vulnérabilité des systèmes d'information (MELISA) [22], and the Central Computer and Telecommunications Agency (CCTA) risk analysis and management method (CRAMM) [23]. These more global methods sometimes include a broader view of information security and may cover related aspects, such as physical and organizational security. These methods are therefore capable of providing a broader picture of how operational risk is being managed. This is useful within the context of global risk management, as it helps ensure that risks are correctly prioritized across the enterprise. These methods are usually based on questionnaires, which are helpful in that they provide a structured approach, but there are obvious limits on the extent to which such

Figure 2.1 Different responses to identified risks.

questionnaires can be updated to reflect recent developments. The major drawback associated with these methods is the amount of time and effort it takes to derive the final result; this can be a major factor in deciding the level of acceptance by those involved. It is interesting to note that the Club de la Sécurité des Systèmes d'Information Français (CLUSIF) has responded to some of these issues with the methode harmonisée d'analyse de risques MEHARI method [21].

Other interesting approaches include The Risk Management Guide for Information Technology Systems [24] published by the National Institute of Standards and Technology (NIST), the INFOSEC Assessment Methodology (IAM) published by the National Security Agency (NSA) [25], and the Information Security Forum's (ISF) Security Status Survey [26]. The methods developed by NIST and the NSA have the advantage of being designed specifically for assessing and mitigating risks affecting IT systems. The Security Status Survey is only available to members of the ISF and is described by the latter as a benchmarking exercise, enabling organizations to focus attention on issues related to best practice. An added advantage provided by the ISF approach is the provision of an analysis tool, which permits members to compare their results against other organizations [26].

Fast risk analysis (FRA) methods are ideal for analyzing risks affecting individual systems. These methods do not aim to provide a global picture of risk, but concentrate on specific IT-related risk. For a more in-depth discussion of FRA techniques, see the appendix of this book.

Due to the need to react rapidly to business requirements, it is recommended that organizations that do not currently have a formalized approach begin with *fast risk management* techniques and aim to supplement this approach later with an annual global risk analysis and resulting action plan. Whichever method is chosen, the key to success is involving the right people in the process and ensuring that the residual risk is well understood and accepted.

More mature organizations should consider defining a set of key risk indicators (KRI) for regular publication to executive management if this is not in place. Such indicators are a valuable component of an efficient reporting mechanism, as they enable management to track the issue of most importance—how much risk is being taken in this area. Because they are destined for executive management, KRIs should satisfy the following criteria to be useful:

- They should be easy to understand conceptually.
- They should allow for comparison between one period and another in order to allow the ability to pinpoint trends.
- They should facilitate decision taking (i.e., the management response to a change in an indicator should be evident).

KRIs are extremely useful within the context of global risk management, and it is worth expanding considerable effort in developing this concept. If the indicators are well chosen, they will allow management to spot and react to trends before they become a problem. This is therefore a useful tool in transforming a reactive approach into a proactive one.

2.4 Strategy and planning

An old engineering method for controlling changes to any established system is to start by defining the current situation and the target situation. Once this has been done, it is much easier to define how the transition will occur. This simple, but nevertheless powerful, approach is one of the most efficient ways to go about defining an information-security strategy.

The strategy itself is one of the key elements in ensuring the long-term success of the information-security approach, as it contains a consolidated vision of the present and the future. Defining an information-security strategy, however, requires a thorough understanding of the following issues:

- Strong and weak points of the current approach;
- Current and projected trends in the areas of incidents and vulnerabilities;
- Probable evolution of security software;
- Business and IT strategy of the organization;
- Level of commitment to reducing risk and available budget.

The first and second points reflect the level of understanding of the current situation, and the remaining points need to be taken into account when defining the target situation. Other things to consider when developing the strategy include:

- It is suggested that the strategy should cover a period of 3 to 5 years. This is long enough to implement significant changes, but short enough to reasonably predict technological evolution.
- The resulting strategy should be accompanied by personal strategy. The purpose of the personal strategy is to gain acceptance within the organization and to be recognized as a leader capable of implementing the strategic vision.
- For managers taking up a position within a new organization, it is probably wise to foresee a consolidation period before defining the strategy. This allows time to develop a feeling for the company culture and way of doing things. If the strategy cannot be delayed, consider including such a period as the first phase.
- Use a phased approach and define milestones so that progress can be checked.

Further details on this subject are to be found in Chapter 5.

The strategy document will provide the high-level roadmap for the next few years. It has already been noted that it is a good idea to provide timescales for executing the different planned phases and using milestones to track key achievements. On the contrary, it is not a good idea to include any kind of more detailed planning in the strategy document, as this will draw attention away from the strategic vision and necessitate regular updates as the plan changes.

Nevertheless, correct planning and tracking is essential for executing the strategy, and many organizations will standardize the requirements and tools in this area. In most organizations, the strategy document will not serve as a license to spend money, but will need to be supplemented by internal proposals (or some similar mechanism) in order to unlock the required budget. This being the case, it helps to decompose the strategy into a series of major activities, each of which can be planned and executed more or less in isolation.

A few words regarding planning and planning tools are in order here. The purpose of planning is to allow us to achieve the following:

> Produce the deliverables defined by the initiative according to the agreed timescales and budget;

> Reprioritize short-term issues without losing invested work;

> Maintain a vision of progress and problem areas via tracking techniques;

> React to changes due to internal or external constraints by modifying the plan accordingly. This may include changing the scope, the budget, or the planned duration of the project.

The last point stresses that the project plan is an instrument to be used to assist in making decisions. As organizations do not remain static, and the planning assumptions at the beginning of a project often prove to be inaccurate later on, plans that do not change with time should be the exception and not the rule. In fact, a plan that does not change with time is often a sign that the project is not being tracked correctly.

Producing and using project plans is not the subject of this book, but it is worth mentioning a few principles that will help to ensure a successful approach:

> Managers should have an idea of what percentage of team effort needs to be dedicated to day-to-day activities, such as ongoing administration, and what percentage can be allocated to project work.

> Projects exist in order to produce certain deliverables. Plans should recognize this fact by building on a work breakdown structure (WBS) geared towards the production of these deliverables. That is, the deliverables should be the focus of the plan.

> Synergies should be exploited wherever possible. This is extremely useful when implementing infrastructure, as it may be difficult to obtain budget for something that is not directly related to a business requirement. This is why it is important to have an understanding of the business and IT strategy when writing the information-security strategy.

- Prioritization is essential, as it permits the most efficient use of limited resources. This is particularly appropriate when budgets are low. FRA is a useful tool for deciding priorities.

- Using a phased approach for larger projects divides the task into manageable chunks and provides checkpoints for verifying progress. This approach can also be used to define points at which the project can sensibly be suspended if it is required to move resources to higher priority issues. The work can then be resumed at a later date.

Finally, managers should try to align staff development plans with project activity in order to motivate and develop staff. Where it is necessary to use external consultants, the impact on permanent staff needs to be managed. This may involve explaining why the decision to use external resources was taken and planning for a transfer of knowledge from external to internal staff. Indeed, such a transfer is often necessary to enable the unit to support systems after their implementation.

2.5   Policy and standards

Many experts view the information-security policy as the definitive source of guidance for taking decisions related to information security, and they build the entire information-security approach on the requirements of this document. This book takes a different approach and considers the policy a statement of the way information security should be carried out, as long as there is no major conflict with the requirements of the problem under analysis. According to this model, therefore, the policy provides general guidelines and helps ensure a coherent approach to common problems across the enterprise.

When policy recommendations are incompatible with the requirements of the problem at hand, a more flexible approach is required, and the benefits of a standard approach have to be weighed against the need to reduce risk for a particular situation. As such conflicts are inevitable, it is a good idea to distinguish between policy requirements that really are mandatory and those that are to be respected on a best-effort basis. If this approach is adopted, any exceptions to mandatory policy requirements should then be authorized by the policy owner (e.g., by granting a waiver). This has the advantage of allowing flexibility but preventing abuse by imposing an arduous process on those seeking waivers.

The information-security policy is usually quite a high-level document, which concentrates on major issues and avoids unnecessary detail. There are many reasons for this approach:

- This limits the overall size of the document, keeping it focused and readable.

- The content is simplified, and specific expertise is not required to understand it.

‣ By avoiding details, the expected lifetime of the policy is increased, and it is not necessary to update the text frequently to reflect technical progress.

This is a good strategy as far as policy is concerned, but the price paid for this simplicity is a lack of detail. Consequently, where day-to-day problems are concerned, it is often tremendously difficult to judge whether a particular approach to securing information is compliant with policy. Equivalently, when faced with a concrete issue, policy may provide few guidelines on how to solve it. For this reason, it helps enormously to plan a structured documentation set consisting of documents of different levels of detail and dedicated to different aspects of information security. Chapter 6 presents a set of criteria for defining a document set and provides an example.

Irrespective of the details of how the documentation set is organized, there will be a requirement for mapping high-level policy statements to lower level implementation details. Where technology is involved, such details will probably vary strongly from one type of implementation to another, which implies that there will be many mappings corresponding to any particular policy requirement. IT security standards are an ideal way to control this mapping.

IT security standards are documents that provide a standard way to satisfy a policy requirement within a particular technical context. Examples of suitable candidates for an IT security standard might include how to implement authentication in common request broker architecture (CORBA) environments or the UNIX® security baseline document. These are therefore low-level documents that are expected to be quite volatile in the sense that they will require regular updates in order to keep pace with technological evolution. It does not matter that standards require regular updating because they merely interpret policy and therefore should not change the risk stance of the enterprise significantly.

Apart from the level of detail of the documents, another essential difference between policy and standards is the scope of application. Given the importance of the subject, most organizations write their own security policy to reflect their own culture and approach to risk. There is a lot of published information to help organizations do this (e.g., [27, 28]). Some of this can be cut and pasted (as long as the required thought process has taken place), but it is unusual to take whole policies and implement them unchanged. This is not necessarily true regarding IT security standards. Indeed, one of the advantages of adopting a particular standard could be its widespread adoption. Where IT security standards are concerned, therefore, it is often desirable to select and adhere to established standards—as long as doing so reflects the policy requirement or is justified on the basis of a risk assessment.

One of the best sources of technical information related to the Internet is the series of Request For Comments (RFC) documents, released by the Internet Engineering Task Force (IETF). These documents are the definitive source of reference for Internet protocols (including all the protocols in the

TCP/IP protocol stack), and they contain a wealth of security-related information. Other excellent sources of technical information related to information security include the American National Institute of Standards and Technology [29] and the National Security Agency (NSA) [30]. Useful reference material published by NIST includes the "NIST Handbook" [31] and the Federal Information Processing Standards (FIPS) publications [32]. Similarly, the NSA has published a series of security recommendation guides for common operating systems [33], mainly in the form of configuration guidelines.

The information-security policy and the standards that translate its recommendations within a particular context are therefore useful instruments in defining high-level requirements and standardizing implementation details. This will only happen, however, if they are read and understood by the target audiences and if the latter incorporate their requirements into their day-to-day work. This requires a well-designed process for publication and procedures for updating the documents to take into account feedback. This is discussed in more detail in Chapter 6.

2.6   Processes and procedures

It is quite fashionable these days to model information security as a process. In this context, a process can be thought of as a machine that transforms a set of inputs into a set of outputs.

In the case of information security, the inputs are essentially unsecured data and systems, known threats, untrained staff, the business strategy of the organization, and legal and regulatory requirements. The outputs are secured data and systems, trained staff, and supporting documentation. This process can be decomposed into a set of constituent procedures. Indeed, the process can be thought of as the collection of these procedures together with relevant supporting documentation and the management and coordination actions necessary to ensure that everything works together. This is depicted in Figure 2.2.

In Chapter 4, we will take a look at an important part of this process, the strategic-planning cycle, in more detail. When discussing this point, we will emphasize that the strategic-planning cycle describes only how strategic improvements are made and therefore describes only a part of the overall process.

This approach turns out to be a very helpful approach for a number of reasons:

- For organizations that have defined and documented their core processes, this places information security on the same footing as other processes.

- Using a process-driven approach can help take the focus off technology by focusing on deliverables expressed in terms of risk reduction.

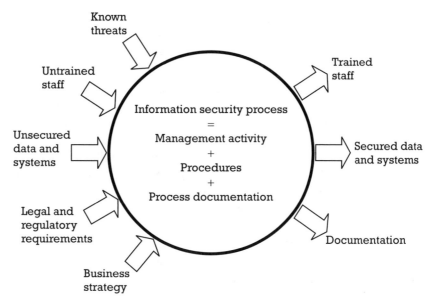

Figure 2.2   Relationship between process and procedures.

> ▸ Using a process-driven approach often makes it easier to integrate with existing quality management systems.

Integration with an existing quality management system is desirable, as security documents will then have the same look and feel as other business documents. This also enables the information-security team to benefit from all of the other advantages of a quality system, including standardized document control procedures and reviews by an independent third party.

It is important, however, that the quality system supports the information-security process and not the other way around. One of the paradoxes associated with an increased awareness of quality issues is that in seeking to achieve better and more accurate documentation, we may actually be reducing the benefit by overloading the intended audience. Documentation that is never read or is not correctly updated does not add much value to anyone. Auditors in particular should take note here—one of the consequences of performing audits on a system-by-system basis is that it is difficult to keep track of scalability issues. Whereas it might be reasonable to require detailed documentation for a particular platform, the same level of detail may not be achievable as a goal for all platforms.

Processes are normally documented by decomposing them into their constituent procedures and describing the latter. Common sense is required when doing this in order to avoid unnecessary complexity, and it is essential to be selective in deciding what gets documented. Organizations should decide for themselves what level of documentation is required for controlled operations, but this should represent a balance between the level of detail of the content and the amount of work required to maintain it.

In some cases, the best approach may be to produce a minimal documentation set. This both increases the probability that it will actually be read and used correctly and simplifies the maintenance process. When compiling the documentation itself, consider the benefit of graphical techniques and checklists as an alternative to normal text. This often makes the content easier to understand for the target audience and reduces the volume of text. Similarly, using references to other documents also helps to reduce the amount of text, while ensuring that redundant information is kept to a minimum (redundant information should be avoided as updating it consistently is problematic). Again, where quality systems already exist, they should provide guidance on these issues.

The process description and detailed procedures specify which activities are carried out and how. These documents, however, do not normally comment on the level of service that is to be provided to particular customers. Defining and agreeing on a level of service with customers (internal or external) is highly recommended, as it helps control user expectations and can considerably reduce the pressure on the help desk or security administrators by reducing unnecessary phone calls. Levels of service to be provided to particular customers are formalized using service level agreements (SLAs).

Defining SLAs can be a lengthy process, particularly if the objectives of the exercise are too ambitious. As usual, to receive the benefits it is important to be pragmatic. Where internal SLAs are concerned, it is neither useful nor productive to try to cover every possible scenario, and both parties should be prepared to be reasonable in interpreting the agreement once it has been made. Without this flexibility, the tendency will be for each side to be over defensive and both parties will lose out. When writing SLAs, it is useful to foresee a mechanism by which the client can prioritize issues or make urgent requests. Similarly, the SLA should allow for a degraded level of service under exceptional conditions. Finally, there should be some way of monitoring the level of compliance to detect problematic situations and react accordingly, although it is probably best to look for simple indicators to start with and to define more sophisticated metrics as experience is gained.

2.7 Methodologies and frameworks

Methodologies and frameworks have been grouped together, as both are used to add structure to processes. Examples of methodologies in the information-security area include the CRAMM [23] and the Common Methodology for Information Technology Security Evaluation [34]. Examples of frameworks include Control Objectives for Information and Related Technology (COBIT) [35] and ISO 17799/BS7799 [36, 37].

As information-security practitioners, we come across methodologies and frameworks in two contexts: those that we impose upon ourselves and those that are used by others. Of the two, the latter are at least as important, if not more important, than the former. This is particularly true in the area of software development and acquisition, where methodologies play an increasingly important role. Few security departments have the power to block a promising business project once it is launched, and if the approach to information security cannot be reconciled with the approach adopted for development or acquisition, the security aspects may simply be bypassed.

Before adopting any particular methodology or framework in the information-security area, in addition to an internal evaluation it is well worth trying to identify other organizations that are using the approach or have used the approach in the past. One of the key elements to look for here is evidence that the approach has stood the test of time. Many of the existing approaches place heavy demands on both IT and business staff, and this may prove unrealistic when resources are limited. This is important, as it is precisely during these periods that IT risk is likely to increase, and any methodology or framework must be able to deliver under such conditions. One of the major challenges facing these more formalized approaches is the requirement to adapt quickly to changing business conditions. This requirement covers not only the need to adapt to structural changes, but also to changes in business strategy or a changing threat environment. Those approaches that do not have this ability to adapt quickly will eventually be abandoned.

One of the best ways to prepare for a stable environment in the future is to integrate the information-security requirements into the development methodology, as this will encourage projects to become more actively involved in the IT security aspects and present them with a unified approach to system development. This is important, as commercial tools can be used to solve a wide variety of architectural issues but are relatively weak when it comes to securing proprietary applications.

Unfortunately, many development methodologies do not address the area of information security in much detail, with the consequence that it usually requires a lot of hard work to integrate security requirements. Guidelines do exist in this area [38], but these must be applied with flexibility if a seamless integration is to be achieved. Success here will depend on the following factors:

- The degree to which other IT staff are involved in the exercise, which includes many groups such as developers, testing teams, production support staff, and customer support;
- The impact on the development and acquisition process;
- The ability of the information-security unit to support the process;
- The way in which such guidelines relate to other important security initiatives, such as the security architecture.

Any attempt to integrate security into the development methodology that does not involve the concerned parties is doomed to failure. This does not mean that the exercise needs to be performed by a committee, either; it is quite acceptable to start with a proposition and to seek opinions and guidance as long as the impacted teams are involved in the exercise and contribute to the final solution. It is important to try and identify and involve all parties, however, and this should include those that rely on the deliverables of the process (as these deliverables will change).

One of the pitfalls in this area is being too ambitious regarding the level of control and signoff to be exercised by the information-security team. While it is reasonable to review and signoff security requirements, high-level design documents, acceptance test criteria, and similar high-level specifications, it is usually unrealistic to expect to be able to review detailed technical specifications, code, and similar low-level deliverables. Setting reasonable goals at the start should enable the team to fill its role correctly.

2.8 Awareness and training

Where information security is concerned, there is no such thing as a totally automated security response. Automated solutions are the product of the human mind, and whereas computers may be able to outperform people in some areas[1], a clever adversary will always have a good chance of finding a flaw in any such system. The most essential part of any security defense mechanism is therefore the human element, and staff must be trained to recognize and respond to problems appropriately.

Getting staff involved in the information-security process requires careful planning and preparation. This preparation should not be limited to *what* is to be said, but should also look at *how, when,* and *to whom* the essential messages are to be passed. People are more inclined to participate actively in activities if they understand why it is necessary and if they agree with the role they have to play.

In deciding what information needs to be passed to the target audience, it helps to distinguish between what is working well and what is not working well. Where problems exist, there is an opportunity to involve the audience and ask their opinion—in which case it helps to have someone present to take note of the points raised. For those who are comfortable speaking in public and who are prepared to face criticism openly, involving the audience from the beginning is a good way to stimulate dialogue and get people actively involved. For those who do not feel comfortable with this approach, an alternative option is to research this beforehand and to present the conclusions. In both cases, it is essential that proposed solutions make it clear what has already been agreed and what is proposed for the future, as staff cannot be expected to agree to perform a new role without having analyzed the impact.

Presentations are the traditional focus of user awareness campaigns and will probably remain so due to the importance of direct contact. The major

---

1. In 1997, the chess grandmaster Gary Kasparov was defeated in a series of matches against the IBM supercomputer Deep Blue. It is interesting to note, however, that he beat the more recent program "Deep Junior" in 27 moves.

advantage of a presentation is that it gives the presenter the full attention of the audience for a certain time, allowing a dialogue to be launched in the absence of other distractions. This, however, is also a disadvantage in the sense that presentations are short events and the objective is to ensure that people remain active over a long period of time. Presentations should therefore be supported by other techniques for passing important messages and maintaining an active dialogue. Suggested techniques include:

> Computer-based training (CBT) and use of video material;

> Workgroups;

> Hands-on demonstrations;

> Use of visual aids, such as posters and mouse pads;

> Local information-security contact points.

A major advantage of both CBT facilities and video material is that staff can use these tools independently and can therefore schedule sessions to suit their own requirements. CBT facilities have additional advantages, notably that they involve user participation. By offering courses on-line, it is also possible to keep a record of progress and arrange for further help if necessary.

Workgroups are useful for looking into particular issues in more detail and constitute one way of responding to difficult issues raised within presentations. Workgroups are helpful as long as they remain focused, but can be counterproductive if they lack direction. A good technique for leading workgroups is to define a clear set of objectives and deliverables for the group while limiting the timeframe. In order to avoid problems, staff participation should be agreed in advance with the responsible line managers. Bear in mind that professional clubs (such as those belonging to the CLUSIX) may organize workgroups to look at particular issues, and this is an alternative to in-house sessions. One of the advantages of attending workshops such as these is that participants often come from a variety of backgrounds and might therefore be able to offer novel solutions.

Hands-on demonstrations of recent attacks can be a very powerful way of making people aware of the current state of the art, but such demonstrations can easily become sensationalist, and without the correct context the right messages may not be passed. Where demonstrations are used, they should be integrated in to a balanced presentation that aims to inform staff about not only the threat, but also their role in dealing with it. One way of achieving this is to select attacks according to the response required by the end user and to carefully explain the correct user response to each type of attack.

Visual aids provide a constant reminder of key messages and help to keep the theme of information security in people's minds. Posters, mouse pads, and brochures are examples of commonly used visual aids. There is considerable room for creativity here, but to remain effective, just as for marketing campaigns, it is necessary to change the material regularly. For those working in international environments, it is as well to remember that humor does not necessarily transcend national boundaries.

Because the information-security team is usually quite small, defining specific contact points within business units for information-security issues often makes sense and can do a lot to improve communications. This represents considerable effort, though, as contact points must be trained and kept up to date with what is happening if they are to be effective. Because they understand both the business issues and the information-security issues, local representatives can present the case for a particular approach in business terms.

Once it has been decided how to conduct the campaign, thought should be given to the timing. Just as it is probably not a good idea to launch a major campaign in the holiday period, it is also unwise to do so in periods of high instability. A campaign that is launched only months before a major reorganization will have to surmount considerable difficulties as the audience will question its validity in the new organization and could reasonably be expected to adopt a "wait and see" attitude.

Finally, the different target groups have to be identified, and the information content and approach needs to be adapted to each group. Clearly, the level of detail should reflect the requirements of the target audience, and the material should support the type of dialogue that needs to be established with that group. Roles and responsibilities should be clearly explained as part of the exercise and verified with management staff. Disagreements here are particularly important, as they are more indicative of fundamental problems.

To summarize, preparing for an information-security awareness campaign involves defining an approach to the following issues:

▸ The way in which staff should be grouped for the purposes of passing the appropriate information;
▸ The information that is relevant for each group;
▸ The manner in which the information is communicated;
▸ The order and timing of information sessions;
▸ The manner in which the initial contact will be followed up;
▸ How the degree of success of the campaign is to be measured.

Whatever methods are chosen to communicate the important messages, it is important to give staff concrete objectives and to implement a mechanism for measuring the impact of the exercise.

2.9 Audits

It may seem strange to include audits in a chapter dedicated to management tools, but audits provide an opportunity to test how well things are working in practice by requesting the viewpoint of a third party. This is particularly useful in guarding against personal prejudices. One word of warning here, however—it is almost never a good strategy to use external audits with the idea of applying pressure on higher management to take a particular decision. The correct way to get decisions made is through good communications, not by putting management in an uncomfortable position.

When dealing with auditors, it is essential to establish a dialogue and to be challenging when observations are deemed to be inappropriate or overly ambitious. This can easily occur, as external auditors have to work within very tight constraints, including short timescales and a rigidly controlled scope. In particular, audits focusing on individual systems may not take sufficient account of architectural controls that compensate for local weaknesses, and therefore they can overestimate the risk. There is usually a lot of added value in the ensuing discussion, as it should involve a confrontation of ideas and require both parties to justify their viewpoints, taking into account all contextual information. It is important for both sides to be demanding here, and contentious points should be settled on the basis of a strong argument and certainly not by unqualified references to books or best practice. Best practice can be rather a nebulous concept at times and equivalently what is best practice for one type of industry may not make sense at all for another.

Some types of audit require special preparation, notably any audit making use of invasive techniques, such as security scanners and penetration testing techniques. There is currently a range of companies offering to perform penetration studies, and many are marketing themselves purely on the basis of technical skills. This is an area, however, in which the management approach is at least as important as the technical exercise itself. Factors to take into consideration when outsourcing this type of study include:

- The need to understand the associated risk and how it will be controlled;

- The ways that any incidents will be managed;

- The value that the study will bring, not only in terms of detecting vulnerabilities, but also in correcting them.

2.10 Contracts

Contracts are an essential part of commercial activity. They are used to clarify and put limits on an agreement and often identify the consequences of not adhering to the imposed terms and conditions. Typically, a contract will specify the governing law and identify how disputes will be resolved.

Where information security is concerned, contracts are the standard way to place restrictions on how data that belongs to the organization can be handled by staff or other third parties. However, as a general mechanism for reducing information security–related risk, contracts are often overlooked. This is unfortunate, because some things can be achieved a lot easier through contractual means than through technical ones. For example, consider an application provided by a financial service provider to a number of banks, enabling the latter to exchange high-value transactions in a secure manner. Given the high level of risk, the application provides for storage of client-side cryptographic keys on a smart card but allows for a less secure software storage mechanism for banks that do not wish to implement external smart card readers. The financial service provider can then use separate contracts to reflect the differing level of risk associated with the solution adopted. In particular, the contractual framework could be used to distinguish under which conditions the organization could be held liable for a security breach in the two different cases.

One area in which contracts are likely to become increasingly important is that of public key cryptography and digital signatures. There is already considerable activity in this field, and organizations that use digital signature techniques or who have deployed a PKI are encouraged to follow this closely. One of the problems in the area of PKI is ensuring that the specific policies and standards in this area, such as the certification practice statement (CPS) and certificate policies (CP), remain consistent with the legal and contractual framework.

2.11 Outsourcing

Outsourcing security has always been a hot discussion topic among professionals. This is understandable, as security may be only one step away from control and not many businesses would like to outsource complete control of their operations. The key to this dilemma is, of course, the degree to which security is outsourced and the way in which this is controlled. In fact, many if not most large organizations are prepared to outsource the security of their buildings to professional security companies, and in real terms this may already provide more access to data than intended. Two points illustrate this:

1. Companies that do not operate a clean desk policy may have confidential information lying unsecured throughout the night. Similarly, sensitive documents are not always removed from printers. Even those that do operate such a policy may use external personnel to enforce it.

2. Some operating systems cannot be adequately secured if the machine is not physically secured. For instance, personal computers can be made to boot from diskette, which provides the opportunity to load an unusual operating system.

The point is that outsourcing security is a risk-based decision like any other as long as legal or regulatory restrictions do not apply. It is to be expected that most companies will aim to retain control over their systems by managing IT security in house or by selectively outsourcing certain activities. Whichever approach is selected, it must be coherent, which involves looking at all sources of risk and not just some of them.

A word on trust here is appropriate. We live in an era where things happen faster and we often accept less thorough controls in return for speed. For many organizations, the approach to recruitment is an example of this compromise, and the degree to which the past history of new recruits is verified may be limited to the most rudimentary checks. As employees, we tend to trust colleagues on the assumption that they have been through the hiring process and we therefore extend considerable trust to people we may not personally know that well [39]. There is little choice in this approach, as it is not possible to know everyone in a big company. However, in this situation, nobody is performing the checks, and the basis for trust is weak. Under these conditions, the advantages of in-house control over outsourcing are somewhat reduced.

In summary, outsourcing selective security services may be a viable option, but outsourcing the entire information-security process is an extreme approach and is not likely to be adopted by most organizations. Where services are outsourced, this should be justified by a clear business case, and the associated risks and proposed way of controlling these risks should be understood and accepted by executive management. Identified control mechanisms should be coherent with those aspects of information security managed in house. SLAs can be used to specify the details of how the service is to be provided.

2.12 Summary

Many of the challenges associated with securing information are management oriented. It therefore makes sense to select management tools with care and to ensure that such tools are being used effectively. At the most fundamental level, the information-security team needs to develop and maintain a pool of experience capable of defining and implementing a long-term strategy while still dealing with day-to-day issues. Managers need to structure and plan their own development in this area. Conferences, training courses, and professional associations are useful for assessing current trends and for establishing a network of peers. The FIRST network develops this idea by managing information related to incidents and vulnerabilities in a global context.

Risk-management approaches are the key to dealing with rapidly changing environments and different methods can be used to achieve different goals. Hence, global methods form a good basis for annual risk assessment and action plan and FRA methods are useful for punctual analysis.

Developing an approach to securing information within an enterprise requires a strategic viewpoint, and this has to be translated into a long-term plan. By considering information security as a process, the accent can be placed on reducing risk rather than on technology. The strategy document and planning techniques are the tools used to transform this vision into reality. In particular, planning and tracking are tools for coping with change, and plans are expected to change as projects develop. The role of the manager is to adapt the approach in the face of change by optimizing the solution for the new constraints. Methodologies and frameworks can be useful in adding structure, but these will not stand the test of time if they are not capable of adapting to changing requirements. For this reason, light-weight methods are to be preferred. Adapting to external methodologies is a good technique for obtaining the buy in of other staff, particularly in the area of development and acquisition.

Policy and standards are important as guidelines for what is acceptable and what is not, but play second role to management decisions based on risk analysis as long as legal or regulatory restrictions do not apply. Policy docu-ments should distinguish between mandatory requirements and those requirements that are to be achieved on a best-effort basis. Standards trans-late policy requirements in particular contexts. User awareness programs not only make staff aware of policy, they seek to involve them actively in the information-security process.

Outsourcing selective security services is a risk-based decision and should be based on a convincing business case that takes account of the associated risk. The associated controls should be well documented and for-mally agreed.

References

[1] "ISSA: Information Systems Security Association," September 2003, http://www.issa.org.

[2] "Information Security Forum," September 2003, http://www.securityforum.org/html/frameset.htm.

[3] "CLUSIF: Nos Homologues à l'International," September 2003, https://www.clusif.asso.fr/fr/clusix/index.asp.

[4] "CISSP Forum Frequently Asked Questions (FAQ)," September 2003, http://www.eaglesreach.com/cisspforum/faq.html.

[5] "New England Information Security User Group (NEISUG)," September 2003, http://www.neisug.com.

[6] "FIRST Member Information," September 2003, http://www.first.org/team-info.

[7] Spafford, S., "The Internet Worm Program: An Analysis," *Purdue Technical Report CSD-TR-823*, December 8, 1988.

[8] "FIRST: Vision and Mission Statement," September 2003, http://www.first.org/about/mission.html.

[9] "CERT Security Improvement Modules," September 2003, http://www.cert.org/security-improvement.

[10] Allen, J., *CERT Guide to System and Network Security Practices*, Boston, MA: Addison-Wesley, 2001.

[11] Orvis W. J., P. Krystosek, and J. Smith, "Connecting to the Internet Securely: Protecting Home Networks, CIAC-2324," September 2003, http://www.

ciac.org/ciac/documents/CIAC-2324_Connecting_to_the_Internet_Securely_
Protecting_Home_Networks.pdf.

[12] Rogers, L. R., "Home Computer Security," September 2003, http://www.cert.
org/homeusers/HomeComputerSecurity.

[13] "Home Network Security," September 2003, http://www.cert.org/tech_tips/
home_networks.html.

[14] "F-Secure Radar," September 2003, http://www.f-secure.com/products/radar.

[15] "Security Tracker," September 2003, http://www.securitytracker.com.

[16] "Security Alert," September 2003, http://www.w3.easynet.co.uk/unitel/
services/alert.html.

[17] "Microsoft Windows Update," September 2003, http://windowsupdate.
microsoft.com.

[18] "Macromedia: Notification Service," September 2003, www.macromedia.com/
devnet/security/security_zone/notification_service.html.

[19] "SANS: The Most Trusted Source for Computer Security Training," September
2003, http://www.sans.org.

[20] Nosworthy, J. D., "A Practical Risk Analysis Approach: Managing BCM Risk,"
Computers & Security, Vol.19, No. 4, 2000, pp. 337–347.

[21] Mannion, C., and A. Dang Van Mien, "The Myth of Quantitative Risk Analysis,"
Strategy, Trends and Tactics, Stamford, CT: Gartner Group, 2002.

[22] "Securite-Informatique.Com: Le Portail de la Sécurité Informatique,"
September 2003, http://www.securite-informatique.com/marion.htm.

[23] "CRAMM from Insight Consulting," September 2003, http://www.cramm.com.

[24] Stoneburner, G., A. Goguen, and A. Feringa, "Risk Management Guide for
Information Technology Systems; Recommendations of the National Institute of
Standards and Technology," September 2003, http://www.cio.gov/documents/
sp800-30.pdf.

[25] "INFOSEC Assessment Training and Rating Program," September 2003,
http://www.nsa.gov/isso/iam/index.htm.

[26] "Information Security Status Survey," September 2003, http://www.
securityforum.org/html/frameset.htm.

[27] "The SANS Security Policy Project," September 2003, http://www.sans.org/
resources/policies.

[28] "The Information Security Policies/Computer Security Policies Directory,"
September 2003, http://www.information-security-policies-and-standards.com.

[29] "National Institute of Standards and Technology NIST," September 2003,
http://www.nist.gov.

[30] "The National Security Agency," September 2003, http://www.nsa.gov.

[31] "Special Pub 800-12—An Introduction to Computer Security: The NIST
Handbook," September 2003, http://csrc.nist.gov/publications/nistpubs/800-12.

[32] "Federal Information Processing Standards Publications (FIPS Pubs),"
September 2003, http://www.itl.nist.gov/fipspubs.

[33] "National Security Agency; Security Recommendation Guides," September 2003, http://www.nsa.gov/snac/index.html.

[34] "Common Evaluation Methodology Documentation: Common Evaluation Methodology," September 2003, http://www.commoncriteria.org/cem/cem .html.

[35] "The Information Systems Audit and Control Association: COBIT," September 2003, http://www.isaca.org/Template.cfm?Section=COBIT6&Template=/ Tagged Page/TaggedPageDisplay.cfm&TPLID=55&ContentID=7981.

[36] ISO/IEC 17799:2000 (Part 1), *Information Technology—Code of Practice for Information Security Management.*

[37] BS 7799-2:2002 (Part 2), *Information Security Management Systems.*

[38] Information Security Forum, "How to Build Security into your Information Systems: Implementation Guide."

[39] Purser, S., "A Simple Graphical Tool for Modeling Trust," *Computers & Security,* Vol. 20, No. 6, 2001, pp. 479–484.

CHAPTER

3

Contents

Technical tools

3.1 Overview

This chapter is concerned with technical tools and how such tools can be used to support various aspects of the information-security process. We have already noted that any realistic approach to securing information within most large or medium-sized organizations must provide a way of managing issues related to complexity and scale of deployment. This can only be achieved if processes are specifically designed to deal with these issues, and these processes will require the support of appropriate tools.

The material in this chapter is complementary to that of Chapter 2 in the sense that solutions to everyday problems usually involve both a procedural component and a technical component, and these two elements should be viewed as different aspects of the same solution. In other words, it does not usually make sense to select a tool to solve a problem without taking into account the procedural aspects of the solution, and, similarly, processes should be designed taking into account the ability of tools to offer the required level of support.

To prepare the way for an overview of the most commonly used tools, we will introduce a classification scheme for IT security software. This scheme will then be used as a basis for presenting the most commonly used tools. In order to retain the focus of the book and avoid unnecessary complexity, this discussion will deliberately be limited both in terms of the tools covered and in terms of the level of detail of discussion. Chapter 8 will build on the material in this chapter by showing how to combine tools and procedures into an effective security architecture.

3.2 Classification of security tools

In order to facilitate the discussion of commonly used security tools, the classification schema illustrated in Figure 3.1 will be used.

Host-oriented tools are distinguished from network-oriented tools based on their focus. The former are designed to improve platform security and are often specific to a particular operating system, whereas the design of the latter is based mainly on network protocol considerations. As a result, although both sets of tools aim to achieve similar goals, the way in which they do this is quite different.

Within each class, tools are further classified to reflect the type of security service that they are designed to support:

▸ Authentication and authorization;

▸ System or network integrity protection;

▸ Access control;

▸ Monitoring;

▸ Data protection services—confidentiality, integrity, and non-repudiation.

Note that the first four services look upon the system or network as a container of data and aim to improve the protection of the container, whereas the last service operates directly on the data.

It is important to understand the difference between system or network integrity and data integrity. System integrity protection measures aim to detect and potentially repair malicious modification of a system component, such as an executable file. Replacement of system executables by modified

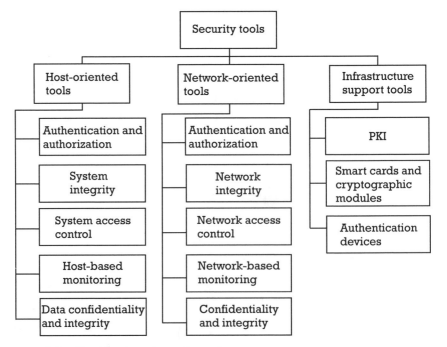

Figure 3.1 Classification of security tools.

versions implementing some form of malicious functionality is a common technique employed by those who attack computer systems. Similarly, network integrity protection measures aim to ensure that the integrity of the network as a whole remains intact. For instance, network integrity protection mechanisms are capable of detecting the presence of unauthorized machines connected to the network.

Data integrity protection, on the other hand, aims to ensure that the integrity of data is ensured. An example of such a service would be a secure protocol that detected any changes made to data while in transit. This example is discussed further in Section 3.3.6.

3.3 Host-oriented tools

3.3.1 Security layers

In discussing the behavior of host-oriented security software, it is necessary to understand how different types of software interact with each other on any given platform. It turns out to be very useful to model these interactions using layers of software, where it is to be understood that a higher software layer receives some kind of service from a lower software layer. Indeed, this type of model is used extensively by network engineers and has been formalized by the ISO in the form of the Open Systems Interconnection (OSI) model [1] (which incidentally has an associated security architecture [2]). This is illustrated in Figure 3.2.

We will only use this type of model to illustrate a few basic concepts, and we will not concentrate too much on the details, as this is not necessary. Given this limitation to our approach, it should be noted that Figure 3.2 could potentially be rearranged, depending on the software packages being used, but this will not affect our discussion.

The most important layer of software is known as the operating system (OS). This is the most important layer because all tasks performed by the system involve its participation. For this reason, the security system associated with the OS usually determines the level of security of the entire system, and once the OS has been compromised it is usually only a question of time before the applications that run on top of it are compromised.

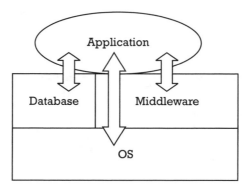

Figure 3.2 Security layers. © 2002 Elsevier Ltd. All rights reserved.

The layer of software above the operating system includes support software and applications that access the OS directly. Support software is implemented on top of the OS and offers certain standard services to a range of applications. Examples of support software include relational database software and middleware (e.g., common object request broker architecture [3]). Because this software uses the services offered by the OS, it is necessarily dependent upon the security of the latter, and if the OS is penetrated, it is usually trivial to bypass the security mechanisms associated with these packages. A concrete example is provided by relational database packages running on mid-range systems. If the super user account associated with the OS is obtained, access to the database administrator account is usually easy to obtain.

In a similar fashion, application layer security is generally dependent on the security of both the underlying support software and the operating system, in the sense that it can usually be undermined if one of these underlying components is compromised.

As an example of why it helps to think in terms of security layers, consider the problems associated with trying to protect data stored on a platform from weaknesses in the platform's operating system. One idea would be to use cryptographic techniques (for instance, by encrypting a database), but such a protection mechanism would have to meet several tough demands to offer real protection:

- Cryptographic keys would have to be used within a tamper-resistant device in order to ensure that they could not be obtained using system tools by someone having administrative rights.

- The design would have to ensure that data never appeared as clear text either in memory or on a secondary storage device.

- The interface between the operating system and the tamper-resistant device would have to be protected using secure protocols to prevent a third party with administrative rights from sniffing exchanges between the database and the device and subsequently using the interface to break the system.

In reality, he who controls the operating system usually controls everything running on top of it, so good security starts with a correctly secured operating system.

3.3.2 The native operating system security subsystem

Just as the operating system is the most fundamental layer of software on any platform, the security subsystem that forms a part of the operating system, which we refer to as the native operating system security subsystem (NOSSS), is the most fundamental layer of security software on the platform. As a result, it is a good idea to make other security software compatible with its requirements rather than the other way around. In terms of a software strategy, therefore, we aim to use the principle of defense in depth to reinforce or complement the features of the NOSSS while taking care not to introduce any security mechanisms that are likely to be in conflict with its requirements.

Features offered by the NOSSS are reasonably standard and usually include such basic protection mechanisms as access control to files and devices, authentication to the OS itself, and logging facilities. Unfortunately, the details of how these features are deployed vary considerably from platform to platform, which complicates the task of defining homogeneous requirements over multiple platforms.

One of the dangers of investing heavily in third-party tools is that it may result in a change of focus away from the NOSSS, leading to underutilization or even neglect of the basic security mechanisms. Equivalently, although they offer many advantages, one of the disadvantages of tools that offer security management functionality over a wide range of heterogeneous platforms is that they deskill the administration process and may discourage the use of facilities offered by the NOSSS but which they do not support.

It is worth mentioning that certain vendors include *trusted operating systems* in their commercial offering. Trusted OSs are evaluated according to formal criteria such as Trusted Computer Systems Evaluation Criteria (TCSEC) and can add value in certain circumstances. However, when deploying a trusted OS, it is important to understand the criteria against which the system is being evaluated and therefore the type of risk that is being mitigated. Furthermore, this risk needs to be evaluated in the context of the system under scrutiny. Finally, extra security often comes at the expense of reduced functionality, and some applications may simply not execute on such operating systems. As an alternative to using a trusted OS, consider "stripping down" the system and using a host-based security scanner to check the final configuration.

3.3.3 Authentication and authorization

3.3.3.1 Authentication

Authentication is the process by which a user (which may be a person or a piece of software in this context) proves their identity to a system or application offering a service. By requiring authentication, systems are able to restrict their services to those authorized to use them. Access control techniques can then be used to further restrict access as appropriate. Note, however, that access control relies on the authentication process to verify the identity of the user.

Because most people in today's organizations access systems and applications over local area networks (LANs) or via remote access connections, authentication is usually considered a network issue. As such, authentication protocols and network authentication schemes will be presented in Section 3.4.1. Authentication devices, such as biometric devices and hand-held tokens, are discussed in Section 3.5.3.

3.3.3.2 Privilege managers

Privilege managers allow system administrators to give users in a controlled fashion the ability to run selective commands under an administrator account. This effectively removes the requirement to share the administrator account between several administrators. Privilege managers are therefore used to secure the operating system and do not operate at the support software or application layers.

Privilege managers have had the biggest success in the UNIX world, where they are often used to exercise more control over use of the root account (the UNIX root account is the super user on the system and has virtually unlimited powers). Probably the best-known privilege manager is the sudo utility, which dates back to the early 1980s, although it was not released into the public domain until 1986 [4]. This functionality is also available from commercial software suppliers.

Privilege management software enables the system administrator to define under what conditions a user, or group of users, can execute a limited set of commands under a different user account than their own (usually, but not necessarily, the root account). In order to execute commands under a different account, the user submits these commands to the privilege management software using a modified command syntax. The latter then parses the command, evaluates it against a set of predefined rules stored in a configuration file, and executes the command on behalf of the user if the rules are not transgressed. In addition, the details of the interaction are logged.

As an interesting aside, note that the privilege management software itself needs to have the privileges associated with the root account to achieve this. On UNIX systems, this is achieved by making the root account the owner of the executables and setting the set user identity (SUID) bit. As a general rule, executables that have the SUID [or less commonly the set group identity (SGID) bit] set should be subject to more stringent controls (see [5] for details).

In a multiplatform environment, users will use client software to send commands to the privilege-management software residing on a separate machine. The latter will authenticate the user, verify that the command is permitted, and instruct a process running on the target machine to execute the command under the required user account. This scheme therefore involves three different machines: the client machine, the secure server, and the target machine. In this configuration, it is usual to protect the network communications using a secure protocol.

3.3.4 System integrity

3.3.4.1 Security scanners

Security scanners essentially come in two flavors: host oriented and network oriented. Host-oriented scanners are discussed in this section and network-oriented scanners are discussed in Section 3.4.2.1.

Security scanners work by periodically monitoring the actual configuration of the platform under scrutiny and comparing this with the desired target configuration as specified by a predefined security baseline. For the purposes of this discussion, a security baseline is a technical definition of the ideal security configuration for any given platform or network. Although security scanners are capable of operating at all layers illustrated in Figure 3.2, in practice commercial scanners capable of operating at the application level are relatively rare, as they require detailed knowledge of the application they are scanning. For similar reasons, the availability of scanners for database, middleware, and other components depends on the popularity of the software in question. In reality, therefore, the main use of vulnerability scanning software is to secure the operating system itself.

Security scanning is used mainly in mid-range environments because the security of mid-range systems usually depends on the correct setting of a large number of configuration options. Depending on the operating system, it may be possible to store important configuration files in a variety of locations. As a result, these options tend to be complex and difficult to track manually. Unfortunately, small changes to many of these options can have a drastic impact on the overall level of security of the system, and such changes can occur due to a variety of reasons:

 ‣ *Through human error*. This often happens when system administrators are working under pressure.

 ‣ *Through ignorance*. For instance, users of UNIX systems are able to install certain files in their home directories in order to allow other users to access their account (these files are known as .rhosts files and are a well known source of problems for system administrators).

 ‣ *As a consequence of installing new software*. It is not uncommon for application software to require undesirable configuration options to be enabled in order to function correctly.

In medium-to-large environments, it is almost impossible to manage such complexity without having recourse to automated tools.

Figure 3.3 illustrates how security scanners are used to secure complex environments. A typical deployment involves agent software running on a series of target platforms, a management station, and user interface software. The agent software performs the actual scanning and makes the results available as a report to the management station, which collates the data for the entire network. The administrator uses a client interface to access the results of the scan.

The agent software is specific to the operating system and usually comes with a preconfigured database of common vulnerabilities and a selection of predefined policies. These vulnerabilities and policies are used as a starting point for defining site-specific security baselines and scanning policies. Typically, the vendor will offer periodic updates to the database (or an on-line method of obtaining such updates) as part of the support contract. Tools

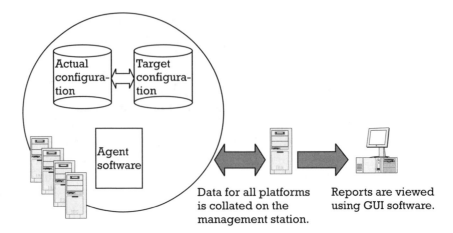

Data for all platforms   Reports are viewed
is collated on the   using GUI software.
management station.

Agent software verifies actual
configuration against target configuration.
Discrepancies are published as a report.

Figure 3.3   Using vulnerability scanners to secure mid-range systems.

may also offer additional features, such as simple password cracking software and the ability to monitor changes to file content (e.g., by storing a keyed hash of files).

Most commercial security scanners are capable of presenting detected deviations from the target baseline in the form of a report, often making use of powerful graphical presentation tools. This ability to summarize data describing vulnerabilities in terms of high-level reports containing graphical displays is extremely useful when creating reports for higher management. Some tools also offer the capability of "correcting" the situation automatically, but this type of functionality should be used with great care, as correcting security vulnerabilities can have a major impact on the way in which systems function. It is therefore advisable to estimate the impact of such changes before carrying them out.

The key point about security scanners is that the degree to which they are effective in reducing risk is linked to two factors:

1.   The extent to which the underlying security baselines represent the desired risk profile of the organization;

2.   The efficiency of the correction process following discovery of vulnerabilities.

If these two factors are correctly managed, security scanners are capable of bringing a lot of additional control into distributed environments.

3.3.4.2   Antivirus software

Computer viruses and other objects implementing malicious code constitute a threat to system integrity, as, for the most part, they operate by installing themselves on the local platform and then use this as a base for propagating further.

The concept behind antivirus software is simple to understand. Every time a piece of malicious code is discovered, it is examined with the aim of identifying some part of its structure that is particular to itself. This element of structure can therefore be regarded as a sort of *signature*, which can be used to detect its presence at a later date. Simply put, antivirus software operates by searching for these signatures and executing a set of removal instructions once the signature is found. In reality, however, the job of antivirus software is considerably more complex than this because the writers of malicious code have found various ways to defeat this simple defense mechanism. These techniques include infecting hitherto untouched objects and using new programming techniques (such as the use of encryption to hide the signature).

As a result of these developments, current antivirus software is designed to operate at both the application layer and the operating system layer, and it is capable of scanning a wide range of objects, such as memory, files, file attachments, e-mails, and boot sectors. In addition, scans are no longer limited to simple detection of the signature. They may involve a number of more advanced techniques, such as decryption and execution in an isolated environment. For a more detailed discussion on how antivirus software works, together with tips on how to identify a good scanner, see [6].

3.3.4.3 Content scanners

Content scanners complement traditional antivirus software by analyzing the content of messages, e-mails, or downloaded code; evaluating this against a predefined security policy; and performing some action when content is detected that does not meet the policy requirements. Because content scanners usually inspect objects that are in transit between one system and another, they operate at the application layer. This approach is potentially more powerful than signature-based detection, as it can incorporate rules based on a variety of criteria and is not limited to recognition of what are essentially static properties of malicious code objects.

Content-filtering software varies largely in scope and sophistication. This ranges from simple e-mail content scanners, which are able to perform lexical analysis and quarantine mail containing certain words or phrases, to sophisticated content-scanning engines capable of performing real-time inspection of incoming messages and code downloaded from Internet sites. At least one product is capable of analyzing the behavior of downloaded code and evaluating this against policy statements that reflect acceptable behavior. This is particularly useful for performing security checks against mobile code (Java, JavaScript, and ActiveX).

Most content scanners provide several ways of dealing with a policy violation once detected and allow the administrator to configure the appropriate action on a rule-by-rule basis. In the case of e-mail content scanners, options may include quarantine of the mail, removal of infected attachments followed by delivery of the text message, or dropping the mail completely. Content scanners analyzing mobile code may block the download, transmit the suspicious content to a third party for analysis, perform varied levels of logging, and potentially send an alert to the user.

In order to add more value to the end user, content-filtering products are continually evolving to incorporate new features. Certain Web filters now have the ability to recognize and respond to content, e-mail filters incorporating antivirus agents already exist, and antivirus software is starting to incorporate some of the features associated with content scanners. The net result is likely to be a convergence of these product areas in the near future.

3.3.5 System access control

3.3.5.1 Access management tools

Access management software is used to manage the rules according to which users may access resources. We distinguish between mainframe access control facilities and multiplatform solutions. The former are limited to mainframe systems, as most other OSs include this functionality in the NOSSS. The latter, also known as enterprise user administration (EUA) tools, are capable of interacting with existing NOSSS features for a variety of platforms and aim to enable centralized access management in a distributed environment.

Mainframe access control software is among the most mature security software in the market at the current time. Access control facilities for mainframe OSs secure objects recognized by the operating system and therefore improve the security of the OS layer of software. Such facilities are necessary, as the OS does not offer such facilities natively (whereas mid-range systems usually include this functionality as part of the NOSSS). These packages have dominated the mainframe security landscape for the past 25 years and are likely to maintain this position for the foreseeable future. Given the stability of such products, together with the fact that their mode of operation is well understood, we will quickly summarize the main functionality of such packages and concentrate on multiplatform solutions.

Access control software for mainframe operating systems typically covers the following functionality:

- Authentication of users;
- Provision of a framework for the protection of resources—this framework allows administrators to define the access rights of users or groups of users to particular resources;
- Provision of an interface allowing applications to interact with the software and to make use of the authentication and access management functionality;
- Verification of level of authorization and access control;
- Generation of audit trails.

In contrast to mainframe access control facilities, EUA software was developed to solve the problems associated with managing access rights across a range of operating systems, databases, and applications, each equipped with its own security model. These problems include:

▸ Difficulty in obtaining an overview of access control data spanning several machines and software products;

▸ The need to carry out changes to user account details and access rights on each system—this is both time-consuming and prone to error;

▸ Limitations in moving administrators from one type of system to another, due to the need to develop administration expertise for each particular system;

▸ An inefficient authorization workflow associated with a low level of automation.

EUA software therefore aims to provide a single point of administration for managing access rights at all software layers and across multiple platforms. It is important to realize that EUA software provides a management interface to a diverse array of existing access control mechanisms. It does not directly implement the underlying security control mechanisms itself.

The most common architectural solution is similar to that used by host-oriented security scanners and involves agent software running on the target platforms, a management application capable of communicating with the agents, and user-interface software. Once the solution has been deployed, the creation, modification, or suppression of accounts or related access control information can usually be carried out either directly on the target platform or via the single point of administration associated with the EUA. The consistency of the central database maintained by the EUA system is assured by the dialogue between the EUA agent and the management application. Details of how this synchronization process works vary from product to product and may involve real-time or batch processes. In the latter case, there is a "window of risk" during which time target systems are not synchronized with the central database, which could lead to incorrect administration decisions.

The agent software is usually installed as an application, which runs on top of the NOSSS of the target platform (or the external access control facility software in the case of mainframe operating systems). As with security scanning software, this agent is specific to the underlying OS. Support for database, middleware, and application software is also provided through agent software, but this may involve deploying several agents. Some software packages offer an applications programming interface (API) to enable the support of proprietary applications. One consequence of using remote agent software is that particular implementations may not support all of the functionality of the native system. This being the case, it is worth analyzing in detail how the agent software interacts with the NOSSS, as any weakness here could potentially be used to defeat the system.

Communication between the central management system and the agents is usually protected using cryptographic techniques to prevent modification of the data in transit. Depending on the level of sophistication of the product, updates from the central server may be protected using standard transaction-protection mechanisms. The possibility to store incomplete transactions and initiate retries at regular intervals is useful when changes need to be made over several platforms but one of the target servers is down.

An alternative approach to using EUA software is to adopt metadirectory software to centralize access control data. This option is likely to be more attractive for organizations that have already invested in such a directory. While such a solution provides a centralization of data, it does not segregate security-related data from other personal data, and metadirectory software is unlikely to offer integration with current systems in the way that EUA software does. Such an approach may therefore require extensive customization and may lead to an overreliance on scripts that are locally developed.

3.3.6   System security monitoring

3.3.6.1   Host intrusion detection systems

Intrusion detection systems (IDS) are used to recognize indications of an intrusion attempt and to either warn the operator or execute corrective actions.

There are two broad classes of intrusion detection systems: network intrusion detection systems (NIDS) and host intrusion detection systems (HIDS). Both NIDS systems and HIDS systems analyze event data for signs of an attack, but the way in which they do this and the type of information they process is very different. The advantages and disadvantages are similar to those cited for security scanners (i.e., network-oriented tools will in general give greater scope of information but in less detail). Host-based tools will not provide a lot of information about the big picture, but will be capable of providing a detailed report for a specific host. Obviously, NIDS systems cannot respond to attacks that make no use of the network, which includes all attacks launched directly on the target system through a local interface.

In addition to classifying IDS solutions in terms of their operating environment, they are sometimes classified in terms of the detection principles they use [7]. This scheme distinguishes between systems using signature-detection techniques, systems using anomaly-detection techniques, and compound detectors. Signature-based systems are based on pattern-matching techniques and typically involve comparing log entries corresponding to events on the host with known attack signatures. Anomaly-detection systems search for anomalies in system utilization patterns.

HIDS systems may use a variety of mechanisms to detect possible intrusions. Currently, this software tends to use techniques such as pseudoreal-time analysis of audit trail information and integrity checks carried out against files. Certain products combine signature and anomaly-detection mechanisms and allow for rapid update of the signature database. HIDS software is usually designed for a particular operating system, which renders more advanced functionality possible, such as direct interception and interpretation of system calls. For products that rely heavily on audit trail information, the configuration of the local logging mechanisms will obviously have a big impact on the ability of the software to detect events. For systems such as these, attacks that provide access to the logging information itself may be capable of modifying the data on which the HIDS depends, which could prove to be a major limitation on the effectiveness of the overall approach.

Note that HIDS systems do not in general have to cope with encrypted data, and any remote attack using an encrypted tunnel to the target host will be decrypted before being processed by the host operating system.

Both NIDS and HIDS systems tend to be equipped with high-quality reporting mechanisms, including the ability to generate reports of varying levels of detail and generating graphical displays of information.

3.3.6.2 Log management tools

Log management tools are used to provide selective access to log information. In multiplatform environments, such tools can help to sensibly combine logging information collected on different platforms, which in turn enables administrators to follow attacks or suspicious events that affect more than one host. Because most software these days is able to provide log information, log management tools are used to secure all software layers.

Getting value out of audit logs in medium to large organizations is extremely difficult. Collecting the information is not usually a problem, although careful thought needs to be given to which events should be written to the audit log for any given application. Assuming that this has been done correctly, we are faced with a number of problems when trying to exploit the information contained in the resulting logs:

- There will usually be a large volume of data to be analyzed.
- Clear rules are required indicating which data needs to be analyzed proactively and which data will only be analyzed in response to a suspected incident.
- The possibility to place audit trail information in a multiplatform context is required in order to follow suspicious activity as it propagates through the network.

These problems have been recognized for some time within the industry and the Computer Operations, Audit, and Security Technology (COAST) Audit Trail Reduction Group at Purdue University was established to develop techniques for resolving them [8].

Log management tools can help to reduce the scale of the problem associated with the volume of data by providing the ability to use filters. Filters implement a set of rules for selecting a subset of data out of the data pool of interest and can be of great help if used correctly. The risk associated with using filters is that important data might be inadvertently "filtered out," and this may hamper the ability to detect and recognize events of importance. One of the problems with filtering data in a multiple platform environment is related to how this data is represented. Different platforms use different syntactical notations to represent the same type of event, and log management software must be intelligent enough to recognize this as an issue and deal with it accordingly. Ideally, the industry will eventually agree on a standard representation of audit data; this is indeed one of the goals of the COAST Audit Trail Reduction Group [8]. The existence of such a standard notation is important not only from a technical point of view, this will also help administrators concentrate on the problem at hand rather than requiring them to translate the raw data before interpreting it.

The second problem is a management issue, and tools are not likely to add much value here, although it might be interesting to be able to label audit trail data as destined for proactive or retroactive analysis.

The third problem turns out to be quite complex. In many environments, the clock time of the various platforms making up the environment is only approximately synchronized. There are protocols for achieving time synchronization across several platforms (such as the network time protocol (NTP) [9]), but these are not always implemented. However, in order to be able to organize logging data into the correct chronological order, it is necessary either to synchronize time across platforms to a suitable level of precision or to measure the offset and clock drift rate of the different platforms relative to some agreed point of reference. When the latter approach is adopted, the chronological order can be calculated. Small differences in timing may not make much difference for most attacks, but in some cases such a difference may prove to be important for determining the correct sequence of events. Time synchronization problems can also have an impact on the data presented by filters.

At the current time, most commercial solutions provide only a partial solution to these problems. In particular, many tools providing multiplatform support are integrated into more complex system management frameworks and cannot always be deployed as stand-alone components. It is interesting to note that tools for Web site log analysis and reporting are becoming quite sophisticated. Unfortunately, the emphasis is not on security events but on analyzing and displaying information related to customer site visits.

3.3.7 Data confidentiality and integrity

3.3.7.1 Cryptographic tools

Cryptography is essentially the art of concealing information by transforming it in such a way that a certain group of people can retrieve it in its original form and everyone else cannot. This is achieved by using some kind of key to effect the transformation. Those that are allowed to retrieve the original information are then provided with another key (which may be the same key or another related key) to undo the transformation. In modern commercial cryptographic implementations, the security is always in the key and not in the algorithm. Among other things, this is in recognition that it is practically impossible to keep algorithms secret in the commercial world, whereas keeping individual keys secret is a manageable problem. Readers who are interested in cryptography and how it works are referred to Bruce Schneier's book [10]. This section will assume a basic knowledge of modern cryptography and concentrate on how it is applied in practice.

Cryptography is used within security architectures to implement certain specific security services, notably authentication, confidentiality, integrity, and non-repudiation. Where host security is concerned, cryptographic tools are used mainly to protect the confidentiality and integrity of data. Requirements for cryptographic authentication and non-repudiation are more common in network environments.

Perhaps the most intuitive use of cryptography is the use of encryption techniques to ensure the confidentiality of data. In fact, although cryptography can be used to implement other security services, such as authentication and non-repudiation, it is always this property of rendering something inaccessible that is acting behind the scenes. Encryption techniques can range from encryption of the entire hard disk (often used to protect the data stored on portable computers in the case of loss or theft) to more selective approaches such as database encryption and file encryption. Finer granularity is also possible, but the finer the granularity, the more effort it takes to implement the requirement (as the software performing the encryption needs to determine when a piece of data meets the criteria for encryption).

A less obvious use of cryptography is to protect the integrity of data. The idea here is to create a fingerprint of the data to be protected (this is usually achieved using a message digest or hash function) and to encrypt and store this information in a safe place. Should any unauthorized persons succeed in modifying the file, they will not be able to recalculate the encrypted hash, as they do not possess the necessary key. Hence, when a bona-fide user verifies the integrity of the file by recalculating the encrypted hash and comparing it against the stored value, the two will not match and it will be evident that the file has been tampered with. Security scanners often use this technique to detect when files have been modified.

3.3.7.2 Content scanners and e-mail filters

Content scanners and e-mail filters are able to analyze the content of downloaded mobile code or e-mail messages to detect potential security violations and to carry out actions in response to the threat. In Section 3.3.4.3, we explained how such functionality is useful in protecting the integrity of the OS. In this section, we note that the same functionality can be used to directly protect the integrity of data.

Consider, for example, an employee exchanging pornographic material with a series of contacts outside the enterprise. One way to do this would be to simply embed the images or text in e-mail messages. Content scanners are able to detect both embedded images and inappropriate text and to quarantine the mail for further analysis. In this example, the content scanning software is directly concerned with the security of the data itself.

3.4   Network-oriented tools

3.4.1   Network authentication and authorization

3.4.1.1   Authentication protocols

One of the major problems associated with existing TCP/IP networks is the ease with which data traveling over the network can be captured and analyzed. This problem has little to do with the TCP/IP protocols themselves, but is related to the way the underlying LAN protocols work. The result is the same, however—data traveling as clear text over TCP/IP networks is exposed to prying eyes. As a consequence, any authentication mechanism relying on clear text passwords, or indeed any predictable exchange of data, is not secure in a network environment.

Securing network equipment is part of the solution to this problem, but it does not address the fact that third parties can often use their own equipment to access a network and run *sniffers* and similar tools. Similarly, where wide area networks, and particularly the Internet, are concerned, we cannot rely on others to implement and maintain security mechanisms that we think are appropriate. It is therefore necessary to incorporate the security mechanisms into the data exchange itself, and the usual way of doing this is to make use of standard authentication protocols. Note, however, that authentication is not the same as establishment of a secure session, and any connection that does not employ additional measures, such as encryption or integrity-protection mechanisms, could be open to hijacking techniques [11].

In the simplest case, user authentication may involve entering a password over an established secure session [such as a secure sockets layer (SSL) session]. This method of authenticating users is often used for Web applications on the Internet. This is not really an example of an authentication protocol, however, as it is the underlying protocol that is protecting the transport of the password.

Most authentication protocols are based on the idea of a challenge-response protocol. The basic idea is that the system requiring proof of identity and the user will initially use some out-of-band mechanism to share a cryptographic secret. When the user wishes to gain access, they will identify themselves to the system, which will respond with a *random* challenge. The user will transform this challenge using their secret and send it back to the system, which will use the same secret to undo the transformation and retrieve the original value. This is indeed proof of identity, as the assumption is that the user is the only person having access to the secret required to perform the necessary transformation. Note that if the challenge were not random, a third party could masquerade as the target system, issue a future value of the challenge to the user, retrieve the transformed challenge, and use it to gain access.

Authentication protocols are a subject in themselves, and secure protocols tend to be quite complex and difficult to devise. An example of this complexity is provided by the Needham-Schroeder protocol used by Kerberos [12] (even here, D. E. Denning and G. M. Sacco identified a flaw that would enable an attacker to reuse an old key [13]).

3.4.1.2 Authentication and authorization servers

Authentication servers are used to centralize the authentication process in a network environment. Authorization servers go one stage further by associating a set of privileges or access rights with the authenticated entity. While authentication and authorization servers are not necessarily associated with accessing systems from a remote network location [a Windows primary domain controller (PDC) effectively acts as an authentication server for Windows clients on the local network], they are most commonly used to support this requirement.

Authentication and authorization servers provide corresponding services to a series of clients following a client-server architecture. They are capable of securing all layers of software depicted in Figure 3.2 as long as the client is equipped with the appropriate interface and is configured correctly. Servers may optionally offer accounting functionality, usually with the intent to support the billing process rather than to offer additional security. Cisco refers to servers that offer authentication, authorization, and accounting as AAA servers [14].

A typical example of how authentication and authorization servers work involves a remote user dialing in to the organization's networks over the PSTN. A device known as a network access server (NAS) receives the connection from the PSTN and allows the connection to the requested internal host after having verified the identity of the user and after applying any access restrictions. The NAS can therefore be thought of as a device that talks to the PSTN on one interface and the LAN on the other. In order to authenticate the user and apply access restrictions, the NAS can either use a local database or, more commonly, it can use the services of a dedicated authentication or authorization server.

In the latter configuration, the NAS plays the role of an intermediary between the user and the server by passing on any request for information from the server to the client and returning the response to the server. As the next section explains, the NAS often uses another intermediate server to do this, rather than talking directly to the server—this enables an NAS to use a single point of contact to dialogue with several authentication or authorization servers. When the server has enough information to accept or deny the request, it sends its response to the NAS, which executes the decision by rejecting the connection or allowing it according to a set of predefined rules.

The details of the authentication method to be used and how access rights will be managed are under the control of the local organization, which enables this architecture to support a variety of technologies including simple passwords, tokens, and smart cards.

The flexibility of being able to support a variety of authentication and authorization methods is achieved by deploying standard, application-level protocols between the NAS and the security server. These protocols are designed to support a generic exchange between the NAS and the server that is not dependent on the details of the authentication or authorization process. There are two major protocols in common use today: the RADIUS protocol [15] and the TACACS+ protocol [16]. Apart from minor details, these two protocols are functionally very similar [14].

Figure 3.4 illustrates how the RADIUS protocol is used by an NAS to allow a remote user access. The sequence of events is as follows:

1. The user initiates a dial-up connection to the NAS. The latter prompts for a user name and password, which the user submits to the NAS as the user request.

2. The NAS, acting as a RADIUS client, sends an Access-Request message to the RADIUS server.

3. The RADIUS server passes the authentication data to the authentication server. This may involve the use of proprietary protocols.

4. The authentication server allows or rejects the request.

5. The RADIUS server responds to the NAS using an Access-Accept or an Access-Reject message, depending on the results of the authentication.

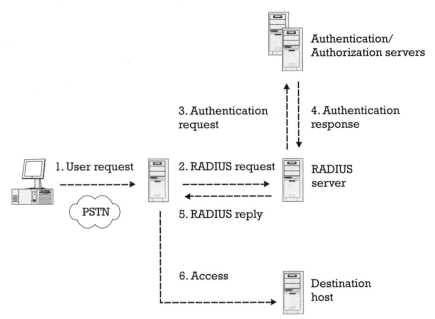

Figure 3.4 The RADIUS protocol.

6. If the authentication was successful, the NAS server allows access to the destination host.

The use of authentication and authorization servers can considerably enhance the security of remote access solutions, but the actual level of security achieved is dependent on the details of the particular authentication and authorization methods implemented. As such, simple password-based mechanisms probably do not add much security, whereas a cryptographic challenge-response mechanism would represent a considerable barrier to an attacker. The choice of the appropriate mechanism will depend on the level of risk the organization associates with the use of PSTN lines (for instance, if the incoming connection passes through a private automated branch exchange (PABX), the degree to which it is possible to secure this device will enter into the risk assessment). However, even assuming a highly secure implementation, the techniques of authentication and authorization do not protect the data exchanged between the user and the internal system once the connection has been allowed. For this reason, it is often appropriate to go one step further and deploy a secure protocol between the end user and a suitable termination point behind the NAS. Depending on the protocol deployed, this will allow not only protection of the data, but may also protect the integrity of the session itself.

Extranet access management (EAM) software is a relatively new development in this area and is concerned with providing authentication and authorization services in an extranet context (as opposed to remote access). EAM software is particularly associated with Web-enabled applications and is typically designed to support a high degree of scalability.

3.4.2 Network integrity

3.4.2.1 Network security scanners

Network security scanners are similar in concept to host security scanners. Their purpose is to scan the network looking for things that shouldn't be there and for potential vulnerabilities.

The simplest network scanners do little more than provide a map of what devices are on the network by using simple probes, such as the Internet Control Message Protocol (ICMP) echo request message (commonly known as *ping*). One level up from these simple command-line utilities are simple tools capable of performing port mapping; by probing individual TCP or User Datagram Protocol (UDP) ports on detected hosts, these tools can both map out the network and identify which network services are operating.

Commercial tools, while using similar techniques, are much more powerful and come equipped with databases containing information on known vulnerabilities. Network-oriented security scanners are based on similar principles to host-oriented scanners (i.e., they compare the actual configuration of the network and hosts to a predefined target situation and report on the differences). In general, network-oriented scanners are capable of providing greater breadth of information (as they are not limited to a single platform), but they may not offer the level of detail that host-oriented scanners are able to offer.

Network vulnerability scanners tend to follow a common architectural approach involving a module responsible for carrying out the scans, a database containing information on known vulnerabilities, a module responsible for report generation and presentation, and user-interface software. Typically, the scanning engine is policy driven, allowing the administrator to tailor the scanning process to particular requirements. The output of the scanning engine is checked against the vulnerability database in order to identify current vulnerabilities. Finally, the results are available via a reporting interface. This is illustrated in Figure 3.5.

The effectiveness of network security scanners depends on similar factors to host-oriented scanners:

- The extent to which the vulnerability database represents the current threat environment, which in turn depends on how frequently it is updated by the supplier;

- The location of the scanning machine in the network topology—in particular, the location of scanners with respect to devices capable of blocking network traffic (such as firewalls and filtering routers) needs to be carefully planned;

- The appropriateness of the scanning policy;

- The efficiency of the correction process following discovery of vulnerabilities.

The last point is, of course, the most important. Knowing where the vulnerabilities lie is certainly a step in the right direction, but removing them is what makes the difference!

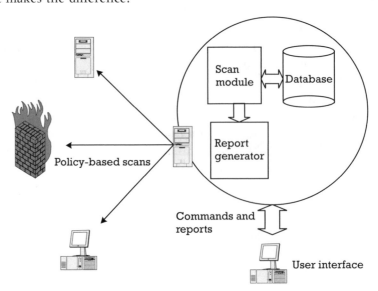

Figure 3.5 Network security scanners.

3.4.2.2 Telephone scanners

Telephone scanning software is the commercial evolution of what is known as war dialing software in the hacking and phreaking community [17]. It is used to identify potential security weaknesses accessible through the telephone system.

Telephone scanning is conceptually quite similar to network vulnerability scanning (see Section 3.4). The idea is to use specialized software to dial a series of phone numbers to perform a certain number of security checks and report on the results [17]. As such, telephone scanners can be used to construct a security map of the organization's telephone system, much as network security scanners can be used to construct a map of the LAN environment using IP mapping techniques.

Telephone scanners are used to detect vulnerable paths into the enterprise network that are accessible from the PSTN. In particular, they are used to detect unauthorized or unknown modems present on the LAN and able to accept incoming calls. In terms of the type of vulnerability they detect, current scanners use probing techniques in combination with recognition of prompts to report on weaknesses at the OS level (e.g., a UNIX system with a weak password) and at the application level (e.g., a remote access system with no password).

As the control of modems is often achieved through procedural solutions (although certain software, notably asset management software, may be used to detect the presence of modems automatically), telephone scanners offer considerable scope for improving the detection rate of unauthorized installations by automating the detection process.

Current commercial software is extremely sophisticated and offers a range of configuration options, enabling the operator to tailor the scan to specific requirements. In particular, considerable flexibility is provided for specifying which numbers are to be dialed and under what conditions. The numbers to be scanned can be entered individually or in ranges, and dialing prefixes can often be used to simplify the configuration rules (numbers can also be omitted where necessary). Scans can be programmed to occur at certain times of the day, and it is possible to further control the scanning process by defining a set of logical constraints on the scan process itself. Typical logical constraints include the ability to stop redialing occupied numbers after a certain number of retries, to use sequential or random dialing, and to define the period of lapsed time between calls.

Certain tools also support different modes of operation, allowing the operator to choose between passive identification of the computer system answering the call or a more aggressive penetration attempt. The latter typically involves trying common username/password combinations but has the potential to evolve into complex penetration scenarios determined by the type of software detected. This potential for evolution can be appreciated by comparison with the Security Administrator Tool for Analyzing Networks (SATAN) network security tool [18]. This particular tool, which essentially operates as a network security scanner, includes an inference engine capable of modifying the scan process itself to take into account the results of data already processed [18] (and this feature has since been incorporated into certain commercial tools).

Depending on the particular solution selected, a distributed solution may also be supported. Such solutions allow for the deployment of a series of remotely installed dialers under the control of a central management station and may allow for encrypted communications between the remote and central components. This feature could be used to carry out a series of parallel scans from different locations, thereby decreasing the time required to perform a complete scan. At least one commercial offering has developed this architectural approach by integrating a firewall-like device, capable of exercising some degree of access control on connections.

In most cases, these features are supported by an easy-to-use GUI. Similarly, current tools offer the ability to produce several different types of reports and may also allow the operator to customize reports to his or her own requirements. In particular, if the scan data is stored in a relational database, it may be possible to access it using Structured Query Language (SQL). Of particular interest here is the ability to produce difference reports, indicating what has changed since the last scan was carried out. This facility can considerably decrease the time required to analyze the important information.

3.4.3   Network access control

3.4.3.1   Firewalls

A firewall is a device, or a combination of devices, that enforces an access control policy between two or more network segments. In this book, the word firewall is always used to refer to a collection of devices, compatible with the idea that firewalls are architectural solutions incorporating the idea of defense in depth. The term *commercial firewall* will be used to refer to firewall products.

As there are many excellent books on firewall technology, this section will be limited to a very brief description of what firewalls are and what they do. Interested readers are pointed towards more specialized texts for a more complete description [19–22].

Firewalls allow or deny connections from one network to another based on a set of rather low-level rules expressed in terms of protocol data. This data is taken from layers 3 to 7 of the protocol stack as defined by the OSI model [1]. In the TCP/IP world, we normally think of layers 5, 6, and 7 as being part of the application, so rules for allowing or denying access are based on network layer, transport layer, and application-level information. Firewalls do not in general recognize non-TCP/IP protocols, and they have to be specially configured to recognize and deal with application-level traffic. From this brief description, it should be evident that firewalls have a very limited set of data with which they can work, and this places limits on what they can reasonably achieve. In recognition of this limitation, most modern commercial firewalls now include functionality for authenticating users, which is a major step forward, as this enables us to relate a network connection to a person rather than to a network address.

Two important classes of commercial firewall software operate using different principles but achieve similar results. Commercial firewalls using the stateful filtering approach route IP packets from one network interface to the other directly. Stateful filtering mechanisms build on simple packet-filtering techniques [23]. The firewall software intercepts packets at the network layer as they are being routed and analyzes protocol information from layers 3 to 7, together with information describing the "state" of the connection in order to determine whether the packet should be dropped or allowed to proceed on its journey. For connectionless protocols, such as UDP, this is achieved using a *virtual session* concept in which state information is stored by the firewall software even though the protocol itself is stateless.

Application-level firewalls, also known as application-gateway firewalls or proxy firewalls, do not directly route packets. Incoming packets are processed by the communications software and handed to a specialized application capable of understanding the particular high-level protocol being used. Because they enforce controls at the application layer, proxy firewalls are application specific, which means that every time a new protocol is developed, a new proxy is required to secure it. In reality, most proprietary protocols do not have an associated proxy, and proxy servers are used mainly to control standard, RFC-based Internet protocols such as file transfer protocol (FTP) and hypertext transfer protocol (HTTP).

The mode of operation of stateful filtering firewalls is compared with that of application-gateway firewalls in Figure 3.6.

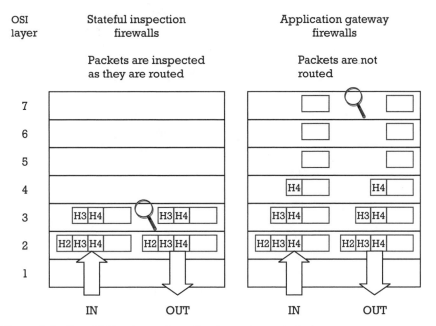

Figure 3.6 Stateful filtering and application-gateway techniques.

In the last few years the distinction between the two technologies has been somewhat blurred due to many vendors now marketing hybrid solutions, incorporating features from both types of model.

3.4.3.2 Proxy servers

Proxy servers are only mentioned briefly here, because, as far as security is concerned, they function in a similar way to application-gateway firewalls [24]. Whereas firewalls are concerned with network access control for both inbound and outbound traffic, the focus of proxy servers is on controlling connections that originate within the enterprise. In this capacity, proxy servers are able to add value by requiring authentication of the end user, restricting communication to a defined set of protocols, applying access control restrictions, and carrying out auditing and logging.

It is important to note, however, that generalized proxy servers, and in particular Web proxy servers (which are probably the most common type of proxy server in deployment these days), are not used for security alone. For instance, one of the most important functions of Web proxy servers is that of caching data to improve performance. Strictly speaking, therefore, proxy servers are not security tools and are more correctly regarded as multifunctional tools, which nevertheless implement important security functionality.

3.4.3.3 Web filters

Web filters are used to control access of internal employees to Web sites. These tools allow the administrator to selectively block access to certain types of Web sites based on a local policy.

Web filtering products permit or block access to external Web sites on the basis of a locally defined policy. In reality, these tools are used as much to control employee productivity as to increase site security. Web filters do, however, help control Internet risk by preventing users from accessing sites that are likely to host inappropriate content or malicious code.

The decision to allow or block any particular request is made by consulting an underlying database of potentially problematic Web sites, which is maintained and regularly updated by the software vendor. Certain products also support agent software, which is used to analyze which Web sites are being accessed by the organization and to update the database accordingly. This allows organizations to develop a database customized to meet their particular requirements.

As the interpretation of "problematic" varies considerably from organization to organization, sites are classified by topic, providing the administrator with the flexibility to define which sites are acceptable for a particular implementation. The degree to which this can be fine tuned varies from product to product, but tools will typically include the ability to block certain categories of sites, apply time-of-day restrictions, and define the way in which attempted accesses are monitored.

Web filter products are used not only to deny access to certain categories of Web sites, but also to monitor activity by providing reports on usage. Tools that support the notion of users and groups are able to provide statistics showing which groups of users are accessing which categories of sites and information relating to individuals. This can be useful for following certain types of suspicious behavior but may also have implications for privacy. The major commercial offerings provide a range of predefined reports and the ability to create customized reports.

3.4.4 Network security monitoring

3.4.4.1 NIDS

Most NIDS systems operate at layer 2 of the OSI model. Software solutions place the network interface card (NIC) in promiscuous mode (which is a privileged operation on most systems), thereby gaining real-time access to all network traffic that this interface receives. It is important to realize that this is not limited to frames destined for the NIC in question because the IEEE 802.3 (or *Ethernet* protocol) is a broadcast protocol [25]. This is exactly how network analyzers and sniffing tools work [26]. However, the widespread adoption of switching techniques within LANs has effectively limited the visibility that any particular NIC has of traffic that does not cross the same network segment, with the result that the location of NIDS software within the network topology is a critical design decision. Another factor to be taken into account when deploying NIDS technology is the ability of such software to handle high throughput, which has been an issue for high traffic volumes in the past [27].

NIDS systems are complementary to HIDS systems in that they are capable of retrieving and analyzing protocol information that is not available to the host and would not therefore be picked up by HIDS systems. That they operate at the network layer also renders such systems OS independent, enabling them to protect a wide range of target platforms.

Because of the similarities in the way they work, NIDS software also shares several limitations with current firewall technologies. Just as a firewall has to understand a protocol in order to make access-related decisions based on the information it contains, NIDS software cannot detect protocol anomalies without such an understanding. Obviously, neither firewalls nor NIDS systems can interpret encrypted data, and any security architecture combining firewalls, network encryption, and NIDS software should take these limitations into account.

Network intrusion detection software can also play an important role in managing malicious code in that it can be configured to recognize certain signatures and take some predefined action. This is extremely useful in the period between the initial description of a malicious code attack and the availability of the first pattern files. Network intrusion detection software can also be configured to prevent infected objects from passing out of the organization, which is a useful mechanism to prevent malicious software spreading to third parties in the unfortunate event of an uncontrolled internal infection.

The response of an NIDS system to an identified event may be a simple notification, some form of active countermeasure, or a combination of the two. Notification techniques include reporting the problem to the monitor screen, generating Simple Network Management Protocol (SNMP) alerts, dialing pagers, and similar responses. Active countermeasures include such actions as terminating connections by interacting with the firewall software. Active countermeasures should be deployed with extreme care, as there is considerable potential to cause interruption of normal service. In the case of *false positives*, the resulting action might prevent a valid business transaction from occurring.

3.4.5 Data confidentiality and integrity

3.4.5.1 Cryptographic tools and protocols

The most interesting use of cryptography is in securing data when traveling over networks. Cryptography is extremely valuable in this context, as there is usually no realistic alternative. In particular, the concept of access control, as it is applied to host-based resources, does not exist in the same sense for networks. Techniques such as packet filtering in the TCP/IP world and the establishment of closed user groups in the X.25 world can be used to control access between two networks, but neither of these techniques can be used to protect data while it is traveling "on the wire."

To secure data traveling over potentially hostile networks, specially designed secure protocols are used. These protocols implement one or more of the following network security services:

- Authentication;
- Protection of confidentiality;
- Protection of integrity;
- Non-repudiation.

Of these services, authentication protocols are associated more with users and devices than with data, although both digital signatures and message authentication codes (MACs) can be used to authenticate the origin of the data they protect[1].

Protection of confidentiality of network data is accomplished using encryption. For performance reasons, the standard approach is to use public-key cryptography to agree on a symmetric key and to use this symmetric key for the duration of the session to perform the bulk encryption.

---

1. Note however that MACs are based on symmetric cryptography, so this binding is not absolute because the key is shared (and therefore cannot be irrefutably linked with the sender). This is not important from an authentication perspective, as the party that shares the key is the authenticating party. It is, of course, important in the context of non-repudiation.

For this reason, the symmetric key is often known as a session key. There are two main techniques for agreeing on a session key: use of a key-establishment protocol such as the Diffie-Hellmann protocol [28] or generation of a symmetric key and transfer under the protection of the public key of the remote party [29]. This sensibly combines the advantages of asymmetric and symmetric algorithms by using asymmetric algorithms to simplify the key distribution process and symmetric algorithms to perform the encryption.

Protection of integrity within network environments is complicated by the fact that we need to consider two different types of integrity—data integrity and session integrity. The concept of data integrity is easy to understand—we aim to ensure that information arrives at its destination in the same state that it left the sender (i.e., that the data has not been modified in any way). Protocols handle data integrity by using techniques such as MAC and digital signatures [10].

Session integrity aims to ensure that the characteristics of the communications session are not modified in any way. In particular, techniques for ensuring session integrity aim to protect against insertion, deletion, or reordering of packets. Although this concept is not quite as intuitive as that of data integrity, it is not hard to appreciate that the ability to "replay" an instruction to transfer money from one account to another could have serious repercussions for a banking system. Similarly, military instructions arriving in the wrong order could have a major impact on the course of action. Techniques for ensuring session integrity are usually based on the inclusion of sequence numbers or timestamps in protected messages.

Non-repudiation services are the least intuitive of all and are concerned with preventing participants in an exchange from denying (or "repudiating") the actions they carried out within the exchange at a later date. It turns out to be more difficult to prevent the receiver of a message from repudiating their role than it is to prevent the sender from doing so. In order to be in a position to prove that the sender sent a particular message, the receiver must require that the sender systematically sign messages before sending them. If the sender later tries to repudiate a message, the receiver simply produces the signed message as irrefutable proof that the sender did in fact send that particular message. Should the sender wish to be able to prove that the receiver received a particular message, they must require that the receiver systematically generates a receipt acknowledgment for every message sent and that this acknowledgment is signed. If the receiver later tries to repudiate having received a message, the sender produces the signed receipt. Note that the distinction between a read acknowledgment and a receipt acknowledgment might be important here.

Examples of protocols that implement network security services include the SSL and the transport layer security (TLS) protocols [30], which are the preferred security protocols in Web environments and the IPSec protocol, which is the preferred protocol for implementing virtual private networks (VPNs) [31].

3.5 Supporting infrastructure

3.5.1 PKI

Public key cryptography, also known as asymmetric cryptography, is one of the essential components of modern network security for many reasons. First, it scales better than symmetric cryptography, as each participant needs only one pair of keys to communicate with everyone else (as opposed to sharing a key with each participant). Second, it *partly* solves the key distribution problem associated with symmetric cryptography. Finally, asymmetric cryptography is exactly that—asymmetric. By associating a unique and private key with each participant, public cryptography provides a way for secure protocols to link actions to individuals, thereby enabling digital signatures and non-repudiation.

The Achilles heel of public key cryptography lies in the second point. In order to reap the benefits of public key cryptography, we need to *trust* the relationship between any participant and their public key. While we do not need to go to extreme lengths to keep public keys from prying eyes (which is required when distributing symmetric keys), the price we pay is the difficulty in associating these keys with their true owners. The most common way of associating public keys with their owners is to use certificates. A certificate is an electronic document that links a public key to the name of the owner in a secure fashion by using a trusted third party [known as the certification authority (CA)] to guarantee the relationship.

A PKI is a coherent implementation of technical, procedural, and legal components aimed at allowing relying parties (those who rely on certificates when participating in a transaction) to trust the binding between a public key and the name of the owner. The extent to which users can rely on this binding depends on the process that the organization issuing the certificates uses to verify the identity of the person to whom the certificate is issued. For the record, a PKI does not in general tell us anything about the trustworthiness of the subscriber or how he or she is likely to react to any trust we extend to them by using their certificate. While the checks carried out by the issuing authority prior to issuance of a certificate *may* provide relying parties with indications as to how trustworthy the subscriber is, this is by no means a requirement. Examples of such checks might be the verification that physical persons have not been in trouble with the law or ensuring that commercial organizations are operating within the framework of legal and regulatory requirements expected of them.

In order to help relying parties make an informed decision about whether to use a certificate, the CA typically describes the practices and processes that it uses to carry out its daily business in a document known as the certificate practice statement (CPS). In addition, the rules and limitations associated with the use of any particular type of certificate are set down in the associated certificate policy document. There is a wealth of standards and guidelines in this area, but unfortunately different sets of standards are not always coherent with each other. Interested readers are referred to the Internet "PKI Page" [32] for a list of useful references and to the core PKIX standards [33–35] as an example of a coherent standards framework.

In terms of technical components, most PKI implementations include a CA component, a registration authority (RA) component, and a directory [X.500 or lightweight directory access protocol (LDAP)]. It is somewhat unfortunate that the term CA is sometimes used to describe the organization running the PKI as a whole and sometimes to describe a particular highly specific technical component. In reality, however, the correct interpretation is usually evident from the context. In addition to these components, PKI implementations may deploy other optional components, such as hardware security modules (HSMs) and smart cards for secure key storage, cryptographic accelerators to increase performance, OCSP responders (if the on-line certificate revocation protocol is being used), transaction validation software, and other support software.

The different PKI components, along with comments explaining how they work together, are shown in Figure 3.7.

The CA is the most important component, as it is the CA that signs certificates and revocation information. In order to limit risk, it is standard to deploy a root CA, which is the trust anchor of the whole infrastructure. The root CA has a self-signed certificate, and the key is published in several available repositories to provide several reference sources (the idea being that if any repository is compromised, this will be quickly recognized by comparing the key information with that held by the other repositories). The root CA signs certificates of other "signing" CAs, which may then be used to sign subscriber certificates or to sign certificates for CAs lower in the

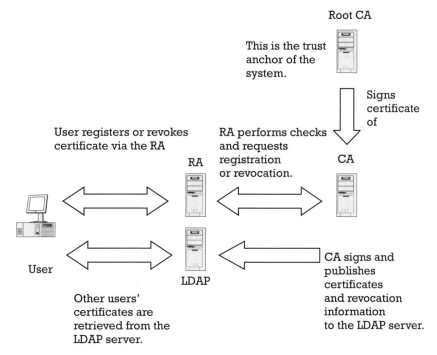

Figure 3.7 PKI components.

hierarchy of trust. The root CA limits the depth of the resulting hierarchy by defining a parameter known as the basic constraint. This parameter defines how many sub-CAs can be created vertically below the root CA.

The RA supports the CA by taking care of most of the administrative overhead associated with issuing and revoking certificates. As such, the RA acts as an intermediary between the subscriber and the CA. The core functionality of the RA is as follows:

- To accept correctly formatted registration and revocation requests either from the RA operator (if this is being done face to face) or over a network interface (if remote registration and revocation is being used);
- To verify this information and carry out any additional checks to verify identity; other checks, such as verifying possession of the corresponding private key, are also made here;
- To accept or reject the request—if the request is accepted, the certificate or revocation information is forwarded to the CA for signing, and if the request is rejected, the subscriber is made aware of the problem.
- Once the CA has signed the certificate, it returns a copy to the RA, which forwards it to the subscriber. In the case of a revocation request, the revocation information is published according to the agreed methods and timescales.

The detailed functionality of the RA is not standardized, but typical functionality includes:

- Network authentication of the end user in the case that remote registration is being used;
- Initialization and distribution of hardware devices;
- Key generation and key management;
- Control over the assignment of names;
- Reporting related to registration and revocation activity.

While certificates are nearly always stored in directories, there is no hard and fast requirement to do so. However, it is to be expected that applications developed to take advantage of PKI infrastructures will use the LDAP protocol to retrieve certificate information. The function of the directory is simply to publish certificate and revocation information.

3.5.2 Smart cards and cryptographic modules

Where IT security is concerned, smart cards and cryptographic modules are used to protect cryptographic secrets.

Smart cards were first manufactured in the late 1960s but did not enjoy commercial success until the introduction of telephone cards in 1984 by the

French Postal, Telegraph, and Telephone (PTT) [36]. Viewed in terms of their physical operation characteristics, there are three major classes of smart card:

- Contact cards, which require physical contact with a card reader [37–39];
- Contactless cards, which do not require physical contact and can be divided into those that operate by capacitive coupling (very short range) [40] and those that operate by inductive coupling [41];
- Dual technology cards, which offer both modes of operation.

For more information regarding the details of how such cards operate, see [36]. Although weaknesses have been published in recent years (for example, differential power analysis [42] and optical fault induction attacks [43]), smart cards are generally recognized as a highly secure, client-side storage environment for cryptographic keys and other secret information. Although the personalization and distribution aspects require considerable investment, the fact that this is not prohibitive from a commercial point of view is born out by the high number of smart card devices already in circulation in the form of banking cards. In particular, smart card technology was an important enabler for the realization of the electronic wallet concept [44]. One factor that may encourage widespread adoption of smart card technology in the future is the increasing capacity to offer support for several applications, although from a security perspective it will be important to check that coexisting applications make sense and do not introduce additional risk.

In using smart cards for secure key storage at the client side, we usually protect access to the card by requiring a PIN to unlock the interface, thereby implementing two-factor authentication to the target system. In this case, users require something they have (the smart card) plus something they know (the PIN) in order to correctly authenticate to the system. A subtle advantage of using smart cards for key storage is that the users do not have access to the key themselves. This prevents a user from performing a transaction and subsequently denying it by deliberately revealing the key and claiming that it was someone else.

Cryptographic applications tend to use smart cards in one of two ways. *Memory cards* are simply used for key storage, and any cryptographic operations to be carried out are not performed on the card. When using memory cards, the keys are read into the application and the latter performs the operations on the host platform. On the other hand, *microprocessor cards*, also known as *cryptocards* in this context, permit secure key storage and also enable the cryptographic calculations to be performed on the card. Applications interact with smart cards via application programming interfaces (APIs). As several different interfaces are defined (example interfaces include PKCS#11, PC/SC, OCF, and CDSA; see [36] for details), the final choice of interface adopted will probably reflect the favored development model of the organization.

For secure applications, cryptocards are to be preferred, as the keys never leave the secure environment and are therefore not prey to attacks that can exercise control over the operating system (such as *remote administration trojans* [45]). However, care is required when implementing such solutions—to be coherent, the PIN should not pass through the operating system, and this requires the presence of an external PIN pad. Figure 3.8 illustrates this principle.

Smart cards are a viable choice for securing access to cryptographic at the client side, but they are not usually an appropriate choice for server-side operations (although they are often used to store the keys that administrators use to gain access to a secure server—Here, however, the administrator is playing the role of a client). At the server-side, keys tend to be stored in specialized devices, collectively known as *hardware storage modules* (HSM). The important standard in this area is the Federal Information Processing Standards (FIPS) 140 standard, Security Requirements For Cryptographic Modules, which covers a total of 11 areas relating to the design and implementation of cryptographic modules. The original FIPS 140-1 standard has been recently updated to FIPS 140-2 [46].

The FIPS 140 standards are used to rate security devices against four levels of protection, known as level 1 to level 4. Security level 1 provides the lowest level of security, and level 4 provides the highest. Cryptographic modules are rated using a series of tests called the *derived test requirements* (DTR) for FIPS PUB 140-2, which are published on the National Institute of Standards and Technology (NIST) site together with a list of all validated cryptographic modules [46].

The possibility of carrying out business on the Internet, where the potential number of clients is almost limitless, has led to new requirements for application scalability, and this has in turn led to new demands on the scalability of cryptographic solutions. Cryptographic accelerators are specialized modules aimed at providing increased performance for cryptographic applications. In reality, cryptographic accelerator functionality is often provided as a specialized HSM, therefore combining secure key storage with high-performance cryptography. For this reason, specific cryptographic

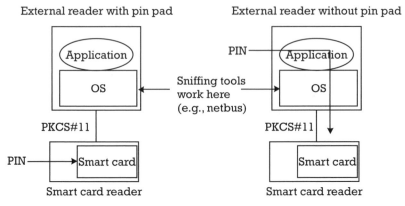

Figure 3.8 Using cryptocards with external card readers.

accelerators may offer the ability to run in FPS 140–compliant mode, where the former will be limited to FIPS-approved algorithms.

3.5.3 Authentication devices

Authentication devices are used to support authentication systems by providing the user with some object that is required to successfully complete the authentication process. Currently, most authentication devices fall into one of the following categories:

- Smart cards;
- Biometric devices;
- Tokens.

Smart cards were discussed in the previous section. As the applicability of this discussion to authentication scenarios is obvious, we will not cover these devices here.

Biometric devices verify identity on the basis of one or more physical attributes. Obviously, the attribute or combination of attributes selected as the basis for identification must be unique to the individual. Current methods use a variety of techniques, including fingerprint recognition, retinal and iris scanning, keystroke analysis (based on the fact that the way people use the keyboard is highly specific to themselves), voice recognition, and facial scanning.

Although the idea of authenticating users based on physical attributes is certainly appealing, there are a number of problems associated with the use of biometrics:

- It is very expensive, due to the requirement for specialized material.
- Psychological factors constitute an important barrier to the introduction of certain techniques (such as retinal and iris scanning).
- Measuring physical characteristics is difficult and subject to errors. The percentage success rate may not be acceptable.
- Biometrics cannot be used to authenticate nonhuman entities, such as automated processes.

In addition to these issues, there are serious doubts as to the ability of several of these systems to withstand a deliberate attack [47–49].

Tokens fall into two categories: those that act as secure storage devices for cryptographic information and those that serve as handheld devices. The former can be considered an alternative to smart-card technology, and similar considerations apply to these devices.

Handheld devices are equipped with a small display and keyboard and do not in general need to be connected to the user's workstation. The device is configured with the authentication server before being issued to the user, which enables the server and token to share a secret as a basis for authentication. In a typical logon scenario, the target system will interact with the authentication server and present the user with a request to authenticate himself or herself. The user accesses the handheld token by entering a password or PIN, and the token displays the authentication information required by the server. This information is entered at the workstation prompt, thereby enabling the user to complete the authentication process.

Although the details of the authentication protocol itself vary from device to device, a distinction can be made between time-synchronized approaches and approaches that do not rely on such methods. Time-synchronized authentication methods rely on the synchronization of the clock in the device with the clock on the authentication server. Most systems can tolerate a certain clock drift and will correct this each time the user makes use of the token. However, tokens that are not used for long periods can result in desynchronization and necessitate special procedures to revalidate the user.

Asynchronous devices usually use challenge-response protocols to authenticate the user (see Section 3.4.1.1) and are therefore not sensitive to clock drift within the device. As for all challenge-response systems, the security of the solution depends on the ability of the authentication server to generate sufficiently random challenges.

3.6 Summary

Technical tools play an essential role in securing information in electronic form. These tools support the core processes by providing scalability and reducing complexity. However, tools alone do not achieve anything, and successful approaches to securing information will ensure that procedures and tools are viewed as two aspects of the same solution.

A simple classification scheme for security tools has been presented. According to this scheme, a distinction is made between host-oriented and network-oriented tools due to the different focus of these tools. Whereas host-oriented tools are geared towards securing layers of software, network-oriented tools either secure network data flows by working at the protocol level or secure objects visible on the network. Despite this distinction, both host-oriented and network-oriented tools can be further classified according to the type of security service they offer:

- Authentication and authorization;
- Integrity protection;
- Access control;
- Monitoring;
- Data protection services—confidentiality, integrity, and non-repudiation.

This area will be revisited in Chapter 8, which is concerned with building security architectures.

References

[1] ISO/IEC 7498-1: *Information Technology—Open Systems Interconnection—Basic Reference Model: The Basic Model,* 1994.

[2] ISO/IEC 7498-2: *Information Technology—Open Systems Interconnection—Basic Reference Model—Part 2: Security Architecture,* 1989.

[3] "Common Object Request Broker Architecture: Core Specification," version 3.0.2, December 2002.

[4] Miller, T. C., "A Brief History of Sudo," August 2003, http://www.courtesan.com/sudo/history.html.

[5] Garfinkel, S., and G. Spafford, *Practical Unix and Internet Security,* Sebastopol, CA: O' Reilly and Associates, 1996, pp. 118–128.

[6] Grimes, R. A., *Malicious Mobile Code: Virus Protection For Windows,* Sebastopol, CA: O' Reilly and Associates, 2001, pp. 447–455.

[7] Axelsson, S., "Intrusion Detection Systems: A Taxonomy and Survey," Technical Report 99-15, Dept. of Computer Engineering, Chalmers University of Technology, Sweden.

[8] "COAST: Audit Trail Reduction," August 2003, http://www.cerias.purdue.edu/coast/projects/audit-trails-reduce.html.

[9] Mills, D. L., "Network Time Protocol (Version 3): Specification, Implementation and Analysis (RFC 1305)," August 2003, http://www.ietf.org/rfc/rfc1305.txt.

[10] Schneier, B., *Applied Cryptography: Protocols, Algorithms and Source Code in C,* 2nd Ed., New York: John Wiley and Sons, 1995.

[11] "Internet Security Systems: Session Hijacking," August 2003, http://www.iss.net/security_center/advice/Exploits/TCP/session_hijacking/default.htm.

[12] Needham, R. M., and M. Schroeder, "Using Encryption for Authentication in Large Networks of Computers," *Communications of the ACM,* Vol. 21, No. 12, 1978, pp. 993–999.

[13] Denning, D. E., and G. M. Sacco, "Timestamps in Key Distribution Protocols," *Communications of the ACM,* Vol. 24, No. 8, 1981, pp. 198–208.

[14] Wenstrom, M., *Managing Cisco Network Security,* Indianapolis, IN: Cisco Press, 2001, pp. 127–151.

[15] Rigney, C., et al., "Remote Authentication Dial In User Service (RADIUS)(RFC 2138),"August 2003, http://www.ietf.org/rfc/rfc2138.txt.

[16] Carrel, D., and L. Grant, "The TACACS+ Protocol (draft-grant-tacacs-02.txt)," August 2003, http://casl.csa.iisc.ernet.in/Standards/internet-drafts/draft-grant-tacacs-02.txt.

[17] Garfinkel, S. L., "Advanced Telephone Auditing with PhoneSweep: A Better Alternative to Underground 'War Dialers,'" *Matrix News,* Vol. 8, No. 12, 1998.

[18] "SATAN (Security Administrator Tool For Administering Networks)," August 2003, http://www.porcupine.org/satan.

[19] Curtin, M., and M. J. Ranum, "Internet Firewalls: Frequently Asked Questions," August 2003, http://www.interhack.net/pubs/fwfaq.

[20] Ranum, M. J., "Thinking About Firewalls," Proceedings of Second International Conference on Systems and Network Security and Management (SANS-II), 1993.

[21] Zwicky, E. D., S. Cooper, and D. B. Chapman, *Building Internet Firewalls*, Sebastopol, CA: O'Reilly and Associates, Inc, 2000.

[22] Cheswick, W. R., S. M. Bellovin, and A. D. Rubin, *Firewalls and Internet Security: Repelling The Wily Hacker*, Reading, MA: Addison Wesley, 2003.

[23] "Stateful Inspection Technology," August 2003, http://www.checkpoint.com/products/downloads/Stateful_Inspection.pdf.

[24] Luotonen, A., *Web Proxy Servers*, Englewood Cliffs, NJ: Prentice Hall PTR, 1997.

[25] Tanenbaum, A. S., *Computer Networks*, Englewood Cliffs, NJ: Prentice Hall PTR, 2002.

[26] Tanase, M., "Sniffers: What They Are and How to Protect Yourself," August 2003, http://www.securityfocus.com/infocus/1549.

[27] Bandy, P., M. Money, and K. Worstell, "Intrusion Detection FAQ—Can the Volume of Network Traffic Get High Enough to Exceed the Capability of the Detectors?" August 2003, http://www.sans.org/resources/idfaq/network_traffic.php.

[28] Rescorla, E., "Diffie-Hellmann Key Agreement Method (RFC 2631)," August 2003, http://www.ietf.org/rfc/rfc2631.txt.

[29] Sirbu, M. A., and J. Chung-I Chuang, "Distributed Authentication in Kerberos Using Public Key Cryptography," Symposium on Network and Distributed System Security, San Diego, CA, February 10–11, 1997.

[30] Thomas, S., *SSL and TLS Essentials: Securing The Web*, New York: John Wiley and Sons Inc., 2000.

[31] Doraswamy, N., and D. Harkins, *IPSec: The New Security Standard for the Internet, Intranets, and Virtual Private Networks*, Englewood Cliffs, NJ: Prentice Hall PTR, 1999.

[32] Kelm, S., "The PKI Page," August 2003, http://www.pki-page.org.

[33] Housley, R., et al., "Internet X509 Public Key Infrastructure: Certificate and CRL Profile (RFC 2459)," August 2003, http://www.ietf.org/rfc/rfc2459.txt.

[34] Adams, C., and S. Farrell, "Internet X509 Public Key Infrastructure: Certificate Management Protocols (RFC 2510)," August 2003, http://www.ietf.org/rfc/rfc2510.txt.

[35] Chokhani, S., and W. Ford, "Internet X509 Public Key Infrastructure: Certificate Policy and Certificate Practices Framework (RFC 2527)," August 2003, http://www.ietf.org/rfc/rfc2527.txt.

[36] Ferrari, J., et al., "Smart Cards: A Case Study," August 2003, http://www.redbooks.ibm.com/redbooks/pdfs/sg245239.pdf.

[37] ISO/IEC 7810: *Identification Cards, Physical Characteristics*.

[38] ISO/IEC 7811: Parts 1–6: *Identification Cards, Recording Techniques*.

[39] ISO/IEC 7816: Parts 1–10: *Identification cards, Integrated Circuit(s) Cards with Contacts*.

[40] ISO/IEC 10536: Parts 1–4: *Identification Cards, Contactless Integrated Circuit(s) Cards, Close-Coupled Cards.*

[41] ISO/IEC 14443: Parts 1–4: *Identification Cards, Contactless Integrated Circuit(s) Cards, Proximity Cards.*

[42] Kocher, P., J. Jaffe, and B. Jun, "Differential Power Analysis," August 2003, http://www.cryptography.com/resources/whitepapers/DPA.pdf.

[43] Skorobogatov, S., and R. Anderson, "Optical Fault Induction Attacks," August 2003, http://www.ftp.cl.cam.ac.uk/ftp/users/rja14/faultpap3.pdf.

[44] "Electronic Jacks-of-All-Trades," *Smart Computing,* Vol. 4, No. 3, 2000, pp. 181–186.

[45] Grimes, R.A., *Malicious Mobile Code: Virus Protection For Windows,* Sebastopol, CA: O' Reilly and Associates, Inc., 2001, pp. 184–186.

[46] "FIPS PUB 140-2: Security Requirements for Cryptographic Modules," August 2003, http://csrc.nist.gov/cryptval/140-2.htm.

[47] Matsumoto, T., et al., "Impact of Artificial Gummy Fingers on Fingerprint Systems," *Proceedings of SPIE, Optical Security and Counterfeit Deterrence Techniques IV,* Vol. 4677, 2002, pp. 275–289.

[48] Schultz, Dr. E., "Security Views: Tests of Biometric Devices Show Numerous Problems," *Computers & Security,* Vol. 21, No. 5, 2002, pp. 385–396.

[49] Schneier, B., "Biometrics: Truths and Fictions," August 2003, http://www.counterpane.com/crypto-gram-9808.html.

Contents

A proactive approach: Overview

4.1 Introduction

Having described the essential tools and techniques that will be needed to define and implement the information-security process, we turn our attention in this chapter to how these tools and techniques can be used to construct a coherent and realistic approach to securing information.

Based on the points raised in Chapter 1, we can summarize the key ideas underlying a risk-driven approach to information-security management as follows:

- We need to develop a framework, which will allow us to react quickly to business requirements at all times. This framework needs to be flexible enough to cope with short-term requirements while still ensuring that long-term goals are met.

- Due to the rapid rate of change associated with both the business model and technical evolution, decisions will also have to be made more rapidly, and this will inevitably involve accepting more risk.

- For most organizations, acceptance of more risk will therefore be a consequence of increased competition, and it will be increasingly necessary to achieve the right compromise between information security and business opportunity.

- Whereas information-security policy and global risk-analysis methods will continue to be important in guiding strategic initiatives, FRA techniques offer an ideal way to rapidly compare differing business scenarios on the basis of risk. Such an analysis is able to take account of contextual information and is therefore more appropriate as a decision-making tool than policy and standards.

Throughout this chapter, we will use The Secure Bank to provide a realistic framework for discussing problems and issues that are frequently encountered when introducing a new approach to managing information-security management. As many of the most commonly encountered problems are related to the management of interpersonal relationships, a lot of emphasis will be placed on the need to successfully develop and manage such relationships within the enterprise.

In order to provide as complete a picture as possible of the different steps required to take control of the information-security process, we will assume that we have just been recruited to introduce a new approach to information security, compatible with the strategic vision of the bank. The first part of this chapter will discuss ways to deal with the period directly following this appointment, whereas the second part presents an overview of the strategic-planning cycle. The strategic-planning cycle is described in more detail in the following chapters.

As we saw in Chapter 1, an important element of the bank's business strategy is to provide innovative solutions to clients in a secure fashion. To achieve this strategy, the executive management of The Secure Bank is keen to make the best use of new technologies where this permits them to gain a competitive edge. Consequently, from day one we use this as a guideline, by favoring solutions that enable the bank to adopt new technologies in line with the IT plan. Where the adoption of such technologies involves increased risk, this will be signaled to the business owner, who will have the choice to accept or reject this extra risk.

4.2   The consolidation period and strategic-planning cycles

At the time we start our mission at The Secure Bank, we have very limited information about the current state of affairs. In fact, the only information we have is that provided during the interview process, where a brief overview of the major problems as raised by a series of recent audits was presented. This information was presented in Section 1.9 of this book, as part of the introduction to The Secure Bank. It is worth emphasizing that at this stage, we only have an outsider's view of the company culture and no view at all of the different personalities with whom we will be working in the future.

It would be premature to launch any major initiatives based on such scanty information. A better way forward is to agree on a consolidation period with executive management. The idea behind the consolidation period is to allow for current activities to be completed in a satisfactory manner and to provide sufficient time to prepare an appropriate strategy for the future. The consolidation period also provides the opportunity to implement any *quick wins,* which are unlikely to conflict with the future strategy. In addition to these published goals, it is a good idea during the consolidation period to develop a personal strategy for gaining acceptance within the management team and becoming integrated into the management process.

In line with this approach, we agree with the executive management of The Secure Bank on a consolidation period of 6 months. At the end of this 6-month period, we will deliver the following:

> • A strategy document, which takes account of the analysis of the current situation;

> • A summary of the status of all initiatives ongoing at the start of the consolidation period;

> • A summary of the current status of all identified quick wins (an action that has a benefit that can be realized quickly and usually at low cost).

Throughout the consolidation period, we are forced to make decisions based on relatively incomplete information. Consequently, initiatives launched during this period tend to be rather limited in scope and based on a "bottom-up" approach. In other words, we try to introduce small improvements to the existing framework, without making any drastic changes to the overall approach. In parallel, we seek to improve our understanding of the current situation and the strategic vision of the organization and to use this information as the basis of a future strategy.

At the end of the consolidation period, the information-security approach should be driven by a series of strategic-planning cycles. Basically, such a cycle involves reassessing the current situation in the light of new requirements and technological progress followed by the definition and execution of a strategy for the next strategic period. Typically, a strategic-planning cycle will take between 3 to 5 years from start to completion and is more likely to be based on a "top-down" approach.

Section 4.5 of this chapter provides an overview of the strategic-planning cycle and the remaining chapters of the book complete this description.

4.3   Deciding on a personal strategy

Defining and executing a strategic approach to information security is not as easy as it might seem due to a number of reasons:

> • Security is often perceived as a necessary evil, rather than as a business enabler [1]. In organizations where the current approach is not working, there may be a tendency to bypass the security unit.

> • A traditional top-down approach starts with the definition of the security policy [2]. Developing and agreeing on an information-security policy is a difficult and time-consuming task [3]. In some organizations, this may be perceived as an intellectual exercise with little practical value.

> ▸ In all organizations, it is important to be seen to be practical and capable of responding to requirements efficiently. At the same time, long-term stability can only be achieved through strategic initiatives, and such initiatives may deliver very little in the short term.

The extent to which these potential issues constitute real problems is dependent on the level of maturity of the enterprise. More mature organizations will have already have achieved a certain level of stability, allowing a greater emphasis to be placed on further strategic development, whereas organizations with a lower level of maturity will require more tactical initiatives to realize their short-term goals. This is illustrated in Figure 4.1.

Figure 4.1 is based on the notion of a *production possibility frontier* (PPF), which is used in classical economics to describe how a limited (i.e., economic) pool of resources can be used to produce two different types of output [4]. In our example, the pool of resources is essentially the staff at our disposal and the possible outputs are strategic deliverables and tactical deliverables. The form of the graph depends on the extent to which the two possible outputs resemble each other. It is convex when outputs are dissimilar and tends towards a straight line as the similarity between the outputs increases [5]. As strategic work tends to be quite dissimilar from tactical work, the convex PPF has been retained here.

As a newcomer at The Secure Bank, we need to make the right impression on fellow colleagues and staff members in order to gain their confidence and to take ownership of the information-security process. For readers who are new to the information-security area and perceive the information-security manager as a position of power, now is probably the time to kill this myth. Successful information-security managers are indeed capable of influencing the IT strategy of the organization for which they

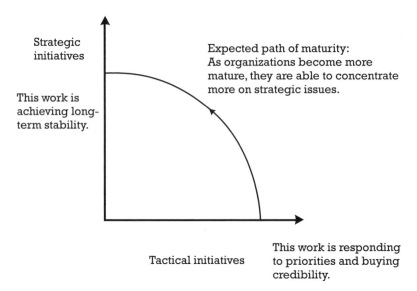

Figure 4.1 Path of maturity.

work, but only by virtue of the confidence that fellow staff place in them. It is therefore critically important to work via persuasion and not by force. As respect is usually gained very slowly but often lost quickly, a lot will depend on how we take over control of the process in the first few months.

To a large extent, the difference between a successful start and a difficult one will depend on our level of understanding of the company culture. Whereas this is largely a question of observation and judgment, we can nevertheless use the information contained in Figure 4.1 to create a personal strategy for assuming control. Based on the information we have at the start of our mission, it would appear that the current approach to information security at The Secure Bank is relatively immature, suggesting that we should initially place more emphasis on tactical initiatives than strategic ones. This conclusion is born out by the fact that the bank has a number of audit points that need to be taken care of in a reasonable timeframe if it is to be able to pursue its strategy of expansion in a controlled fashion. Finally, the company culture strongly reflects the core value of innovation, which staff members often seem to link with speed of response. All of the evidence therefore points towards a personal strategy of achieving a number of significant quick wins to get the buy in of management and staff, followed by a gradual introduction of more strategic projects.

For the purpose of comparison, such an approach might not at all be well received within a more conservative organization having a more mature approach. In such circumstances, we would expect to find less pressing issues and would therefore be able to consecrate correspondingly more time to a strategic approach from day one.

4.4 The consolidation period

4.4.1 Planning

The first major task with which we are confronted during the consolidation period is to create a short-term plan, which will allow us to demonstrate progress to management and to satisfy the expectations of those impacted by this plan.

In the case of The Secure Bank, this plan incorporates the following actions:

- Identifying and developing a working relationship with the major stakeholders in the information-security process;
- Identifying major issues by interviewing business and technical staff;
- Classifying issues into short-term, medium-term, and long-term concerns;
- Providing temporary or permanent solutions to short-term issues and canceling any ongoing activities that are not likely to be in line with the future strategy;

> Identifying any quick wins that can be realized before the strategy document is completed and agreed;

> Implementing initial management-control mechanisms.

The fact that the information-security strategy will be produced during the consolidation period is not included in this list, as this activity will be described in Chapter 5.

4.4.2 Establishing contact with stakeholders

Of these tasks, the most important is the first one, as the way in which the security unit interacts with the different stakeholders in the process is likely to have the greatest impact on the probable success or failure of the approach as a whole [6]. Any approach that is not well understood and that seems to put arbitrary constraints on management and end users is not likely to succeed in the long term. It is therefore important not only to inform the various groups within the organization impacted by the approach, but also to involve them in the decision-making process itself [7].

One way to achieve this is to use the concept of *stakeholders*. A stakeholder in the information-security approach is someone who will be affected by the quality of the result and who therefore has a vested interest to protect. In one sense, all employees are stakeholders, as an IT security event could potentially affect anyone. However, in this context, the requirement to identify and work with stakeholders is linked to the need to obtain approval and budget for initiatives related to information security. For The Secure Bank, the following stakeholders were identified:

> The business lines;

> Internal audit;

> Risk management;

> The legal department;

> The IT department.

Having identified the stakeholders, we are interested in understanding how they perceive the current approach to information security. In particular, we need to identify the positive and negative aspects of the current approach from the perspective of each of these stakeholders.

This is therefore a task that involves more listening than talking, and it is well worth taking the time to prepare meetings with stakeholders in advance. The degree to which this preparation extends is a matter of personal style, but this should include at least a statement of objectives and an agenda to allow stakeholders to prepare themselves.

For managers that prefer a more structured approach to meetings, the use of a questionnaire might be appropriate. When sent to the stakeholders before the meetings, this is a good method for receiving a considered response to a well-chosen set of questions, but the overall result will depend on how well the questions have been chosen. An alternative technique is to just let the stakeholder talk and to guide the conversation using open questions. This tends to result in information that is less structured, but gives more scope to stakeholders to concentrate on their concerns. Both methods have their advantages and disadvantages, and managers should choose the approach that is most suited to their management style.

Whichever method is used to conduct the dialogue, it is useful to close the initial discussion with a summary of what has been said and to explore ways in which the negative aspects could be improved. A word of warning here, however; it is not usually appropriate to commit to any course of action during the initial discussions, as it is possible, and indeed probable, that different stakeholders will have conflicting requirements.

4.4.3   Identifying major issues

At The Secure Bank, the initial discussions with stakeholders revealed a general dissatisfaction with the current process and confirmed the problems listed in section 1.9. All stakeholders agreed that the current approach to IT security was too theoretical and a more hands-on approach was required. Most stakeholders found it extremely difficult to relate requirements back to risk, and almost everyone thought information security was inaccessible due to the high level of complexity and specialized jargon. This latter problem has been recognized by the information-security community for some time and has led to the publication of specialized dictionaries on the Web (see, for example, [8]).

As expected, the initial discussions also revealed a number of new points, the most important of which are listed here:

▸ The Secure Bank has recently expanded the risk-management role to include operational risk management in response to the Basel II requirements. However, no attempt has been made to align the new responsibilities of the risk-management group with those of the IT security department.

▸ The standards imposed by the audit department exceed those required by the existing policy and are often justified on the basis of best practice. This is causing considerable problems for projects, which are under instructions to sharply reduce the time to market for new applications.

▸ For historical reasons, the audit department has retained certain operational responsibilities from the time when the distinction between audit and security was not well defined. In particular, the audit department still administers access rights on the bank's mainframe platforms.

▸ There has been no attempt to align information-security concepts with software development and purchasing activities. As a result, software development and acquisition projects effectively bypass the IT security department.

- Testing is currently carried out in development environments, which are less secure than the production environment. Despite regulatory restrictions protecting the confidentiality of data related to clients, testing cycles use real production data.

- System administrators and production support staff feel that they have little influence on the security of the machines they administer. Several interesting ideas for improving security at a reasonable cost have not been followed up on.

- Several stakeholders pointed out that the overall approach to information security was not coherent. In particular, there has been no attempt to align physical security mechanisms with logical security. The fact that computing equipment and mass storage devices could be transported freely in and out of the organization's buildings was seen as a significant weakness.

- The IT security department was concerned by the recent proliferation of handheld computing devices within the organization. The department has recently tried to prohibit such devices by modifying the existing security policy, but this has been unsuccessful due to poor publication mechanisms and a general lack of awareness throughout the user community.

- The marketing department has recently been looking into providing personalized information to key clients via the Internet Web server. Although they recognize the importance of privacy laws, they are not sure what needs to be done to be compliant with current legislation and cannot identify the person responsible for this issue within the enterprise.

Several other issues were collected during this initial information-gathering phase, but these were judged to be of lesser importance and have therefore not been included in this description.

4.4.4 Classifying issues

The output of the initial series of interviews is as follows:

- The minutes of each meeting, which are distributed to the people interviewed and agreed;

- An internal document summarizing all issues identified, including the name of the person or people that identified the issue and a description of the problem.

At this stage, none of these documents are for general circulation. This is because some of the identified issues are contentious, and different stakeholders have different points of view on what the issue is and how it should be solved. An example of such an issue is the problem of the high standards being set by the audit department and the business need for rapid time to market. Knowing that the resolution of these issues is likely to be a difficult process involving some degree of compromise, we choose to solve this issue by discussion groups and not by circulating analytical documents.

Now that we are aware of the known issues, the next task is to prioritize these in order to decide which issues can be solved quickly and which require a more strategic approach. This prioritization will take account of several factors, including:

> ▸ The risk associated with the issue;
>
> ▸ The estimated timeframe within which a solution can be implemented;
>
> ▸ The extent to which there is likely to be agreement among stakeholders on the issue itself and how to resolve it.

The results of the prioritization exercise are shown in Table 4.1 and include the issues raised in Section 1.9.

At this point it is extremely important to stress that the prioritization presented in Table 4.1 involves professional judgment, and there is no right or wrong solution. Any similar exercise is therefore open to discussion, and indeed such discussion can be very helpful in understanding how different stakeholders perceive risk and the degree to which they are prepared to accept identified risk. In other words, while we strive to impose a structured approach to resolving issues and to use good engineering practice, we also recognize that this is not an exact science. Ensuring that stakeholders feel comfortable with the approach and obtaining their buy in where actions are concerned is as important as carrying out a correct logical analysis of the issues. The examples discussed in the following paragraphs will help the reader understand the factors leading to this prioritization in the case of The Secure Bank.

Starting with the high-priority issues, points I1 and I2 are almost self explanatory. Issue I1 is judged as high priority because the visible support of executive management is a necessary condition for success. Support at this level will also help to assure that information security as a whole is correctly prioritized with respect to other concerns, such as the need to reduce costs. Issue I2 is also of paramount importance, as the approach we wish to introduce puts a lot more emphasis on risk analysis and somewhat less emphasis on policy. Both of these issues can be dealt with in the short term, and neither point is likely to be contentious (although we will need to work closely with the risk-management team where the second point is concerned). Issues I3 and I5 are classed as high priority, as they are contributing to the current negative image of the IT security department. Finally, issue I4 is also classed as high priority, as it is a source of friction between two stakeholders.

Of the high-priority issues, only issue I3, insufficient dialogue between the security department and users, poses a planning problem because this cannot be resolved in the short term. By comparison, issues I16 and I17 are classed as low priority mainly because both require significant investment before any real benefits can be achieved. Where issue I3 is concerned,

Table 4.1 Prioritization of Known Issues for The Secure Bank

Id	Issue	Priority
I1	*Support from Executive Management* Currently, the support for the information-security process by the executive management team is quite passive. Support needs to be more active and highly visible.	High
I2	*Absence of Risk Analysis* The current approach to IT security is almost entirely policy driven and little risk analysis is carried out.	High
I3	*Insufficient Dialogue Between the Security Department and Users* There is little dialogue between the security department and other departments. The main point of contact is a yearly presentation, which is largely out of date.	High
I4	*High Standards Imposed by the Audit Department* The standards currently imposed by the audit department are inconsistent with the restrictions being imposed upon project teams.	High
I5	*Lack of Involvement of Production Support Staff* System administrators and production support staff feel that they have little influence on the security of the machines they administer. Several interesting ideas for improving security at a reasonable cost have not been followed up on.	High
I6	*No Defined Approach to Privacy Issues* Nobody is taking ownership of data privacy, and, consequently, there are no policy statements or guidelines in this area.	High
I7	*Theoretical Approach* The current approach to information security is generally thought to be too theoretical. A more hands-on approach is required.	Medium
I8	*Poorly Defined Responsibilities* Responsibilities are poorly defined and do not match what happens in reality. In addition, the current set of responsibilities in incoherent across the enterprise.	Medium
I9	*Risk Management Not Aligned with IT Security* There is no collaboration between the risk management group and the IT security group.	Medium
I10	*Administration Procedures Do Not Scale* Existing procedures for security administration are based on those originally defined for the mainframe. These procedures do not scale well and are often ignored. There is little automation in place.	Medium
I11	*No Coherent Approach to Information Security* There has been no attempt to create a coherent framework for information security, which covers physical security and personnel issues in addition to IT security.	Medium
I12	*Insufficient Security of Mobile Devices* There is currently no consistent approach to securing mobile computing devices, such as handheld and portable computers.	Medium
I13	*Operational Responsibilities with the Audit Department* For historical reasons, the audit department has retained certain operational responsibilities from the past, notably the administration of access rights on mainframe platforms.	Medium
I14	*No Integration with Software Development and Acquisition* There has been no attempt to align information-security concepts with software development and purchasing activities. Consequently, projects tend to bypass the IT security department.	Medium

Table 4.1 (continued)

Id	Issue	Priority
I15	*Test Environments Use Production Data* Testing is currently carried out in development environments, which are less secure than the production environment. Despite regulatory restrictions protecting the confidentiality of data related to clients, testing cycles use real production data.	Low
I16	*Complex Infrastructure with Little Standardization* In the past, the IT security department has not been able to respond rapidly enough to requirements for securing applications. This problem is compounded by a complex infrastructure and a lack of product standardization.	Low
I17	*No Architectural Approach* In the past, the introduction of security-related tools has been very limited. Existing tools have been implemented as point solutions and economies of scale have not been realized.	Low

however, we can expect to achieve benefits in the short term even though the issue can only be resolved via a strategic approach.

4.4.5   Implementing short-term solutions

Of the issues summarized in the previous section, the medium- and low-priority issues will not be dealt with in the short term, as they are either too complex, too contentious, or will take too long to complete. Consequently, these issues are one of the major inputs into the information-security strategy (the strategic vision of the organization is the other major input). Issues that don't make it into the strategy will be recorded and tracked using an issues-tracking database (see Section 4.4.6).

The high-priority issues will be dealt with during the consolidation period. We have seen that in the case of The Secure Bank, the following issues are judged as high priority:

- Support from executive management;
- Absence of risk analysis;
- Insufficient dialogue with users;
- High standards imposed by the audit department;
- Lack of involvement of production support staff;
- No defined approach to privacy issues.

Resolving the first point is somewhat simplified by the fact that executive management has already recognized that there is a problem. Indeed, in Section 1.9 we explained how a series of unfavorable audits resulted in a decision by executive management to change the management of the information-security process, which is why we are here!

One of the first actions we undertake therefore is to ask executive management to name a representative for issues relating to information security. At the same time, we request that the IT security department be given temporary responsibility for coordinating all aspects of information security on the understanding that this decision will be reviewed at the end of the consolidation period. One of the arguments used to justify this approach was that nobody was prepared to accept responsibility for privacy issues, and this had therefore become a bottleneck to further progress for the marketing department.

Following the agreement of the executive committee and the appointment of a representative, we prepare and agree on a brief statement of support for the information-security process and publish this on the organization's internal Web site. In parallel, we establish an information-security steering committee chaired by the IT security department and consisting of a representative of each stakeholder, including the executive-management representative. The primary goal of the steering committee is to encourage the active involvement of stakeholders and to provide a forum for dialogue. In the future, this steering committee will prove to be a valuable mechanism for depersonalizing issues and avoiding conflicts.

More formally, the responsibilities of the steering committee are as follows:

▸ Review and approve the information-security strategy.

▸ Review and approve information-security policy statements.

▸ Ensure that the information-security approach is aligned with the business strategy of the bank and make recommendations on how to proceed where conflicts arise.

▸ Ensure that the information-security department receives the support it requires from stakeholders in order to successfully complete its mission.

▸ Provide a cross-discipline management forum for discussing security-related issues.

The second issue, the absence of risk analysis, provides us with an opportunity for strengthening the relationship with the risk-management group. During the initial stakeholder meetings, the manager of the group stressed the importance of preparing for the requirements of the Basel II agreement and expressed a certain frustration with the lack of progress to date. Our approach was therefore to actively support the risk-management department in this area in return for their support for the introduction of FRA techniques in the short term. The risk-management department was happy to agree to this approach under the understanding that efforts be made to combine the two methods into a single approach in the long term.

A number of actions will be launched to immediately improve the dialogue with end users:

▸ Creation of an information-security section on the company's intranet server, including a bulletin board where users can ask questions and receive responses from the IT security department;

▸ Modification of current IT help desk procedures to allow security-related problems to be forwarded to the IT security team;

▸ Establishment of a centralized telephone number for reporting security incidents;

▸ Creation and delivery of a short awareness presentation focused on awareness of current threats. The objective of the presentation is to encourage users to think about the possible consequences of everyday actions, particularly where modern technology is concerned.

The problem arising from the high expectations of the audit department is more delicate, as it involves a potential conflict between two important stakeholders. Within The Secure Bank, we were able to resolve this problem by introducing a proposal for a more risk-oriented approach to the information steering committee. According to this approach, the appropriate level of security for new applications will be decided by the business manager, based on a risk analysis performed together with the risk-management team and the IT security department. The steering committee was in favor of this approach because the business manager was in the best position to weigh information-security risks against the risks of late delivery. In addition, the new procedure requires the business owner to accept the residual risk. The role of the audit department is then to ensure that the business managers fulfill this role correctly and to verify that any legal or regulatory requirements are satisfied.

The lack of involvement of production staff is only an issue in the sense that nobody has provided feedback to this group in the past. This is easily resolved by appointing a member of the IT security unit as a point of liaison with administrators and organizing a biweekly meeting to discuss proposals and how to take them forward. As production support staff will be proposing mainly technical improvements, the first task of this workgroup is to define a set of global requirements, which all proposed ideas for improvement must meet in order to be considered as candidates for implementation. By insisting on this preliminary step, we will be able to align this process with our strategic vision for the future.

Finally, following the decision of executive management to temporarily extend the scope of IT security to cover all aspects of information security, we agree to take charge of the privacy issue confronting the marketing department. Work started on this issue at the beginning of the fourth month. Although it took another 3 months to solve this issue, the marketing department was able to resume the project after 4 weeks, following a site visit to a financial institution that had already solved this problem. The final agreed solution was to produce a privacy policy by working together with the legal and audit departments and with guidance from a contact point in the financial institution. The final policy was formally approved by the information-security steering committee in its second meeting (month seven), which meant that the text could be published on the Web site and sent to customers in mailings at the beginning of month eight.

This last issue is worthy of further comment, as the final delay of 8 months was initially unacceptable to the marketing department. However, we were able to use the information steering committee to support this strategy, given the commitment of executive management to improving information security. As a result, the marketing department received the full support of executive management to delay the project until the issue had been resolved correctly.

4.4.6 Identifying quick wins

The consolidation period provides an ideal opportunity for identifying those quick wins having a high probability of success and for which we can agree the way forward without waiting for the strategy to be finalized. However, the extent to which these initiatives can actually be realized will depend on factors such as the available budget and the size of the team.

At The Secure Bank, the following initiatives were identified as potential quick wins:

- Introduction of FRA techniques;
- Implementation of a network-oriented security scanner;
- Implementation of an issues-tracking database;
- Enhanced background checks prior to recruitment of staff occupying sensitive positions.

The first quick win, the introduction of FRA techniques, will be implemented in response to issue I2 as described in the last section; we will therefore not dwell on this point any longer.

The second point was agreed to by the information-security steering committee in month seven, based on the following arguments:

- The low level of security of midrange systems and the lack of automated tools in this area were common themes in recent audit reports, and there was a strong desire to show progress in this area.
- Given the current state of affairs, the IT security department recommended the acquisition of a network-oriented scanner as opposed to a series of host-oriented scanners. In the short-term, the network-oriented scanner provides better value by allowing a more complete vision of vulnerabilities in a shorter timeframe.
- The budget requirements were acceptable and could be funded in part using money set aside for the Internet banking project.
- The technology was judged as being very mature and noninvasive. The probability of implementation problems or negative impact on the production environment was assessed as low.

The implementation of this initiative took 3 months, with the result that the final delivery date was outside the consolidation period. Despite this fact, we can still consider this as a quick win—the delay was due to the fact that it was preferable to wait for the second meeting of the steering committee for approval on this. Pushing the project through without approval was possible but not desirable, as this would have weakened the position of the steering group.

The third point was adopted without discussion, as it could be implemented with minimal effort within the department. Nevertheless, the issues-tracking database will be extremely useful in the future to track ongoing issues and to store information about how previous issues were resolved.

The fourth point was dropped following preliminary discussions with the human resources department, who felt that the introduction of such a procedure would be poorly received by staff. This point will therefore be postponed until a further date and will be introduced as a subject for discussion by the information-security steering committee.

4.4.7 Implementing initial management-control mechanisms

The consolidation period is the ideal time to look into existing planning and reporting methods and implement internal controls to make sure that this information is available as needed. While it is preferable to base these controls on existing procedures where they exist, it is also worth checking that these procedures are sufficiently complete to support decision making within the department.

At The Secure Bank, we ensure that the following procedures are in place by the end of the consolidation period:

- An agreed schedule for internal coordination meetings;
- Procedures for internal reporting;
- Procedures for planning and tracking projects;
- Procedures for the production of basic statistics (where this is possible).

It was agreed that the information-security manager would meet every week with the team leaders within the department. This meeting would focus on planning and resolution of issues. Furthermore, a quarterly meeting would be held with all department staff and will be used to ensure that all staff members are aware of the different initiatives in progress. As part of this latter meeting, staff will be encouraged to train each other by presenting interesting aspects of their work in more detail to other members of the department.

Procedures for internal reporting were introduced at an early stage and were aligned with the existing management reporting cycle. In order to encourage concision and simplicity, internal reports were restricted to a maximum of two pages and required to follow a standard structure.

Introducing planning procedures was somewhat more difficult, due to a certain reticence to the adoption of formal tracking procedures and a lack of knowledge. Completing this step took approximately 6 months, as staff had to be trained on the use of the project-planning tool.

Introducing statistics was the hardest task of all, largely due to the following factors:

> Staff members were worried that the data would be used for other purposes, such as to compile reports on the efficiency of administrators.

> There were no tools for producing statistics, which meant that these tools had to be developed or the data had to be collected manually.

> The production of statistics was seen as an unnecessary overhead.

Following several discussions, it was finally decided that a number of simple scripts would be developed by the team to collect basic statistics and that these statistics would be used to make executive management aware of the scale of certain operations and to support future proposals. Initially, statistics were maintained in the following areas and reported on a biweekly basis:

> Number of requests for access processed per type of operating system;

> Number of problems investigated;

> Number of changes made to the firewall infrastructure;

> Number of virus/malicious code incidents.

This list was retained on the basis that these statistics could be provided with minimal effort and would be useful for supporting future proposals. As an example, the trends indicated by the first set of data were used to successfully defend the proposal for the implementation of EUA software.

4.5   The strategic-planning cycle

4.5.1   Overview

Once the tasks defined in the initial consolidation period have been successfully completed, we effectively enter the first strategic-planning cycle. From this point, the approach should evolve continually to reflect the constantly changing threat environment and any changes in the business strategy of the organization. This idea of constant evolution is depicted in Figure 4.2, which depicts a cycle consisting of four phases:

1.   Definition of a strategy;

2.   Production of a strategic plan;

3.   Execution of the plan;

4.   Monitoring for further improvement.

Although different process models for information security differ in the phases they define, this cyclical process model is very commonly used to

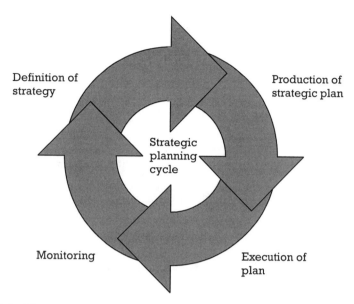

Figure 4.2 The strategic-planning cycle.

describe the strategic approach. (For examples of documented security process models, see [9–12]).

Before providing a detailed description of the strategic-planning cycle, it is important to relate this process back to Figure 4.1, which shows the path of maturity for the information-security approach of a given organization. As we have already mentioned, less mature organizations will be forced to devote more time to tactical issues than to strategic ones, whereas more mature organizations will have day-to-day issues under control and will concentrate their efforts on strategic initiatives. Figure 4.2 takes no account of this distribution of work and only describes the life cycle of strategic initiatives. This is important when producing plans, as the level of maturity will therefore determine the amount of effort that can be dedicated to strategic issues.

Note also that the phases constituting the cycle are depicted as being sequential. For strategic work, this is a reasonable description of the process, but we should keep in mind that Figure 4.2 is a model of reality and, like all models, it should not be taken too literally. In reality, we will not wait until the end of the strategic-planning period to introduce new ideas into the strategy and subsequently implement them; rather, we will place core documentation under change control and update it as part of a controlled process. This, of course, does not stop us from restarting the cycle from scratch at the end of the planning period, and this is exactly the approach we take.

4.5.2 Definition of a strategy

The starting point for a new strategic-planning period is the definition of a new strategy. For the first such cycle, the definition of the strategy occurs during the consolidation period. This activity is described in Chapter 5 of this book.

4.5.3   Production of a strategic plan

The strategic plan translates the strategy into a series of initiatives spread over time. Whereas the strategy says *what* is to be achieved, identifies priorities, and provides a high-level view of planning, the strategic plan says *how* this will be achieved and provides details of timeframe and costs.

One of the key points to bear in mind when producing any sort of strategic plan is that the uncertainty associated with the planning increases as a function of time. In other words, there is more uncertainty associated with actions planned for the distant future than that associated with those planned for the near future. While most people would agree that this is common sense, it is easy to lose sight of this during the planning process.

At The Secure Bank we take account of this fact in the following way:

▸ At any given moment, the strategic plan will consist of a short-term component (6 months), which provides a high level of detail, and a long-term component providing less detailed information in terms of major tasks.

▸ The level of contingency planned into the task will increase with time.

▸ The initial plan will be constructed in a series of iterations over a period of 3 weeks.

The strategic plan was produced as a result of three meetings held at weekly intervals. In the first step, each of the team leaders within the IT security department was given a copy of the strategy. They were then asked to produce a prioritized list of projects and a work breakdown structure for each project without exchanging any information with each other. As expected, this exercise produced very different results, which were discussed in the first meeting and used to arrive at a common structure. In the second step, the same team members were asked to provide estimations for each work breakdown structure, again without exchanging information with each other. These were then compared in the second meeting and used to agree on a draft plan. In the third step, the short-term plan was refined as a group exercise.

In general, this planning technique works very well when team members are sufficiently disciplined to genuinely work in isolation. The major benefit is realized when ideas are compared, forcing participants to reveal and justify their assumptions and methods.

4.5.4   Execution of the strategic plan

Referring back to Figure 4.1, work carried out as part of the strategic plan is moving the organization up the maturity path. Throughout the strategic-planning period, there will be a competition for resources between strategic projects and tactical requirements that are likely to arise at short notice. This problem has been anticipated to some extent during the planning phase, by estimating the likely division of effort based on the level of maturity of the enterprise. However, this only provides an average value and takes no account of peaks and troughs.

To successfully cope with periods of exceptional demand, we require a mechanism for prioritizing initiatives. In particular, when tactical initiatives start to compete for resources with strategic ones, we require a mechanism for deciding where the resources should go. Not surprisingly, the best way to deal with this issue is by using risk analysis. Here, however, instead of analyzing threats and vulnerabilities directly, we need to compare the effect that delaying a strategic activity has on known risk against that of delaying (or canceling) a tactical activity. Given that tactical requirements tend to appear at short notice and require a quick response, there is often insufficient time to organize and perform a risk analysis involving all stakeholders, and this therefore requires judgment. The essential point is that this judgment should be made on the basis of perceived risk, and the way forward should be agreed with the appropriate business managers if the impact is nonnegligible.

When discussing the competition for resources between strategic and tactical initiatives, we are mainly concerned with project-related resources. A more serious clash of interests occurs when the staff concerned has security administration responsibilities. Here, we need to weigh the risks of not performing some particular action aimed at improving the overall level of security against the risks of reducing the operational support for the production environment. For this reason, it is extremely useful to prioritize administration activities and to allow for the possibility of a degraded mode of operation. Although such an extreme measure may not be used very frequently, it is just as well to be able to use such a mechanism in times of need. In this context, it is worth mentioning that some strategic initiatives require considerable input from experienced administrators in order to achieve their goals, and it may be necessary to envisage accepting more risk in the short term in order to provide a stable long-term solution.

One of the benefits of decomposing the strategic plan into a series of projects is that the activity of tracking progress can be delegated. Wherever possible, it is by far the best approach to adopt existing standards for project management and reporting to achieve this, as it is to be expected that these standards will be aligned with the normal reporting process. Where such standards do not exist, there is little choice but to define them for local use. It is also beneficial to have "internal" projects (i.e., those that do not require funding and can therefore be run under the control of the information-security department) comply with these standards, which results in a uniform tracking process. Note that it is the tracking that is being delegated here and not the management of the strategy. Although project managers are expected to manage their own projects, managing the dependencies between projects and planning at the macroscopic level is the role of the information-security manager.

Unfortunately, introducing formal planning and tracking mechanisms into The Secure Bank proved to be rather problematic. Although the executive management had succeeded in creating a culture based on innovation and creativity, this had resulted in a somewhat undisciplined environment with few agreed standards. Planning and tracking was therefore introduced as an initiative internal to the information-security department, and reports to management followed the standard format, largely based on free text. Project-planning techniques were introduced approximately 18 months later by the quality department, with the result that the existing process had to be adapted to meet the new standards.

Following up on the quick win identified during the consolidation phase, it was decided to use the issues database to track project-related issues in addition to those flagged by external parties. This involved a minor change to the database to indicate the origin and scope of the issue. At a later stage, it was noticed that a significant number of issues were due to dependencies on other projects that were not being correctly managed. This observation led to another modification in order to permit the tracking of dependencies. Finally, after a period of 2 years, and following a period of continual improvement in the area of project management overseen by the quality department, The Secure Bank created a project office function. The latter agreed to assist in resolving dependencies on external projects and, over a period of time, took responsibility for negotiating the resolution of external dependencies on behalf of the IT security department.

4.5.5 Monitoring for further improvement

Monitoring the effectiveness of the strategy involves far more than just tracking the projects that make up the strategic plan. Monitoring projects will only provide us with feedback on the implementation issues and will provide no useful information on how successful new procedures and tools are once they have been deployed.

Monitoring the effectiveness of the information-security approach involves monitoring a number of different aspects, all of which provide valuable information on how well the approach is responding to the organization's needs. Useful areas to monitor include:

▸ Effectiveness and efficiency of procedures and mechanisms;

▸ Acceptance within the user community;

▸ Alignment with business strategy;

▸ Alignment with external events.

Where procedures are concerned, a healthy dialogue with stakeholders should result in a continual feedback of the impact of any changes, and this is where any signs of problems are likely to be first picked up. However, it is a good idea to plan for more structured feedback by including checkpoints in the strategic plan. A checkpoint might simply consist of a meeting with the manager or managers impacted by a recently completed project and publication of the minutes, or it might involve speaking to staff directly impacted by the changes and producing a more detailed report. Either way, planning for and using checkpoints is a good way of checking up on how changes are being received in the field.

Feedback on the effectiveness of security mechanisms is more likely to come from technical staff. At The Secure Bank, the biweekly meeting with production support staff will provide a useful forum for discussing the impact of changes to the technical infrastructure.

Monitoring acceptance within the user community should obviously be an ongoing activity and should make use of all possible contacts within the organization. All members of the IT security department were therefore encouraged to regularly request feedback from the people with whom they work and to report any issues via the internal reporting line. Similarly, IT security staff was asked to promote the Web site and the bulletin board as a way of exchanging information with the department. Finally, the awareness presentations were designed to encourage a high degree of participation from the target audience, and a member of the team was designated to accompany the information-security manager to take note of all issues that arose during these presentations.

The business strategy will be monitored within the information-security steering committee. This will be achieved by including a fixed item on the agenda dedicated to this issue. During each meeting, stakeholders will be required to communicate any changes of business strategy likely to have an impact on the approach to information security.

Last, but not least, team leaders within the IT security department will be made responsible for following external events relevant to their area of responsibility. This will include following a number of information sources, including:

- Security alerts and information relating to vulnerabilities;
- Technological trends;
- Studies and reports.

Staff will be invited to make presentations to the department on interesting developments as part of the quarterly department meetings.

4.6   The core deliverables

The remaining chapters of this book analyze particular aspects of the strategic-planning cycle in more detail. These chapters have been organized to reflect the core deliverables of the approach, namely:

- The information-security strategy;

▸ Policy documents and supporting standards;

▸ The IT security architecture;

▸ User awareness material.

As these deliverables are the cornerstones of our approach, we'll describe their significance briefly before proceeding with a more in-depth treatment.

The information-security strategy has already been referred to several times and provides the vision for the next 3 to 5 years. Among other things, the strategy should outline how the other core deliverables will be produced or will evolve during this period.

The way in which policy statements are structured is expected to vary considerably from organization to organization, but in all cases it is important that policy documents be produced as part of a structured documentation set. Failure to do so is likely to result in confusion, particularly when several policy documents coexist. Policy documents provide a high-level statement of requirements in a certain domain. Most organizations are expected to publish an information-security policy, an IT security policy, or both, and some organizations will opt to produce a hierarchy of policies. As will be explained later, we will favor the less complex approach and aim to produce two policies, one destined for end users and the other destined for IT specialists, taking care to ensure that the two policies are consistent with one another. IT security standards are documents that support policy by providing an interpretation of policy statements in specific situations. Standards add value by encouraging a common approach to dealing with specific issues, thereby reducing complexity.

The purpose of designing an IT security architecture is to ensure the optimal use of technology in reducing risk. Using an architectural approach involves taking an end-to-end view of security issues. By designing an architecture that provides a series of mutually reinforcing security mechanisms, weaknesses specific to individual systems can be protected by using compensating controls provided by the architecture.

Finally, user-awareness material provides the bridge between the information-security department and other profiles within the organization. User-awareness material *can* therefore play a critical role in the general scheme of things by providing one of the most important mechanisms for communicating the approach to the end user. However, user-awareness material is generally only effective if it is supported by a coherent approach to the whole issue of communicating with end users. We will discuss this point in some detail towards the end of the book.

4.7 Summary

In order to be successful, any approach to securing information must be aligned with corporate culture and values. Developing a thorough understanding of cultural issues and establishing solid interpersonal relationships take time, but both are a necessary prerequisite to establishing a durable approach; hence, new managers should try to agree to a consolidation period before releasing a long-term strategy.

The main objectives of the consolidation period are to establish a network of contacts and to gather sufficient information to allow the definition of the information-security strategy. Managers are also encouraged to devise a personal strategy for success by taking into account such factors as the maturity of the organization and key corporate values.

During the consolidation period, the current situation is analyzed to identify strong and weak points. This involves identifying the major stakeholders in the security process and listening to what they have to say about the current situation and how it could be improved. Ongoing activities that are unlikely to fit into the future strategy are terminated in an organized manner, and a short-term plan is devised to take care of high-priority issues that arise out of discussion with the stakeholders. Any issues that cannot be handled in the short term automatically become candidates for the strategy.

The end of the consolidation period marks the beginning of the first strategic-planning cycle. From this point on, strategic work should proceed via a series of planned cycles, each lasting from 3 to 5 years. This work will constantly compete for resources with more tactical initiatives, and the extent to which the effort should be divided between the two types of work depends on the maturity level of the organization. All strategic cycles except the first encompass four phases: definition of the strategy, production of a strategic plan, execution of the plan, and monitoring. The first strategic cycle is slightly different in that the first phase is built into the consolidation period.

The strategic approach proposed by this book involves the production of four core sets of deliverables: the information-security strategy, the policy documents and supporting standards, the IT security architecture, and the user-awareness material. Subsequent chapters of this book build on the material in this chapter and show how these deliverables can be used to construct a solid and flexible foundation for information security.

References

[1]   Taite, J., "Security as a Key Business Enabler," September 2003, http://www.scmagazine.com/scmagazine/sc-online/2001/article/035/article.html.

[2]   Harris, S., *CISSP, MCSE, CCNA, All-In-One CISSP Certification: Exam Guide*, Berkeley, CA: McGraw-Hill/Osborne, 2002, pp. 68–69.

[3]   Wan, C., "Developing A Security Policy—Overcoming Those Hurdles," September 2003, http://www.sans.org/rr/paper.php?id=915.

[4]   Parasuraman, N. S., "Production Possibility Frontier (PPF)," October 2003, http://www.geocities.com/parasu41/PPF.

[5]   "The Production Possibility Frontier," September 2003, http://www.netmba.com/econ/micro/production/possibility.

[6] Nellis, R., CISSP, "Creating an IT Security Awareness Program for Senior Management," September 2003, http://www.sans.org/rr/paper.php?id=992.

[7] Pereira, B., "Security Policies: The Right Approach," September 2003, http://www.networkmagazineindia.com/200211/cover2.shtml.

[8] Hinson, G., "Information Security Jargon Buster," September 2003, http://www.cccl.net/information/2000_1_jargon_buster.html.

[9] Wenstrom, M., *Managing Cisco Network Security*, Indianapolis, IN: Cisco Press, 2001, p. 41.

[10] Bayuk, J. L., "Information Security Metrics: An Audit-Based Approach," September 2003, http://csrc.ncsl.nist.gov/csspab/june13-15/Bayuk.pdf.

[11] "Systems Security Engineering Capability Maturity Model," September 2003, http://www.sse-cmm.org/model/ssecmmv2final.pdf.

[12] "The Information Systems Security Engineering Process, IATF Release 3.1—September 2002," September 2003, http://www.iatf.net/framework_docs/version-3_1/index.cfm.

The information-security strategy

5.1 The need for a strategy

For some activities in life, we only have an approximate idea of where we want to go when we set out, and we gradually refine our idea of the ideal destination as we follow the route we have chosen. A typical career path might be a good example of the latter situation. Few people leaving school or college are able to define what they would like to be doing in 30 years time and, even for those that can, the route they choose to get there often influences their final career choice. For many organizations, finding the right approach to information security will be a similar experience. First ideas will probably be incomplete and may prove to be completely inappropriate in the long term, but the approach that is best for the organization will gradually reveal itself as experience is gained from implementing these ideas.

Although many organizations will initially be unable to precisely define the ideal target situation where information security is concerned, they will almost certainly be able to identify improvements to the current situation and these improvements can be used to define an intermediate goal. This is the situation at The Secure Bank, where the organization as a whole has not yet made any attempt to define what the term *appropriate security* means and has not given any consideration to how much risk it is willing to take in exchange for business opportunities. In this case, therefore, the analogy of the career path is probably a good one and we will need to make a first educated guess at the target situation and expect to learn a lot while trying to get there.

As a result of these observations, the first core deliverable we produce at The Secure Bank is the information-security strategy. Note that we do not aim to rewrite the security policy as a first step, because it will take a lot of time to discover what the most appropriate policy should look like. The production and agreement of the information-security policy will, however, be one of the activities comprising the strategy. Equivalently, we do not try to derive the ideal target situation from the existing security policy, as we know that there are problems with this document.

The information-security strategy is the roadmap for the foreseeable future and details how the organization intends to progress along the path of maturity illustrated in Figure 4.1. The strategy therefore provides a consistent and coherent framework for improvement and ensures that the organization remains focused on the most important issues. In order to achieve this, however, the strategy must take account of all activity in the information-security domain. In particular, successful strategies recognize that a certain amount of tactical work is inevitable and take account of the likely impact of such work.

In the rest of this chapter, we illustrate the steps that were taken to produce and agree on the strategy at The Secure Bank. The resulting strategy is probably too simple for a real-life situation, but complexity will be avoided where it is not needed. This will enable us to concentrate on the method while still supplying enough detail to illustrate where and when trade-offs need to be made.

5.2 Planning

At The Secure Bank, the information strategy was developed as a series of steps:

> • Analysis of the current situation;
> • Identification of business-strategy requirements;
> • Identification of legal and regulatory requirements;
> • Identification of requirements due to external trends;
> • Definition of the target situation;
> • Definition and prioritization of strategic initiatives;
> • Distribution of the draft strategy;
> • Agreement and publication of final strategy.

The first four of these steps concentrated on identifying strategic requirements. Discussions with stakeholders indicated that such requirements were most likely to arise in one of these four areas. In each case, major issues were identified and requirements were derived from these issues. In step five, these requirements were consolidated and verified for coherency. The complete list of strategic requirements was then used to define the target situation.

The next step, definition and prioritization of strategic initiatives, involved identifying and prioritizing the strategic initiatives that would have to be undertaken in order to satisfy the strategic requirements. Initiatives were designed to resolve logically related groups of requirements and initially prioritized by cost and ability to mitigate risk. Finally, the prioritization of initiatives was reviewed by taking into account the provisional planning for future projects and exploiting obvious synergies. The result of this step was a high-level planning of the strategic initiatives.

The strategy document was produced and agreed on with stakeholders as a result of the last two steps. Following approval, the strategy document was published on the organization's intranet.

The timeline illustrating how this was achieved at The Secure Bank is shown in Figure 5.1.

The strategic-planning effort was started at the beginning of the second month. The first four steps were carried out in parallel and took a total of 3 months to complete. The definition of the target situation and the prioritization of initiatives took a further month, which resulted in the publication of the first proposal at the end of month five. The final proposal was published at the end of month six after having incorporated comments from stakeholders and was approved by the information-security steering committee in month seven.

5.3   Analysis of the current situation

Of all the defined tasks, the analysis of the current situation took the longest to complete. This was due to a number of factors:

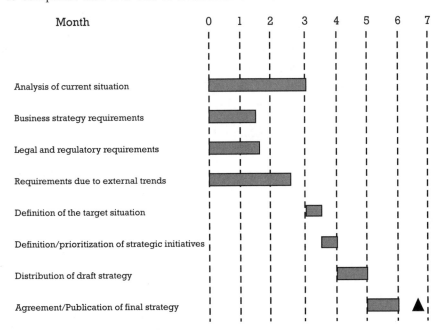

Figure 5.1   Producing the information-security strategy.

▸ The overall standard of documentation was poor. Many documents had either been lost or not produced in the first place. Where documents did exist, they were often out of date.

▸ Stakeholders were initially cautious in their observations, but became more open as the initiative developed.

▸ Many of the staff that had contributed to the earlier initiatives had since left the organization.

▸ Despite efforts to present the exercise as an objective analysis, staff from the IT security unit clearly felt exposed to criticism and tended to react defensively to identified issues.

In addition to confirming known issues, this analysis revealed a wealth of minor details, most of which were subsequently tracked using the issues database. Table 5.1 lists the only three new major issues that were defined.

The first issue was rated as medium priority because a temporary solution was identified in agreement with the IT department. The other two issues were causing a certain level of inefficiency, but neither was business critical. Equivalently, there were good arguments for implementing solutions to these problems as soon as possible, hence the rating of medium priority.

The final deliverable of this exercise was the list of strategic requirements summarized in Table 5.2. These requirements were formulated to cover the medium and low priority issues identified in Chapter 4 (for which no corrective actions have yet been defined) and the three issues identified in Table 5.1. In addition, a strategic requirement was added in the area of user awareness, as the work carried out in the consolidation period in this area only provided a short-term solution to an important problem.

In Table 5.2, strategic requirements have been mapped back to issues by referring to the identifiers of the latter. Although this has been done here by referring to a section in the previous chapter of this book, in reality, this

Table 5.1 New Major Issues

Id	Issue	Priority
I18	Whereas there was a clear IT owner for most types of technology, certain types of systems (notably the more recent additions, such as the application server) had not been designated an owner. As a result, many necessary security enhancements had not been made to these systems.	Medium
I19	Although the point was not specifically raised by any of the stakeholders, a review of past events demonstrated a clear requirement for a secure e-mail implementation for certain groups within the enterprise. This mainly affected executive management, human resources, and audit.	Medium
I20	Several departments had experienced difficulties in transferring information from the public Internet workstations to the internal network. Many users had a clear business requirement to do this, as information that was previously distributed on storage media (such as compact discs) was now only available over the Internet.	Medium

Table 5.2   Strategic Requirements Arising Out of Analysis of Current Situation

Id	Strategic Requirement	Underlying Issue
R1	The organization shall design, agree on, and implement a new approach to information security, which is in line with business expectations, pragmatic and capable of dealing with day-to-day issues, and aligned with the approach to physical security and human resources.	*Issues I7 and I11, Section 4.4.4* The current approach to information security is generally thought to be too theoretical. A more hands-on approach is required. There has been no attempt to create a coherent framework including physical security and personnel issues.
R2	The organization shall ensure that all responsibilities within the area of information security are agreed on and documented.	*Issues I8 and I13, Section 4.4.4 plus I18* Responsibilities are poorly defined and do not match what happens in reality. In addition, the current set of responsibilities is incoherent across the enterprise. Also, certain IT systems have no designated owners.
R3	The organization shall define, agree on, and implement an approach to risk management in the information-security domain.	*Issue I9, Section 4.4.4* There is no collaboration between the risk-management group and the IT security group.
R4	The organization shall ensure that current security administration procedures are modified and/or automated to ensure sufficient scalability for projected requirements.	*Issues I10 and I13, Section 4.4.4* Existing procedures for security administration are based on those originally defined for the mainframe. These procedures do not scale well and are often ignored. There is little automation in place. Administration of access rights on the mainframe is currently carried out by the audit department.
R5	The organization shall design, agree on, and implement an IT security architecture capable of providing core security services in an efficient manner.	*Issues I16 and I17, Section 4.4.4 plus I20* The current IT infrastructure is complex and there is little product standardization. The existing deployment of security tools is very limited and economies of scale have not been realized. In addition, transferring information from Internet workstations to the internal network is problematic.
R6	The organization shall design, agree on, and implement an approach to integrating information security into the product development and acquisition life cycle.	*Issues I14 and I15, Section 4.4.4* There has been no attempt to align information security with software development and purchasing activities. In addition, testing is carried out in less secure environments using production data.
R7	The organization shall design, agree on, and implement a secure mail solution for those groups having a requirement for confidential mail exchanges.	*Issue I19* Certain groups within the enterprise require confidentiality protection of mail. This mainly affected executive management, human resources, and audit.
R8	The organization shall design and execute an information-security training program with the aim of making staff aware of the important issues and the approach the organization will take to resolving them.	*Issue I3, Section 4.4.4* There is little dialogue between the security department and other departments. The main point of contact is a yearly presentation, which is largely out of date.

would involve referencing the appropriate document. This technique of mapping requirements to issues is extremely useful, and initiatives will be mapped to requirements in a similar manner. Throughout the strategic-planning cycle, these references can be used to relate ongoing activities back to the issues they are designed to resolve. This is a good technique both for checking coherence and for keeping an eye on how risk is being mitigated. Similarly, at the end of any given strategic initiative, such references provide a mechanism for measuring to what extent the initiative has resolved the underlying issues.

Of the medium- and long-term issues identified as a result of discussions with stakeholders, issue I12, insufficient security of mobile devices, could not easily be associated with any strategic requirement. This issue was therefore resolved separately and progress was tracked using the issues database introduced as a quick win in the consolidation period.

5.4 Identification of business strategy requirements

The business strategy of the organization is likely to have a significant impact on future IT requirements and can therefore be expected to have an impact on future information-security requirements also. It therefore makes sense to analyze the business strategy in order to identify changes that need to be applied to the current information-security framework to successfully support the new business model.

Unfortunately, analyzing the business strategy may prove to be extremely difficult in practice, for a number of reasons:

- ‣ A documented business strategy may not exist.
- ‣ The business strategy may be under review.
- ‣ The business strategy may be inaccessible.

A business strategy that is under review is difficult to interpret unless it is clear which parts of the strategy are being reviewed and which parts remain stable. If this is not clear, or if no documented strategy exists, the best way to proceed is to convince business managers of the need to identify plans that are likely to have a significant impact on the information-security frame-work. While there may be no formal strategy, there certainly should be some form of future planning, and the goal is then to obtain as much information as possible through meetings with stakeholders.

For those organizations that have defined a strategy, most are likely to regard the content as highly sensitive information, if only because knowledge of the strategy would presumably be extremely valuable to competitors. Although some organizations publish a version of their business strategy on the Internet (see, for example, [1, 2]), this is almost certainly only the part of the strategy that the organization is willing to render public for marketing purposes. For these reasons, the business-strategy document may not be accessible to the information-security manager. Once again, the best way of dealing with this is to solicit the important information from stakeholders.

At The Secure Bank, we are informed by executive management that a business strategy does exist, but that this information is strictly restricted to the board of directors and those business managers that have a need to know. Our approach is therefore to set up meetings with each of the business lines. The results of these meetings identified several key strategic initiatives, but also some gray areas, where stakeholder opinions differed on the business goals to be achieved. The following strategic initiatives were identified as those most likely to have an impact on the information-security process:

▸ Development of private banking activities;

▸ Introduction of a range of financial services over the Internet;

▸ Restructuring of the branch office network;

▸ Closure of operations in Asia and the Middle East.

The biggest impact is linked to the first business objective, which is to aggressively develop the private banking side of the business. The target is to increase the customer base in this sector by 50% over the next 3 years. Revenue increases will be achieved not only as a result of the increase in the number of customers, but through the introduction of a range of financial services tailored for private-banking clients and available over the Internet. As these services are aimed at private-banking clients, the average amount associated with any transactions is expected to be quite high.

The risk associated with the systems implementing these services is therefore also expected to be high and the technical infrastructure should therefore be modified to take account of this change in risk profile. This is achieved by updating the issues underlying the strategic requirement R5, design and implementation of an IT security architecture. This is a better way to proceed than defining new technical requirements, as requirement R5 is sufficiently global in scope to cover these modifications.

Quite apart from any technical impact, it is clear that a significant increase of activity in the private-banking sector will necessitate modifications to the way in which customer data is currently handled. The business manager charged with developing this sector of activity believes that private-banking customers will be very demanding in terms of discretion and confidentiality and that many will be prepared to pay for special services, such as anonymous accounts. However, this type of service will only be a viable proposition to clients if the underlying security framework is capable of enforcing the required level of confidentiality throughout the IT infrastructure. This therefore merits the definition of a separate requirement.

The restructuring of the branch office network and closure of operations in Asia and the Middle East will require considerable activity to consolidate operations within a lesser number of larger branch offices situated at strategic locations. As there will be a lot of changes made to the existing network infrastructure, there is a possible synergy in replacing leased line connectivity by Internet connectivity at the same time. Although we have not yet looked in any detail at the question of implementing a security architecture, a move towards Internet connectivity for branch offices would be logical given the bank's innovative culture and clear commitment to getting the most out of new technologies. Introducing Internet connectivity would also result in significant cost savings, as the existing leased lines could be decommissioned. Once again, this technical requirement is bundled into requirement R5.

In speaking with stakeholders, it is clear that the decision to restructure the branch offices and to close down operations in Asia and the Middle East is expected to result in redundancies. The manager responsible for the branch office network thinks that there may be opposition in some countries, mainly in the form of strikes, but does not rule out a more extreme response, such as sabotage. As many branch offices store customer information, this constitutes a risk to the reputation of the bank. If data were rendered public, this may also result in lawsuits against the organization. As a result, it is imperative that the information-security department works closely with the business to ensure that the bank's data and systems are protected against these threats.

In summary, the strategic requirements arising out of the business strategy are summarized in Table 5.3.

As an aside, requirement R9 will almost certainly have an impact on the way in which future applications will be designed and configured. This is

Table 5.3 **Strategic Requirements Arising Out of the Business Strategy**

Id	Strategic Requirement	Underlying Issue
R5	The organization shall design, agree on, and implement an IT security architecture capable of providing core security services in an efficient manner.	*New issues supporting requirement R5:* *Issue I21:* The existing system and network architecture must be modified to enable the bank to offer financial services associated with a high degree of risk over the Internet. *Issue I22:* Regional offices must be connected to the central site using standard Internet protocols in order to lower costs and to enable a common approach to network security throughout the organization.
R9	The organization shall implement measures to protect the confidentiality of data relating to customers and their banking operations that are compatible with the requirements of the private-banking sector.	*Issue I23:* The business strategy is to significantly increase activity in the private-banking sector. This will result in a need for greater confidentiality for data associated with such customers.
R10	The organization shall ensure that an approach to securing systems and data is agreed on as part of the preparation for the restructuring of branch offices and closure of operations in Asia and the Middle East.	*Issue I24:* The plans to restructure the branch office network and close down operations in Asia and the Middle East may result in social unrest and disruptive actions in some countries.

therefore an excellent starting point for a dialogue with project development and acquisition teams. By launching the dialogue at this early stage, we are able to provide requirements for the future long before the business lines request work begin on developing new systems.

5.5 Identification of legal and regulatory requirements

Legal and regulatory requirements usually place restrictions on what the organization is able to do with its systems and data. These requirements can therefore have a major impact on the information-security strategy, and it is important to identify and thoroughly understand these requirements before formulating the latter.

Examples of legal requirements that are likely to have a significant impact on the way in which data and systems are secured include:

- Data protection laws;
- Privacy laws;
- Laws relating to banking secrecy;
- Laws limiting the use of cryptographic protection mechanisms.

For all of these issues, the appropriate point of contact within the enterprise is likely to be the legal department, and defining an approach to ensure compliance with legal requirements will normally require a joint effort involving both the legal department and the information-security department.

Data protection has been an important issue for many years, and many countries have introduced legislation in this area. In Europe, the European Commission's Directive on Data Protection came into effect in October 1998 [3], and most European Union countries have implemented this directive since by passing national legislation. In the United Kingdom, for instance, at the time of writing, the latest data protection act was passed in 1998 [4] and came into effect in 2001. This act, and the related Freedom of Information Act [5] passed in 2000, are under the supervision of the Information Commissioner [6], an independent authority who reports directly to the U.K. parliament.

By means of comparison, the approach to data protection in the United States is based less on legislation and more on regulation. Nevertheless, there have recently been moves to introduce legislation in this area, and two competing database protection bills have been recently submitted to Congress:

- The Consumer and Investor Access to Information Act of 1999 (H.R. 1858 [7]);
- The Collections of Information Anti-Piracy Act of 1999 (H.R. 354 [8]).

A decision on these bills is still pending. More recently, SB 1386 became effective in California in July 2003. This bill requires custodians of information relating to individuals to disclose any security incidents that are likely to have resulted in the unauthorized acquisition of personal data to those concerned [9].

As a result of the different approaches to data protection adopted by European Union nations and the United States, the European Commission and the U.S. Department of Commerce developed the *Safe Harbor* framework [10] to allow U.S. organizations to be compliant with European privacy laws. U.S. companies likely to be affected by the Safe Harbor agreement should therefore consider adapting their information-security strategy to ensure compliance with this framework [10].

Just as approaches to data protection vary considerably from country to country, so do approaches to ensuring privacy [11]. In Europe, the European Union Directive on Privacy and Electronic Communications [12] was adopted by the European parliament in July 2002. With the notable exception of the Children's Online Privacy Protection Act (COPPA) [13], efforts to introduce similar global legislation covering the private sector in the United States have so far been unsuccessful [10]. In the public sector, however, legislation dates back to 1974 [14], and there have been some interesting developments in particular sectors of activity, such as the Health Insurance Portability and Accountability Act (HIPAA [15]). The Electronic Privacy Information Center publishes updates to the status of bills related to privacy, speech, and cyber liberties in the United States [16].

Within certain countries, notably Luxemburg [17] and Switzerland [18], financial institutions may also be subject to further restrictions as a result of banking secrecy laws. In both of these countries, current legislation is aimed at protecting the confidentiality of customer data, including contact details and details of financial operations.

Finally, there has been a lot of activity in recent years related to the use of cryptography, although legislation varies greatly from country to country [19–23]. This is important for international organizations that require secure communications with entities in foreign countries, as the legislation in effect at the remote location may limit or disallow the use of strong cryptography.

For organizations that are subject to regulatory control, such as government and financial institutions, the regulatory body may define further constraints or, alternatively, specify in greater detail how legal requirements are to be satisfied. Examples of regulatory requirements taken from the finance industry include:

‣ Requirements to conform to particular security standards;

‣ Requirements relating to the protection of customer-related data;

‣ Requirements relating to business continuity.

Organizations affected by regulatory issues often designate a compliance officer, whose function is to ensure that the organization satisfies the requirements of the regulatory body. Even if the compliance officer does not exist, there will normally be some point of contact with the regulatory body in question, and this person is the appropriate contact point for resolving any issues in this area.

A common approach adopted by regulatory bodies is to require the adoption of certain standards. As an example, U.S. federal agencies are expected to adopt the FIPS published by the NIST [24]. Regulatory bodies in the financial sector may require compliance with internationally accepted standards, such as Trusted Computer Security Evaluation Criteria (TCSEC) [25] or Information Technology Security Evaluation Criteria (ITSEC) [26]. Because modern enterprises typically require solutions to be put in place quickly, and the majority of business-related software is not developed with such considerations in mind, complying with such standards can be difficult and may well have a bearing on the strategic plan.

Where The Secure Bank is concerned, the important legal requirements are in the areas of privacy and data protection. The Secure Bank has branch offices in many different countries, and national legislation on privacy and data protection differs considerably from country to country. We therefore define requirements to clarify what needs to be done within each country in order to be compliant with the national legislation and to implement appropriate controls. In addition, the central office is required to be compliant with local banking regulations, which in this case means that procedures and mechanisms used to enforce appropriate security must be compatible with criteria published by the regulatory body. These requirements are summarized in Table 5.4.

As we will see in later chapters, these requirements will not be easy to meet and will require extensive changes to current procedures. As an example, to be compliant with these requirements, it will no longer be possible to use production data in development and test environments without implementing additional controls.

As a final check, we verify our understanding of the key requirements as stated here with the internal audit department. Once confirmed, these requirements are documented and will influence our choice of strategic initiatives.

5.6   Identification of requirements due to external trends

So far, our approach to defining a strategy has taken into consideration requirements arising out of an analysis of the current situation, legal and regulatory requirements, and requirements associated with the business strategy. None of these reflect changes in the threat environment or the associated risk due to external factors. Interestingly, it is precisely this type of change that is likely to have the biggest impact on any approach to information security in the long term.

Examples of external factors that would be expected to result in new or modified threats include:

Table 5.4 Strategic Requirements Associated with Legal and Regulatory Stipulations

Id	Strategic Requirement	Underlying Issue
R4	The organization shall ensure that current security administration procedures are modified and/or automated to ensure sufficient scalability for projected requirements.	New issue supporting requirement R4: *Issue I25:* Procedures must be compliant with the criteria published by the regulatory body.
R5	The organization shall design, agree on, and implement an IT security architecture capable of providing core security services in an efficient manner.	New issue supporting requirement R5: *Issue I26:* The infrastructure that supports security-related functionality must be compliant with the criteria published by the regulatory body.
R11	The organization shall implement measures to ensure that the privacy of data relating to staff and other third parties is managed according to the requirements of the legislation of the country in which the data is stored.	*Issue I27:* Branch offices store data on customers and other third parties on local servers. Privacy laws governing how such data should be managed vary significantly from country to country.
R12	The organization shall implement measures to ensure that data relating to staff and other third parties is managed in line with data protection requirements of the legislation of the country in which the data is stored.	*Issue I28:* Branch offices store data on customers and other third parties on local servers. Data protection laws governing how such data should be managed vary significantly from country to country.

> • Changes in the economy;
>
> • Political events;
>
> • Mergers and acquisitions;
>
> • Technological evolution.

Of these examples, the first two could be expected to modify the threat environment as a consequence of their social impact. It is obvious that disgruntled staff members are more likely to constitute a threat than motivated ones [27]. Similarly, when acquired rights and benefits come under threat as a result of economic considerations, it is not uncommon to witness disruptive action by staff. In the latter case, this can take many diverse forms, ranging from legal and orderly protest to deliberate sabotage. Indeed, the most significant change in the global threat environment of the last decade, that of terrorism, has its origins in changes in the political environment [28]. However, the impact of social and political changes is not limited to changes in the threat environment. Such changes may also have a negative impact on staff motivation and therefore introduce new vulnerabilities into the security framework.

Consequently, to the extent to which it is possible to predict changes in the economic or social climate, the likely effects of such changes should be factored in to the information-security strategy. As this book is being written, the Bush administration in the United States is taking steps to ensure that the approach to security at the national level is adapted to reflect the events of September 11, 2001, and their consequences [29]. In parallel, many organizations are adapting their approach to security to take account of the increased probability of terrorist attacks.

Mergers and acquisitions can also be emotive events for those concerned and often involve important changes in company culture [30]. In many cases, risk is likely to rise quite sharply in the immediate period following the event for a variety of reasons. These include the effect on staff, who are likely to experience doubt about the future, a period of reduced control during which processes and procedures are harmonized across the organization, and, most likely, restrictions on spending as the organization strives to demonstrate increased profitability.

Unlike changes in the economy, political events, and mergers and acquisitions, technological evolution is easier to predict in the sense that we know that it will happen, and we often have advanced warning of major changes. It is therefore easier to plan a response to this type of evolution. The key to understanding and reacting to technological evolution is to have an organized approach to gathering and processing information. Because the ability to follow trends in the external marketplace is so critical to managing risk, it is a good idea to establish a *technology watch* within the team to take care of this. This will turn out to be one of the strategic initiatives identified by The Secure Bank. The mission of the technology watch function is not restricted to following changes directly related to information security (such an approach would not be very proactive, as security concerns do not typically drive technological innovation). Nevertheless, the person or people carrying out this function would be expected to make maximum use of the information sources described in Section 2.1 of this book.

At The Secure Bank, technological evolution was thought to be the only significant external factor that would lead to the definition of strategic requirements at the time the strategy was developed. Here, a number of areas of increasing risk were identified including:

▸ Spam;

▸ Malicious code;

▸ Web security;

▸ Privacy and trust;

▸ Wireless communication;

▸ Home working;

▸ Use of mobile computing devices.

Given the significant gap between the current state of the security framework and the threats associated with recent technological developments, it was decided to include a strategic initiative to analyze the impact of these developments in more detail and to provide recommendations on how to proceed. In parallel, the identified areas of increasing risk would be monitored as part of the design and implementation of the security architecture to ensure that the final architecture does not prevent the deployment of new software in these areas.

Finally, given that the lack of communication with staff was identified as a major issue, it was decided to launch an initiative to build on the small Web site developed during the consolidation period.

The strategic recommendations, which were formulated due to external factors, are summarized in Table 5.5.

5.7   Definition of the target situation

At The Secure Bank, the target situation is defined in terms of a series of strategic requirements on the current approach. If we manage to satisfy these requirements, we can reasonably claim that we will be where we want to be at the end of the strategic-planning period.

In fact, there is one last strategic requirement that needs to be added to the list of requirements identified so far (see Table 5.6). This is due to a management decision that was taken in month three of the exercise: to reduce expenditure globally by 25% over the next 18 months. This decision came about as the result of a study commissioned by the board of directors in which the bank's profitability was benchmarked against the industry standard. As a result, all departments will set a target for cost reduction. However, at the time the strategy was compiled, this target was not known for the information-security department. Although this decision has not yet become part of the business strategy of the bank, it is clear, that it will have major repercussions on the way in which the bank operates. We therefore treat this as a strategic requirement.

Table 5.5   Strategic Requirements Related to External Factors

Id	Strategic Requirement	Underlying Issue
R5	The organization shall design, agree on, and implement an IT security architecture capable of providing core security services in an efficient manner.	New issue supporting requirement R5: *Issue 129:* There is a significant gap between the current state of the security framework and the threats and opportunities associated with recent technological developments.
R13	The organization shall perform an analysis of threats and opportunities associated with recent technological developments and recommend how to proceed.	*Issue 129:* There is a significant gap between the current state of the security framework and the threats and opportunities associated with recent technological developments.
R14	The organization shall design, agree on, and implement effective communications channels for ensuring that all staff are appropriately informed about information security–related matters.	*Issue 13:* There is little dialogue between the security department and other departments. The main point of contact is a yearly presentation, which is largely out of date.

Table 5.6   Last Strategic Requirement

Id	Strategic Requirement	Underlying Issue
R15	The organization shall reduce expenditure related to information security in line with management directives.	*Issue 130:* Management's decision to reduce expenditure globally by 25% over the next 18 months.

To summarize, the target situation at the end of the strategic-planning period is one in which the current situation has been modified to satisfy the strategic requirements R1 to R15. The next step consists of analyzing exactly how this will be achieved (at the macroscopic level) and how long it will take.

5.8   Definition and prioritization of strategic initiatives

A simple approach to defining the initiatives that make up the strategy would be to define one initiative per strategic requirement and to prioritize them according to some predefined criteria. This, however, is unlikely to be the most efficient strategy, as such a method takes no account of other activities that will be ongoing during the same period. A better approach is to gather information on future projects and to define and prioritize initiatives in such a way as to obtain as much benefit as possible from possible synergies.

At the Secure Bank, not only are we not allowed to see the strategy document, there exists no centralized control over project activity (although this was introduced later in the form of a program management team). Hence, it is necessary to piece together a project roadmap for the future based on information we can glean from stakeholders. The result is far from ideal but will allow us to order some initiatives so as to take advantage of likely synergies. The project roadmap we derived is displayed in Figure 5.2.

A few comments are in order at this point:

▸ The "Introduction of New Tariffs" and "Implement New Accounting Rules" projects have no impact on information security and can therefore be ignored.

▸ Apart from the cost-cutting exercise and the initiative to offer personalized information to private-banking customers over the Web, dates are only a best guess based on discussions with stakeholders.

▸ There is a high degree of uncertainty associated with the planning of the last project, to the extent that no sensible date could even be guessed at this point.

Although the possibilities are rather limited, some synergies can be realized here. To start with, we decide to begin work on designing the architecture immediately, even though we do not yet have a budget, in order to be

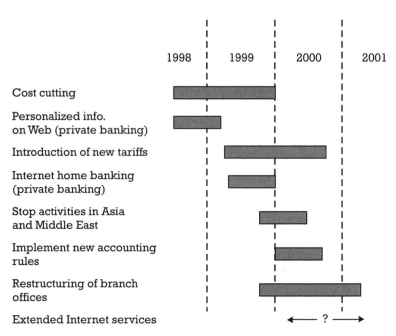

Figure 5.2 Derived project roadmap for The Secure Bank.

ready to contribute to the Internet home banking initiative when it starts in the second quarter of 1999. This is realizable, as the design stage can be achieved with a small team and costs can be absorbed as part of daily business. As designing an IT security architecture typically takes from 3 to 6 months, this will allow us to develop the essential ideas before the home banking project begins.

The resolution of requirement R15, reduction of expenditure, must start immediately, as the planning for this has been fixed by executive management. This is an example of a strategic initiative for which there is absolutely no flexibility in terms of planning. The same is not true, however, for requirements R9, R11, and R12, all of which are concerned with confidentiality and privacy issues. The resolution of these issues is planned to start in the first quarter of 1999 to take advantage of the work that has been carried out with the marketing department regarding the privacy issue.

Requirement R10 is effectively preparation for the plans to close down operations in Asia and the Middle East and to restructure the branch office network. It therefore makes sense to plan to do this work in the second quarter of 1999. This date is chosen to coincide with other preparation activities that will be ongoing at this date. For the remaining requirements, there is little to be gained from planning around this vision of future projects, so these initiatives will be prioritized based on their degree of difficulty, likely cost, and likely impact on risk.

We note in passing that this prioritization results in the production of the information-security policy almost a year after we start our mission. The reason that this doesn't really result in any problems is that we introduced risk analysis as an essential tool early on in the consolidation period. This approach also has the benefit of encouraging managers to think in terms of risk first and policy afterwards, which leads to more conscious decision making.

With this last exercise completed, we finally have enough information to define and prioritize the initiatives that collectively comprise the strategy. In order to further simplify tracking, it is a good idea to group initiatives into themes or *tracks*. The successful completion of a track should represent the termination of a logically connected series of projects. At The Secure Bank, we define the following tracks and initiatives. The strategic requirements satisfied by each initiative are listed in parentheses following the name of the initiative. Note that some requirements are satisfied using a stepwise approach. For instance, requirements R9, R11, and R12 are resolved by first defining suitable policy statements (initiative 2.1) and later describing how these policy statements are to be satisfied in particular situations (activity 2.2).

Track 1: Consolidation

1.1 Consolidation

1.2 Architectural design (R5)

Track 2: Framework initiatives

2.1 Policy (R1, R2, R9, R11, R12)

2.2 Standards (R6, R9, R11, R12)

2.3 Risk-management methodology (R3)

2.4 Information-security training (R8)

2.5 Administration procedures (R4)

2.6 Technology watch (R13)

Track 3: Technical initiatives

3.1 Secure mail solution (R7)

3.2 Information-security Web site (R14)

3.3 IT security architecture (R5)

3.4 Analysis of technical developments (R13)

Track 4: Operational initiatives

4.1 Support for restructuring/closure of operations (R10)

4.2 Cost control (R15)

A high-level plan, showing how the four tracks are spread over time, is shown in Figure 5.3. Although the consolidation period is not strictly a part of the strategy, it has been included for completeness. When the final document is produced, a short description of the initiatives carried out during the consolidation phase will help readers understand the background to the remaining activities. We show the planning details here to illustrate the method, but this level of detail will not be included in the strategy document itself. Of course, this high-level planning provides the basis for the strategic plan as explained in Section 4.5.3.

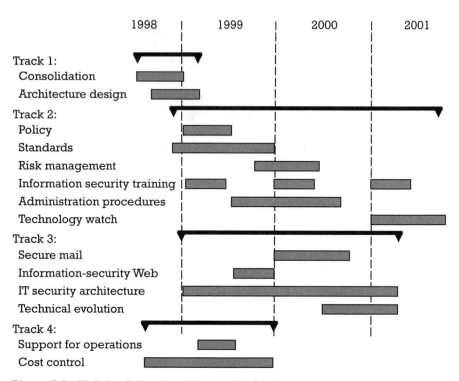

Figure 5.3 High-level planning of strategic initiatives.

When finalizing the strategy, it is important to remember that resource constraints have not been taken into account. The high-level plan that underpins the strategy is therefore an ideal. This fact will emerge when this high-level blueprint is turned into a strategic plan and, for some initiatives, it will be necessary to either reschedule the activity or request additional resources at the proposal stage.

5.9 Distribution of the draft strategy

The final strategy pulls all of this information together into a coherent, high-level description of the strategic objectives and how they will be achieved.

A suggested structure for the strategy document is as follows:

- The introduction;
- The mission statement of the information-security department;
- The major objectives that the strategy is designed to achieve;
- A description of each track in global terms;
- A description of the initiatives in each track;
- A summary.

The introduction should provide any background information that the reader needs to know in order to put the strategy in context. The introduction can also be used to explain how the document is structured and the information it contains.

The mission statement is optional, but it is useful to state it if it has been prepared. At The Secure Bank, no effort has been made to date to prepare a mission statement, and so the strategy does not contain this section. Well-defined mission statements are useful, however, as they capture the essence of what the information-security department is striving to achieve and can be used to make clear any limitations. Consequently, we will aim to include such a statement in future strategy documents (although this is already looking towards the next strategic-planning cycle).

The objectives simply restate the requirements in a generic fashion, without entering into details, and are followed by a description of the four streams or tracks of activity that we will undertake to achieve these objectives. The purpose of organizing initiatives into tracks is to group together all activities leading towards a common goal. In our case, we have defined four streams of activity: those activities associated with the consolidation period, activities aimed at defining the policy and procedural framework, activities required to construct a robust architecture, and activities required to support operations.

For each identified stream of activity, the strategy document should contain a short description of each of the defined initiatives. Where appropriate, it is useful to cross reference other initiatives, as this reveals interdependencies and illustrates how the strategy is being used to construct a coherent framework as opposed to defining a set of point solutions.

The summary recapitulates the main arguments by listing the main issues and showing how the strategy results in their resolution.

5.10 Agreement and publication of final strategy

Once the strategy has been produced, we need to ensure that it is formally adopted. As we have used a consultative approach to create the strategy, we do not anticipate too many difficulties here, but given the importance of obtaining the necessary approval, we will manage this aspect carefully.

The first step in this process is to distribute the document to stakeholders for comment, allowing a reasonable time for them to provide their feedback. Common mistakes here include asking for feedback too quickly or trying to impose implicit signoff after a certain date. Asking for feedback too quickly would be a sign of bad management on our part—if the planning slips, it is better to negotiate an extension to the deadline rather than try to cut corners at the expense of others. Implicit signoff is hardly ever a good idea, especially where important deliverables such as this are concerned. A better approach is to remind reviewers that have not responded a certain number of days before the deadline and to suggest a meeting to discuss problems if appropriate.

In addition to planning for a reasonable delay to receive comments, it is also necessary to plan for a delay to introduce the necessary modifications. On the contrary, it is reasonable to require a rapid response for the amended version of the document, as this should only require a quick verification that the required modifications have been carried out. At The Secure Bank, we allowed stakeholders 2 weeks to respond with comments, and we planned for a further 2 weeks to introduce the modifications. Stakeholders were then given 1 week to approve the final version.

The approved document was submitted for approval by the information-security steering committee, who approved the document in the second meeting in month seven. Following this final step, the strategy document was published on the organization's intranet.

5.11   Summary

The information-security strategy is the blueprint for the current strategic-planning period. The strategy identifies and describes those initiatives that contribute to moving the enterprise up the path of maturity (see Figure 4.1). For less mature organizations, first attempts to define a strategy may be hampered by an inability to predict the impact of initiatives that modify cultural values or significantly change working practices. For such organizations, the experience gained in trying to get to the final goal may be as valuable as the effort to define that goal.

There are several inputs into the information-security strategy. One of the most important inputs consists of a summary of the strong and weak points of the current approach to securing information. In this chapter, we have concentrated on weak points, but it is evident that any strengths should be retained when introducing a new approach. The business strategy also provides valuable input by identifying the direction that the business as a whole is taking. Modified business plans can lead to significantly different requirements for protecting data and systems. Similarly, a modified strategy can require major changes to the IT infrastructure and supporting applications, thereby indirectly affecting the approach to securing information.

Legal and regulatory requirements often have a major impact on information security. Commonly encountered legal requirements include data protection laws and privacy laws, and some sectors may be subject to further legislation. In the financial sector, certain countries have passed legislation relating to banking secrecy, and this is often interpreted by regulatory bodies.

Finally, a coherent strategy should take into account events happening in the outside world, such as economic and political events and technical evolution. Mergers and acquisitions present special challenges, as they are likely to force staff to question core values and often modify corporate culture.

The final strategy defines a number of strategic initiatives, which collectively satisfy requirements arising out of an analysis of these areas. The strategic initiatives are prioritized according to a set of predefined criteria, typically reflecting the degree to which they mitigate risk, degree of difficulty, and cost. The final prioritization will also take into account any synergies that can be realized with other defined activities. While it is a good idea to construct a high-level plan in order to derive the prioritization of initiatives, the plan itself is not part of the strategy. However, the strategy is the major input to the strategic plan, which is described in Section 4.5.3. This approach is adopted to keep the strategy document free of volatile information (i.e., information that is likely to change regularly).

It is important to carefully plan the approval process, as failure to do so is likely to result in reduced commitment from stakeholders. In particular, suitable time should be planned to allow stakeholders to correctly review the document and request modifications. Similarly, it is important to allow time to make the necessary changes once feedback has been received.

Following approval, the information-security strategy should be published in a location visible to all staff. The company intranet is an ideal channel for achieving this.

References

[1] Katoh, T., "Bank of Tokyo-Mitsubishi Announces New Business Strategy, News Release, Bank of Tokyo-Mitsubishi, Ltd. (1999)," August 2003, http://www.btm.co.jp/html_e/news/news_53e.htm.

[2] "Bank's Strategy 2002," August 2003, www.kookmin.lu/page3.html.

[3] "Directive 95/46/EC of the European Parliament and of the Council of 24 October 1995 on the Protection of Individuals with Regard to the Processing of Personal Data and on the Free Movement of Such Data," September 2003, http://europa.eu.int/smartapi/cgi/sga_doc?smartapi!celexapi!prod!CELEXnumdoc&lg=EN&numdoc=31995L0046&model=guichett.

[4] "Data Protection Act 1998,"August 2003, http://www.dataprotection.gov.uk/dpr/dpdoc.nsf.

[5] "Freedom of Information Act 2000," August 2003, http://www.hmso.gov.uk/acts/acts2000/20000036.htm.

[6] "Information Commissioner: Responsible for Data Protection and Freedom of Information," August 2003, http://www.dataprotection.gov.uk.

[7] "The Consumer and Investor Access to Information Act of 1999," September 2003, http://thomas.loc.gov/cgi-bin/query/D?c106:2:./temp/~c106CvLWUH::.

[8] "The Collections of Information Anti-Piracy Act of 1999," September 2003, http://thomas.loc.gov/cgi-bin/query/D?c106:2:./temp/~c1062J7m15::.

[9] "Bill Number 1386 Chaptered: Bill Text," September 2003, http://info.sen.ca.gov/pub/01-02/bill/sen/sb_1351-1400/sb_1386_bill_20020926_chaptered.html.

[10] "Welcome to the Safe Harbor," August 2003, http://www.export.gov/safeharbor/index.html.

[11] Cowles, R. and M. S. Singh, "Internet Privacy Issues: How Should They Be Resolved?" Gartner Note, 2002.

[12] Directive 2002/58/EC of the European Parliament and of the Council concerning the processing of personal data and the protection of privacy in the electronic communications sector (directive on privacy and electronic communications), September 2003, http://europa.eu.int/eur-lex/pri/en/oj/dat/2002/l_201/l_201 20020731en00370047.pdf.

[13] "Children's Online Privacy Protection Act of 1998 (COPPA)," August 2003, http://www.cdt.org/legislation/105th/privacy/coppa.html.

[14] "The Privacy Act of 1974," August 2003, http://www.usdoj.gov/04foia/ privstat.htm.

[15] "The Health Insurance Portability and Accountability Act of 1996," August 2003, http://aspe.hhs.gov/admnsimp/pl104191.htm.

[16] "The Electronic Privacy Information Center," August 2003, http://www.epic.org.

[17] Thiel, L., "Le Secret Bancaire Démystifié," August 2003, www.uae.lu/Secret_ demystifie.pdf.

[18] Aubert, M., "Swiss Banking Secrecy: General Extent and Recent Developments," Geneva Financial Center Foundation, 1997.

[19] Koops, B. J., "Crypto Law Survey," August 2003, http://rechten.uvt.nl/koops/ cryptolaw/index.htm.

[20] Van der Hof, S., "Digital Signature Law Survey," August 2003, rechten.kub.nl/ simone/ds-lawsu.htm.

[21] Sylvestri, M., "European Links," August 2003, http://www.wowarea.com/ english/help/cryeuro.htm.

[22] "E-Commerce Law Resources," Baker and McKenzie Global E-Commerce Law Website, August 2003, http//www.bakerinfo.com/ecommerce.

[23] Merrill, C.,"PKI Law: Public Key Infrastructure and the Law," August 2003, http://www.pkilaw.com.

[24] "Federal Information Processing Standards Publications: FIPS Home Page," August 2003, http://www.itl.nist.gov/fipspubs.

[25] "Department of Defense Trusted Computer System Evaluation Criteria (1985)," Department of Defense Standard, DoD 5200.28-STD.

[26] "Information Technology Security Evaluation Criteria," August 2003, http://www.cesg.gov.uk/site/iacs/index.cfm?menuSelected=1&displayPage=18.

[27] Boni, W. C., MBA, CISA, "The Dark Side of E-Commerce—The Threat of Cyber Sabotage," August 2003, http://www.shockwavewriters.com/Articles/WCB/ dark7.htm.

[28] Roberts, A., "September 11 in Context: The Changing Faces of Terrorism," August 2003, http://www.bbc.co.uk/history/war/sept_11/changing_faces_01. shtml.

[29] Hasson, J., and D. Frank, "Bush Budgets $52 Billion for IT," August 2003, http://www.fcw.com/fcw/articles/2002/0128/web-budget-02-01-02.asp.

[30] "Why Do Mergers and Acquisitions Fail to Create Synergy? Is the Situation Redeemable?" August 2003, http://mworld.mce.be/artPrint.php?article_id=449.

Policy and standards

6.1 Some introductory remarks on documentation

Policies and standards provide a framework for information security by defining rules and guidelines for handling everyday situations. Policy statements essentially define high-level requirements, which are sufficiently generic to be applicable in a variety of circumstances. Standards and procedures translate these high-level requirements into implementation details. However, although policies and standards are important tools, they are not the whole story. Most information-security departments have to manage a relatively complex set of documentation, including items such as:

- Contracts;
- Legal and regulatory documentation;
- Plans and reports;
- Financial plans and budgets;
- Vendor-supplied documentation;
- Nondisclosure and similar agreements;
- User guides;
- Project-related documentation.

Efficiently managing such a diverse set of documents is no easy task. Documents need to be stored in such a way that they can easily be retrieved. Updates need to be carefully controlled, and there needs to be a simple way of identifying the latest version. References between documents need to be managed and updated when documents are changed. International organizations may also have the additional burden of managing documentation in several different languages. Simply put, the document-management system needs to be user friendly while ensuring that the content of the entire document set remains accurate, up to date, and coherent.

Before writing any document, it is essential to know how the content relates to related documentation. If this is not decided in advance, there is a risk that certain information will be included in several documents and other information will be missed or forgotten entirely. Omitting information is obviously problematic, but creating redundant information can also lead to serious problems. Not only is this inefficient, but introducing changes can become a complex activity, as changes have to be carried out in several different places.

Consequently, before thinking about the information-security policy, it is appropriate to think about the documentation set as a whole and how the policy will relate to other documentation. By doing so, we will avoid problems later on.

6.2   Designing the documentation set

Following the discussion of the last section, it is clear that a well-designed documentation set that is kept up to date to reflect reality is an extremely valuable asset. On the contrary, poorly designed documentation or documentation that is out of date can prove to be more a liability than an asset and can result in a lot of unnecessary work. The problem is that the terms *well designed* and *poorly designed* only have meaning when the criteria for separating one from the other are clear, and these criteria are likely to differ from organization to organization.

Despite this fact, it is not too difficult to define a set of criteria that should apply to most organizations. For our purposes, a good documentation set has the following characteristics:

- Easy to use;
- Easy to maintain;
- Accurate and up-to-date information;
- Appropriate for target audience;
- Only relevant and essential information.

At The Secure Bank, we undertake the task of designing the documentation set as the first task of the information-security policy initiative. This decision is motivated by the fact that the content of the policy will be influenced by the structure of our documentation set, so we need to have the structure of the documentation set in the back of our minds as we write the policy document.

Given the existing company culture, where actions are judged as being important and documents considerably less so, we will aim to limit the documentation in the short term and to build up the document set gradually. For similar reasons, the design and implementation of document-control procedures will initially be carried out as an internal activity. Documents destined for other departments, or for the organization as a whole, will ultimately be published on the information-security Web site. Consequently, the details of the document-management system and the structure of the entire documentation set will be transparent to staff members outside the information-security department. This approach enables us to impose a certain level of rigor without running the risk of being seen as too theoretical.

The design of the documentation set is illustrated in Figure 6.1.

According to this schema, all documents owned by the information-security department will be classified as being internal or external. Any document that is published to staff outside the department is automatically an external document.

Internal documentation consists of all documents that are necessary for the correct functioning of the department, but are not for an external audience. Internal documentation also includes a range of documentation that is used by, but not owned by the information-security department.

Referring to the examples presented in Section 6.1:

▸ Management documentation includes contracts, plans, reports, and documents relating to budgets and financial plans. Nondisclosure agreements are also considered management documentation, as they are under the control of the department manager.

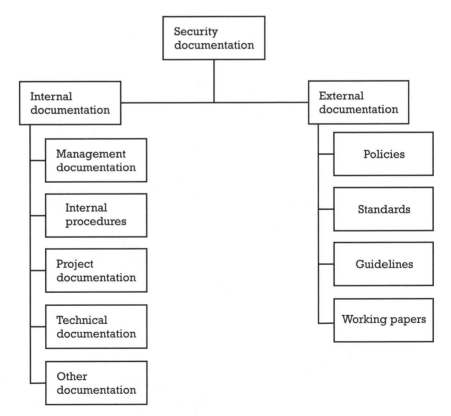

Figure 6.1 The information-security documentation set.

- Internal procedures cover aspects such as internal reporting and local administration procedures. In particular, the procedures managing the documentation set itself (such as change-control procedures) are contained here.

- Project documentation includes all documentation produced within the scope of internal projects (i.e., projects that are exclusively under the control of the information-security department and have minimal external impact—an example might be the implementation of a security scanner).

- Technical documentation includes vendor-supplied documentation, technical reports, and similar material.

- Other documentation includes any other documents of interest, organized by subject, including legal and regulatory documentation, training material, and conference proceedings.

Note that legal and regulatory documents are not typically owned by the information-security department and are therefore stored under *other documentation*. User guides appear nowhere in this list because they are destined for end users and are therefore an example of external documentation.

External documents produced by the information-security department are organized into a hierarchy to help staff appreciate the type of information they contain. This hierarchy represents the organization's view of published information and is illustrated in Figure 6.2.

As far as published documents are concerned, the most authoritative document is the information-security policy (ISP) document; other policy documents, such as the IT security policy, are required to be consistent with the requirements of this policy. Standards are authoritative in a particular well-defined area and translate policy requirements within a specific context. Finally, guidelines and working papers have no authority whatsoever, but are produced as a useful aid to implementing security requirements.

In the rest of this chapter, we will look at the documentation produced by the information-security department from this latter perspective.

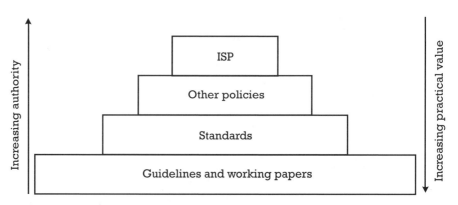

Figure 6.2   Hierarchy of published documentation.

6.3 Policy

6.3.1 The purpose of policy statements

Policy statements describe in very high-level terms how an organization has chosen to deal with a particular issue. As such, they essentially distinguish what is acceptable or appropriate from what is unacceptable or inappropriate. In Section 6.3.3, we define what we mean by the terms *acceptable* and *appropriate* very carefully, as this ultimately leads to a useful way of introducing a certain degree of flexibility into policy statements. There exists a wealth of material on policy statements and how to create them (for example, [1–4]). The purpose of this section is not to summarize this material, but to supplement it by illustrating the role of policy statements within the approach outlined in Chapter 4.

Policy statements are important for several reasons:

▸ They provide guidance.

▸ They form the foundations of the control framework.

▸ They define roles and responsibilities.

▸ They document the organization's stance with respect to the issues addressed.

First and foremost, albeit at a high level, policy statements provide guidance by stating how things should be or how things should be done. In order to achieve this, policy statements are designed by taking a number of different factors into consideration, including known risks, legal and regulatory requirements, and cultural values.

Policies must be unambiguous and easy to understand, as they form the foundations of the control framework (i.e., the procedures and security mechanisms that are put in place to ensure that the organization is appropriately secured in its day-to-day activities). The supposition underlying most control frameworks is that the policy requirements upon which they rest will not change substantially with time. Indeed, it is common practice to avoid placing volatile information (i.e., information that is likely to change quickly) in policy statements. Control frameworks are a recognition of the fact that we cannot analyze the consequence of routine actions every time we undertake them. They provide a solution by standardizing the way to carry out the action based on an initial analysis.

In contrast, risk-analysis techniques are used to measure risk at a given moment in time. A risk analysis is one of the inputs into the policy design process and can be used at any moment to check that policy requirements make sense in particular circumstances. For this reason, risk-analysis techniques provide a useful mechanism for checking that policy requirements are reasonable in a given context and for overriding policy when this obviously makes sense.

Policy statements are a particularly efficient method for defining roles and responsibilities within a given area and are frequently used for this purpose. The use of roles is particularly advantageous, as the concept of a role is independent of the organizational structure. This allows roles to be mapped to management positions in a flexible manner. This is particularly useful when reorganizations take place. In this area, it is critical that overlaps or dependencies between policy statements are correctly controlled and that the resulting roles and responsibilities are coherent.

Policies also document an organization's way of handling a particular issue. This may be required for a number of reasons, including compliance with regulatory requirements, supporting disciplinary measures in the case of misconduct, and reducing liability. The availability of a coherent set of policies is also likely to prove to be an asset for organizations seeking compliance with external standards, such as ISO 17799/BS 7799 in the field of information security or ISO 9000 where quality systems are concerned.

6.3.2 Identifying required policy statements

Within the information-security domain, there are no hard and fast rules for defining the scope of policies, and sample policy statements are available on the Internet for addressing a wide variety of issues. Examples of sites offering sample policy statements free of charge include the SANS organization [5] and the NIST [6]. Commercial sources of sample policy statements include [7–10]. In addition, many institutions publish their own policy statements on the Internet, and these can be useful sources of inspiration (be aware, however, that these policy statements are invariably protected by copyright laws).

In order to get the most out of this material, it is necessary to give some thought to how policies will be structured, and this will most likely depend on the size and culture of the organization. For smaller organizations, a single policy might be preferable, but larger organizations may find this approach too restrictive and opt for a series of more targeted policy statements. In general, publishing a series of policy documents has the advantage of keeping individual policies short and focused, but it may prove to be difficult to avoid some degree of overlap in scope. Managing these overlaps and the redundant information they give rise to may prove to be difficult. On the other hand, where larger organizations are concerned, publishing all policy statements relative to information security in a single policy tends to produce a forbiddingly large document, different sections of which will be aimed at different groups within the enterprise. It is therefore clear that one of the key decisions to be made when designing policy documents is how such documents should be organized.

At The Secure Bank, we will aim to produce two core policy statements in the first strategic-planning cycle. The first core policy, the information-security policy, will be a relatively short document, summarizing the essential policy statements in a nontechnical manner. The audience for this document is the entire organization. The second policy, the IT security policy, is focused on more technical issues and addresses a number of subjects that are of little interest to the majority of staff members, but which are critically important for technical staff. It is important to realize, however, that the IT security policy does not enter into technical details. The purpose of this policy is to provide high-level policy statements in specialist areas, such as application development or use of cryptography.

Other policy statements will be created if they are really required, but the goal will be to limit the number of policies at this stage in order to concentrate on what is essential. This approach is appropriate for this planning cycle, as it is in line with the company culture and also minimizes administrative overhead. In fact, we have already identified the need for at least one additional policy statement—the requirement for a privacy policy to support the activities of the marketing department was identified during the consolidation period. This document was agreed on by the information-security steering committee in month seven. Consequently, we need to ensure that the core policies are aligned with this existing policy and issue a revised version of the latter if required. In reality, changing the privacy policy will be a solution of last resort, as this has a direct impact on customers.

6.3.3 Design and implementation

Once the decision has been made on how to structure policy statements, work can begin on producing individual policies. As we saw in the last section, it is sometimes necessary to produce policy statements before the structure has been thought out. Under these circumstances, it is best to be proactive and to sketch out a rough model of how policies will be structured before writing the policy. Normally, this will be sufficient to ensure that the final structure is coherent, even if minor modifications to the original rough design are necessary.

Policy statements are likely to be influenced by a variety of factors. All policy statements in the area of information security will need to take into account all legal and regulatory requirements, the threats to which the enterprise is exposed, and the corporate culture. Some policies will also be affected by other factors. As an example, policy statements related to the use of software will probably need to take account of the current state of the art and predicted evolution of security functionality in order to be credible. Pursuing this example, it is of no use to mandate the use of secure cryptographic protection mechanisms if the software to implement them is not available. This is particularly important for international organizations, where it may be relatively easy to satisfy a particular requirement in the country where the parent company resides, but extremely difficult in other countries. Again, this example is pertinent, as the use of cryptography is restricted in many countries.

The most important point to bear in mind when developing policy statements is that it is vital to involve those concerned in the process. Involving people in the development of a policy greatly reduces the chances that it will be rejected during the approval process. This doesn't mean that it is necessary to start with a blank page, either, and most organizations will need strong guidance in producing policies. For organizations that have existing policies in place, even unsuccessful ones, it is worth analyzing these policies to identify those elements that are appropriate. These can then be used as a possible starting point for creating new policies.

One way to involve people is to identify any groups that are likely to be impacted by a policy statement before beginning to develop it and to invite a representative from each group to participate in an ongoing review process. For this type of exercise, it is useful to include a mixture of experience, including management and the staff that actually carry out the work. The latter group can be further split into staff performing business tasks, technical staff, and administration staff, thus ensuring that potential policy statements are reviewed from a variety of different perspectives. The policy can then be developed by regularly circulating incomplete versions of the document for review and taking account of the feedback. Ideally, this process starts with the distribution of a skeleton document, consisting of a list of titles and a brief description of the content of each section. Subsequent versions might be distributed on a weekly basis until the document is completed. Interim meetings can be used to resolve punctual issues, which also helps resolve issues when a participant has particularly strong views.

Identifying the target audience and securing its participation in the development activity helps to ensure that we will receive quality feedback during the policy-development process. The next goal is to ensure that the policy is realistic. In the author's experience, groups producing policies tend to err on the cautious side and produce over-restrictive policies. Over-restrictive policies do not survive because the work has to be done, and staff will always find a way to circumvent something that is obviously unreasonable. Workable policy statements achieve an acceptable balance between efficiency and control.

At the beginning of this section, we emphasized the difference between acceptable and appropriate behavior. This distinction is important, as it leads us naturally to a corresponding distinction between mandatory requirements and requirements that are to be satisfied on a best-effort basis. For our purposes, we therefore define *unacceptable* as some state of affairs or some behavior that will not be tolerated by the organization. The adjective *inappropriate* on the other hand is used to describe a situation or behavior that is undesirable but may prove to be unavoidable. As a result of these definitions, policy statements aimed at preventing unacceptable situations will be mandatory, whereas those aimed at preventing inappropriate situations will be satisfied on a best-effort basis. This simple convention provides us with a way of introducing limited flexibility within policy statements, which in turn enables large organizations to fine tune these policies to particular situations.

In the policy statements we will create at The Secure Bank, we will employ a convention often adopted within RFC documents [11], as published by the IETF, to distinguish between mandatory and best-effort requirements. According to this convention, the word *must* is used in stating mandatory requirements and the word *should* is used for requirements that are to be met on a best-effort basis.

6.3.4 The Secure Bank—Policy statements

At The Secure Bank, the strategic initiative to define and agree on core policy statements began at the end of month six as planned. In order to simplify management of the resulting documents, policy statements were produced in line with a standard template, based on the structure defined for the privacy policy. This template consisted of a document-management section containing change-control information, a section identifying the target audience, an initial introduction, a description of the structure and scope of the policy, a section containing policy objectives, and a glossary. In addition, the final page was reserved for sign off by approvers. This common structure is illustrated in Table 6.1 and is assumed throughout the rest of this section.

The information-security policy was produced and agreed on within the agreed timeframe. The structure and content of the information-security policy are summarized in Table 6.2.

The last section of this policy deserves a special comment. Given that we have deliberately introduced flexibility into the policy framework by distinguishing between mandatory and best-effort requirements, the policy waiver process will be deliberately dissuasive. Obtaining a policy waiver will require a detailed justification and will be signed off at the executive-management level.

The production of the IT security policy took longer than expected, largely due to discussions related to the level of security that should be applied to development environments. The final decision was to segregate development environments from production environments and to allow a more flexible approach to security for development teams. It was agreed that risk would be mitigated by enforcing technical controls at the segregation point and putting procedural controls on the flow of code and data between these two environments. This discussion resulted in a delay of 3 months for the initiative and the IT security policy was finally agreed on in month 15. The structure and content of the IT security policy are summarized in Table 6.3.

The privacy policy was the first policy to be produced, as the marketing initiative was required to provide personalized data to key clients via the

Table 6.1 Common Structure for Policy Documents

Number	Section	Content
—	Document control	Title, author, version, date, amendments
—	Target audience	The target audience for this document
1	Introduction	A brief introduction to the policy statement explaining the context
2	Structure and scope	A description of the scope of the policy and an overview of how the document is structured
3	Objectives	The objectives of the policy
...	...	
...	...	
N.	Glossary	A glossary of terms used within the document
N + 1	Approvers	Signatures of approvers

Table 6.2   Structure and Content of the ISP

Number	Section	Content
4	Statement by executive management	This section reproduces the statement of commitment to information security that was requested of executive management during the consolidation phase (see Section 4.4.5).
5	Common responsibilities	This section presents in bullet-point form the most important responsibilities that apply to all staff and external service providers.
6	Management responsibilities	This section presents a summary of responsibilities that apply specifically to management staff. One of these responsibilities is to ensure that both internal and external staff members are aware of the policy requirements set down in this document.
7	Third-party responsibilities	This is a summary of responsibilities that apply specifically to external staff.
8	Further documentation	This section explains the document hierarchy presented in Figure 6.2 and explains the significance of standards and guidelines.
9	Contacts	This is a list of important contacts. This list makes references to positions of authority and not names.
10	Policy waivers	This is a description of how to request a policy waiver.

Internet Web server. The structure and content of the privacy policy are summarized in Table 6.4.

Together with the method for risk analysis that we agreed on with the risk-management department during the consolidation period, these policies are sufficient to see us through the first strategic-planning cycle. If further policies are required due to some unforeseen requirement, the framework exists for developing such policies.

6.4   Establishing a control framework

The control framework consists of all of the policy statements, standards, procedures, working documents, and technical measures put in place to secure day-to-day operations. Think of the control framework as the slow-moving side of the information-security process and risk management as the dynamic side of things. This framework changes slowly as a result of strategic initiatives, and the extent to which it is capable of successfully responding to the day-to-day needs of the organization is a good measure of the organization's maturity. We have already seen that risk management is the primary tool for verifying the framework in a particular context and for indicating where modifications or tactical solutions are necessary. As organizations become more mature, it is expected that the control framework will be driven more by risk assessment than by policy, reflecting the ability of the organization to quickly react to changes in the business environment. These ideas are illustrated in Figure 6.3.

Table 6.3 Structure and Content of the IT Security Policy

Number	Section	Content
4	Roles and responsibilities	These are detailed roles and responsibilities for information security within the area of IT.
5	Physical security of IT equipment	These are policy statements concerning the physical security of data centers and IT equipment. This section also covers mobile equipment, such as portable personal computers and handheld computers.
6	Use of cryptography	These are policy statements relating to the use of cryptography. This section addresses the use of specialized equipment in addition to providing policy on algorithms and protocols.
7	Authentication	These are policy requirements for authentication. Requirements are provided for a variety of contexts, such as internal connections, remote access, and system-to-system connectivity.
8	Authorization and access control	These are policy statements governing authorization and access control. This section addresses both host-based issues, such as account management, and network access control.
9	Confidentiality protection	These are policy statements related to the protection of confidentiality in both host and network environments.
10	Integrity protection	These are policy statements related to the protection of integrity in both host and network environments.
11	Logging and audit trail	These care policy statements governing the configuration and monitoring of logging systems.
12	Alerts and incident handling	These are policy requirements on how to detect and manage alerts. This section provides definitions of severity and a high-level description of the escalation process.
13	Special considerations for development environments	This section explains how policy is to be interpreted for development environments by referring to the preceding sections of the document.

Because the control framework changes slowly, whereas IT in general and risk in particular evolves rapidly, the control framework always provides an approximation to the best response to any particular problem. For mature frameworks, this approximation is usually sufficient, but the speed with which IT-related risk is growing is putting even the most mature control frameworks under strain. In this context, it is important to note that for most organizations, the control framework usually has dependencies on external partners. This is easy to appreciate for organizations that outsource security-related activities, but more subtle where the dependency is buried in the technology being used to respond to particular threats. Virus-control software provides a useful example here, where organizations are dependent on the ability of the solution provider to quickly release a new pattern

Table 6.4 Structure and Content of the Privacy Policy

Number	Section	Content
4	Information stored	This is a short description of the type of information stored on the bank's systems, together with a description of why this information is required.
5	Methods of gathering information	This is a list of the methods used to gather information about customers and other third parties.
6	Management of cookies	Although cookies are used to gather information, a section is dedicated to their use to ensure that Web site visitors are correctly informed.
6	Access to personal information	This section identifies who has access to personal information and why. It also relates this access to the underlying requirement.
7	Updating personal information	This is a procedure to request an update to or modification of stored information. For customers who use the private-banking Internet package, this will be supported by a secure connection allowing the customers to update their own information.
8	Opting out	This is information on how to request removal of information from the organization's databases or to stop receiving marketing information.
9	Availability to third parties	This describes which third parties have access to personal data under what conditions. For The Secure Bank, the only third parties potentially having access to data include law enforcement agencies, regulatory authorities, and auditors.
10	Further information	This provides contact details for further information.

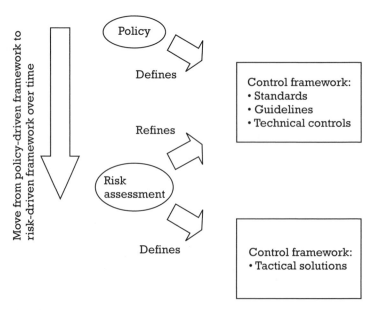

Figure 6.3 Relationship between policy, risk analysis, and control framework.

file when a new threat occurs. One response to this problem is to ensure that the security architecture and associated procedures implement the notion of *defense in depth*, and this will be discussed further in Chapter 8.

Increasingly, however, this is not sufficient, and a successful approach to security should regularly challenge the ideas underlying the control framework. This is what makes auditing IT security difficult—the fact that procedures have not been followed at a particular time does not necessarily indicate that there was a problem. Indeed, not following procedures may have been the best response to a particular risk at the time it occurred. The key question is whether it was appropriate to bypass procedures at this time and whether this was done in the correct manner. This is of course the main theme of this book, managing security-related risk, and we have seen that one appropriate way of achieving this would have been to measure the risk, identify alternatives, and select the alternative of least risk. Where the risk concerned is significant, the proposed way forward should be agreed on with the appropriate business line.

In the last section, we were careful to insist on the difference between mandatory policy statements and those statements that are to be achieved on a best-effort basis. It is now easy to appreciate why this distinction is necessary. Policies that are too rigid will not survive in the corporate world, where the notion of risk changes rapidly and where changing business models may require an organization to modify its position with respect to certain risks at any moment. This is not true of all environments. It makes more sense, for instance, to define more rigid policies within military environments, where the risk model is less likely to change suddenly and the culture is one of strict obedience. This is, of course, one of the reasons that military security models do not translate particularly well into the corporate domain.

The rest of this chapter, together with Chapters 7 and 8 of this book, describe various aspects of the control framework. When reading this material, it is important to constantly remind oneself that this framework starts to grow old the day that it is put into production, and good security managers will continually verify that the assumptions underlying its design are still appropriate.

6.5 Standards

6.5.1 Types of standards

The primary purpose of standards is, not surprisingly, to standardize something. This is advantageous for several reasons:

- Standardization reduces complexity.
- Standards document a preference when there is a choice to be made.
- Standards help ensure interoperability

Standardization reduces complexity by limiting the number of ways in which something can be done (physicists might say that they reduce entropy). Where information security is concerned, we would expect it to be easier to secure a set of computers running identical software than to secure a set of machines having an arbitrary software configuration. By standardizing the configuration of the machines, we reduce the complexity of the problem (assuming, of course, that we don't standardize on a configuration that is particularly difficult to secure). Should we wish to introduce secure communications between these platforms, the software implementing this functionality has to be compatible with only one configuration—interoperability is almost self evident. It is not too difficult to imagine the difficulties in achieving this where several different operating systems and versions of software are concerned.

The term internal standard is used to refer to a standard that is produced by an organization and used exclusively within that organization. An external standard is a standard that is accepted and used by a community. Following this nomenclature, the standard configuration for UNIX platforms within The Secure Bank is therefore an internal standard, whereas the International Telecommunications Union (ITU) [formerly Comité Consultatif International Téléphonique et Télégraphique (CCITT)] X.509 standard is clearly an external standard.

Where internal standards are concerned, a standard can either document the essential characteristics of something or explain how some activity is to be carried out. We make this distinction because describing something that is static, such as an electric plug, requires a different vocabulary and approach than describing something dynamic, such as a procedure. In the first case, we might describe a plug by providing the material it is made of, the geometry and the distance between the pins, and a range of other values. A procedure, on the other hand, might be best described using a graphic technique such as a flow chart or a state transition diagram. Note that this distinction is not made for external standards because we have no control over how such standards are produced.

We will refer to the first type of document as a specification standard and the second type as a procedural standard. This is illustrated in Figure 6.4.

6.5.2   External standards

The intelligent use of standards that are adopted by the international community greatly simplifies the task of securing information in IT environments. This applies to all standards, not only those applying to information security. Advantages of adhering to internationally agreed upon standards include:

- Software implementing such standards will be subject to more testing in the field.

- Security issues are likely to be discovered and fixed more rapidly.

- Experience will be more widely available.

As we are discussing international standards, it is to be expected that software implementing such standards will be installed in a variety of

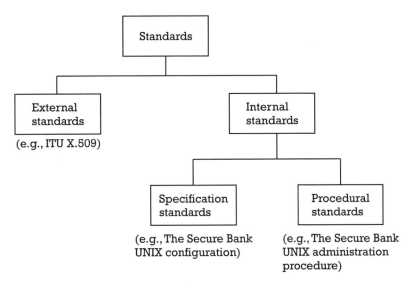

Figure 6.4 Classification of standards.

different environments. In addition, universities and research groups are more likely to study the strengths and weaknesses of popular standards and the software that implements them. This will increase the probability that different options within the software are exercised in some environment, and this in turn should result in a more rapid detection of flaws and bugs. Largely due to the mechanisms discussed in Section 2.2 of this book, information regarding any security issues that are discovered via this process will be quickly made available to the international community as a whole. This not only puts pressure on vendors to implement solutions rapidly, it increases the chances that some interested party will identify and publish a workaround for the issue in the intervening period.

It is clearly not feasible in a book of this size to provide an exhaustive overview of external standards that are likely to be of interest to information-security managers. It is, however, possible to provide a rapid introduction to the subject by quickly identifying some of the more influential standards groups, and this is the approach we have taken. Interested readers are pointed to the Web site of the World Standards Services Network (WSSN) for more information on international, regional, and national standards [12].

Arguably the best-known standards organization in the world is the ISO. The ISO is a nongovernmental institution founded in 1947 and organized as a federation of national standards bodies. At the time of writing, the ISO comprises 147 members [13], including the American National Standards Institute (ANSI) and the British Standards Institute (BSI). Examples of standards published by ISO include the OSI model and related security architecture [14, 15], numerous standards in the area of network and transaction security (of which examples are provided in [16]), and a series of security-related standards published jointly with the IEC.

Other international standards bodies include the IEC and the ITU, which is the parent organization of the former CCITT. Examples of security-related standards published by the IEC include the Code of Practice [17] and the Common Criteria [18–20], both of which were published jointly with the ISO. The ITU publishes a range of extremely important standards related to data communication, including the X.25 [21], X.400 [22], and X.500 standards [23]. Particularly noteworthy in the area of security is the X.509 standard [24], which is widely adopted in the area of PKI.

At the national level, standardization is coordinated by national standards organizations. In the United States, the national standards organization is the ANSI. The ANSI has published a wealth of standards related to information security, which are available via the ANSI electronic standards store [25]. More recently, the ANSI established the Homeland Security Standards Panel (HSSP) in February 2003 [26]. This panel was created to assist the Department of Homeland Security by coordinating standards developed to meet homeland-security requirements. The panel is also charged with ensuring that the public and private sectors are aware of the existence of such standards.

Organizations such as the NIST, the IETF, and the Institute of Electrical and Electronics Engineers (IEEE) produce standards for a specific community. The NIST, for instance, produces standards to meet the needs of the U.S. federal government and industry [27]. In particular, the NIST issues the FIPS documentation, which governs the use of federal computing systems [28]. More security-related standards and a great deal of other useful information are available from the NIST's Computer Security Resource Center (CSRC) [29].

One of the most useful bodies of standards where the Internet or TCP/IP is concerned is the RFC documentation published by the IETF. These standards are extremely important, as they effectively define the TCP/IP protocol stack. Many of the most important security protocols used to protect network transmissions over TCP/IP are also documented in the form of RFC documents. RFC 1539, "The Tao of IETF: A Guide For New Attendees of the Internet Engineering Task Force" [11], provides an excellent introduction to documentation produced by the IETF and provides references to other documentation providing more detailed information.

The important thing to remember when using external standards is that there are a lot of good standards available, but care needs to be exercised in selecting a standards set that is coherent. Wherever possible, the simplest solution is to select a set of standards for use in a particular domain and to stick to it, rather than selecting standards produced by different standards bodies.

At The Secure Bank, we will make extensive use of the IETF RFC documentation within the area of network security. When dealing with legacy applications, it may well be necessary to refer to ITU recommendations, notably those dealing with X.25. In the area of cryptography, use will be made of several important FIPS standards and other relevant NIST standards. In this latter area, we will also make use of the public key cryptography standards [30], which have not been discussed in the preceding paragraphs. Other standards will be used on an as-needed basis, taking care to ensure that the particular group of standards selected is self consistent and can be used as the basis for a coherent approach.

6.5.3 Internal standards

We have seen that, in order to stand the test of time, policy statements must be high level and avoid unnecessary detail. This technique is ideal for capturing the essence of a requirement and making sure it applies in a variety of circumstances, but it is not at all useful for supporting the type of decisions that need to be made on a day-to-day basis. The purpose of internal standards is primarily to interpret policy in particular situations. Consequently, as every organization has policy requirements reflecting its own needs and company culture, standards will also be highly specific to the organization that produces them.

Internal standards are at the core of the control framework. They add value by documenting an agreed upon solution to a particular problem in enough detail to support the normal day-to-day activities and decision making in a particular area. Interpreting policy in this way turns out to be very difficult in some circumstances, and this is why standards are so important—by defining and agreeing on standards, this complex thought process has to occur only once. Once a standard has been agreed on, it can be made available for general use. The price we pay for this approach is that of approximation. A good standard should ensure a reasonable response to the underlying problem in most cases, but there will be occasions where the analysis upon which the standard was designed does not hold; in such cases, supplementary controls or a different approach will be required.

Awareness training provides a partial solution to this problem. Users that are trained to look at security from a risk perspective and that are sensitive to changes in the environment will be capable of challenging procedures and suggesting alternative courses of action when faced with unusual circumstances. However, this level of awareness is usually associated with very mature organizations. For this reason, information-security managers should ensure that standards are regularly examined and challenged by competent personnel. A good audit department will be of considerable help here, and good auditors will look beyond the defined control framework to discover whether it is still providing the most appropriate response to the risk. When challenging the control framework, however, it is important to realize that standards need to be designed and modified with the big picture in mind; otherwise, the overall approach will no longer be optimal. Due to resource constraints, applying an additional control in a relatively secure area can introduce an unacceptable weakness in another part of the organization. This doesn't usually make sense because an intelligent attacker will always seek out and exploit the weakest link.

Returning to The Secure Bank, we follow the convention stated in Section 6.5.1 and classify internal standards as specification standards or as procedural standards. We also decide to manage standards using the same template and document-control procedures that we used to manage policy statements.

Within The Secure Bank, the most important use of specification standards is to define security baselines. A security baseline defines what we consider to be the ideal security configuration of a particular system and is an extremely important concept as far as system security is concerned. As the target configuration for a particular system, the security baseline needs to be realistic. Defining security baselines on the basis of theoretical considerations and taking insufficient account of local needs is a process doomed to failure. Equivalently, erring on the tolerant side and not taking into account sources of important vulnerabilities will lead to unacceptable risk. The design of a good security baseline is therefore an exercise in compromise, and the definition of the most important security baselines (mainframe, UNIX, and Windows server machines) took almost 6 months at the bank. The degree to which systems are compliant with security baselines is usually checked using automated utilities, such as system security scanners (see Section 3.3.4). It goes without saying that the concept of the security baseline only adds value if vulnerabilities identified relative to the baseline are repaired in a timely manner. Chapter 7 will discuss this point in more detail.

Procedural standards define activities and therefore provide a useful mechanism for describing security administration procedures. This is one of the reasons that the strategic initiative to produce security standards started before the initiative to develop administration procedures. By the time the work on administration procedures begins, the standards framework already exists. An important decision was to restrict the documentation of administration activities to a description of the important steps in a given procedure. As such, administration procedures contain no technical details and are therefore not system specific. Where such details are required, the policy of the bank is to refer to vendor documentation and only to document screen shots and other technical details when absolutely necessary. This is then achieved using guidelines.

This last decision is illustrative of an important principle. Security managers should aim to keep the documentation under their control succinct and to the point. Competent administrators can be expected to know what they are doing at the detailed technical level, and it serves little purpose documenting something that should be a part of the skill sets of the administrator. While it remains necessary to document proprietary or "home-grown" solutions, a judicious use of standards should limit this to a minimum.

6.5.4   Agreement and distribution of standards

At The Secure Bank, the strategic initiative to set up the standards framework began in month five but was completely reviewed in month 13. The initial approach to publishing and agreeing standards was based on the idea of a standards working group. The objectives of this group were as follows:

> Review and approve proposals for standards.
> Identify the need for new standards.
> Ensure that standards are consistent with policy.

This group met once per month and consisted of permanent representatives from the information-security, risk-management, and audit departments. Business managers were invited when the standards under discussion involved their business area. Standards would only be considered approved when each member of the working group (including the business manager) had signed off on the document.

As from the third meeting of this group, however, it was clear that this approach was not working. The major problems were as follows:

> Many of the initial proposed standards were in specialist areas and members of the group did not have sufficient experience in these areas to comment on the content. This was particularly true for the security baseline documents.

> Many of the discussions centered on details associated with little risk. Despite several attempts to correct this, the situation had not improved at the end of month 12.

> This tendency to concentrate on details resulted in a sign-off process that was far too slow. At the end of month 12, only four standards had been signed off on. Six standards were in the approval process and three were currently under development.

These issues were discussed at the fourth meeting of the information-security steering committee in month 13, and it was agreed to adopt a different approach. According to the new approach, the information-security department would be responsible for maintaining a list of required standards and for producing such standards. These activities would still involve extensive discussions with stakeholders, but the way in which this dialogue was to take place was streamlined in the following way:

> A summary of the status of the standards initiative would be sent to stakeholders at the end of every month. This summary would identify proposals for new standards and the state of progress for standards that were in progress. Stakeholders would then provide feedback within 5 working days of receiving the document.

> Standards requiring approval would be distributed to the appropriate stakeholders, who would then have a period of 10 working days to reject the document. In the absence of a rejection, the standard would be considered accepted.

> The standards working group would be closed down.

This revised approval process was agreed with stakeholders during the meeting of the information-security steering committee. Under these circumstances, implicit approval was deemed acceptable, as all parties agreed to it. Although there was a real danger that stakeholders might dissociate themselves from the standards process once active participation was no longer required, the existing dialogue proved strong enough to avoid this. As a result of the revised approach, the approval backlog was quickly absorbed, and the initiative was successfully closed according to plan. Furthermore, stakeholders in general and the audit department in particular provided regular feedback on problems and issues, and these were taken into account as part of the normal document revision and publication process.

At the request of the information-security steering committee, the information-security department produced a report analyzing why the standards working group failed. The major conclusion of this report was that the group failed because neither the scope of the exercise nor the responsibilities of the group were well defined. The report recommended that future working groups be required to define a charter statement defining the scope of the work to be done together with the level of authority and responsibilities of the group.

6.6 Guidelines and working papers

Guidelines and working papers either summarize aspects of the control framework or provide further information on specific issues where this is necessary. Guidelines can usefully be used to summarize standards by using simplified graphic representations or checklists, for example. Similarly, a white paper suggesting an approach for securing a new technology would be considered a working paper.

The purpose of guidelines and working papers is to increase understanding without introducing any changes into the control framework. That these documents add nothing new to the framework is what distinguishes them from standards.

6.7 Summary

Successful management of the information-security process requires adequate control over a variety of documentation. Efficiently managing this documentation is not easy and usually requires an organized approach. Organizations are therefore encouraged to design and implement a structured documentation set at an early stage. Distinguishing between documentation that is owned and produced by the department and other documentation is necessary in order to apply correct change-management procedures to the former. This distinction also simplifies the process of publishing documents.

The control framework consists of all of the procedural and automated controls put in place to secure day-to-day operations. Together with a well-defined security architecture, policy statements and standards form the backbone of the control framework. This framework can be thought of as the slow-moving side of the information-security process. Risk-management techniques, on the other hand, provide the ability to rapidly assess the level of risk associated with a particular situation and can be used to verify the framework within a particular context.

Policy statements define in high-level terms how an organization has chosen to deal with a particular issue. As such, they form the foundations of the control framework. Just as the overall documentation structure needs to be well thought out, so does the way in which policy statements are organized. In general, opting for a series of policy statements will result in short, focused policies, but managing dependencies between these policies may become difficult. At the other extreme, a single policy statement is likely to be unwieldy and difficult to comprehend by the different target audiences.

Standards reduce complexity, facilitate interoperability, and document a preference for a particular way of doing things. By adopting external standards, an organization can align itself with tendencies in the outside world, which can have benefits when trying to resolve problems. Internal standards, on the other hand, are likely to be highly specific to the organization and are used principally to interpret policy requirements. Internal standards are further divided into specification standards and procedural standards to reflect that the description of static entities is best achieved using a different vocabulary and different techniques from those used for describing activities.

Finally, guidelines and working papers provide a mechanism for clarifying standards or for discussing new issues without introducing any changes into the control framework.

References

[1]   Guel, M. D., "A Short Primer For Developing Security Policies," August 2003, http://www.sans.org/resources/policies/Policy_Primer.pdf.

[2]   Barman, S., *Writing Information Security Policies*, Indianapolis, IN: New Riders, 2002.

[3]   Fraser, B., "Site Security Handbook," RFC 2196, August 2003, http://www.ietf.org/rfc/rfc2196.txt.

[4]   Danchev, D., "Building and Implementing a Successful Information Security Policy," August 2003, http://www.windowsecurity.com/pages/security-policy.pdf.

[5]   "SANS Security Policy Project," August 2003, http://www.sans.org/resources/policies.

[6]   "Policies," NIST, Information Technology Laboratory, Computer Security Division, CSRC, August 2003, http://csrc.nist.gov/policies.

[7]   "The Information Security Policies/Computer Security Policies Directory," August 2003, http://www.information-security-policies-and-standards.com.

[8] "RUSecure Information Security Policies," August 2003, http://www.information-security-policies.com.

[9] "IT Security Policies and their Implementation," August 2003, http://www.network-and-it-security-policies.com.

[10] Wood, C. C., CISA, CISSP, *Information Security Policies Made Easy, Version 9*, Houston, Texas: Pentasafe Security Technologies, 2002.

[11] Malkin, G., "The Tao of IETF: A Guide For New Attendees of the Internet Engineering Task Force," August 2003, http://www.faqs.org/rfcs/rfc1539.html.

[12] "WSSN: World Standards Services Network," August 2003, http://www.wssn.net/WSSN/index.html.

[13] "About ISO," August 2003, http://www.iso.org/iso/en/aboutiso/introduction/index.html.

[14] ISO/IEC 7498-1:1994, *Information Technology—Open Systems Interconnection—Basic Reference Model: The Basic Model*, 1994.

[15] ISO/IEC 7498-2:1994, *Information Technology—Open Systems Interconnection—Basic Reference Model: Part 2: Security Architecture*, 1994.

[16] "Information Security Standards," August 2003, http://www.diffuse.org/secure.html.

[17] ISO/IEC 17799:2000 *Information Technology—Code of Practice for Information Security Management*, 2001.

[18] ISO/IEC 15408-1:1999 *Information Technology—Security Techniques—Evaluation Criteria for IT Security: Part 1: Introduction and General Model*, 1999.

[19] ISO/IEC 15408-2:1999 *Information Technology—Security Techniques—Evaluation Criteria for IT Security: Part 2: Security Functional Requirements*, 1999.

[20] ISO/IEC 15408-1:1999 *Information Technology—Security Techniques—Evaluation Criteria for IT Security: Part 3: Security Assurance Requirements*, 1999.

[21] ITU-T Recommendation X.25. *Interface Between Data Terminal Equipment and Data Circuit-Terminating Equipment for Terminals Operating in the Packet Mode and Connected to Public Data Networks by Dedicated Circuit.*

[22] ITU-T Recommendation X.400, *Message Handling Services: Message Handling System and Service Overview.*

[23] ITU-T Recommendation X.500, *Information Technology—Open Systems Interconnection—The Directory: Overview of Concepts, Models, and Services.*

[24] ITU-T Recommendation X.509, *Information Technology—Open Systems Interconnection—The Directory: Public-Key and Attribute Certificate Frameworks.*

[25] "American National Standards Institute: Electronic Standards Store," August 2003, http://webstore.ansi.org/ansidocstore/default.asp.

[26] "ANSI Homeland Security Standards Panel," August 2003, http://www.ansi.org/standards_activities/standards_boards_panels/hssp/overview.aspx?menuid=3.

[27] "Standards," August 2003, http://www.nist.gov/public_affairs/standards.htm.

[28] "Federal Information Processing Standards Publications (FIPS PUBS): FIPS Home Page," August 2003, http://www.itl.nist.gov/fipspubs.

[29] "NIST Information Technology Laboratory, Computer Security Division (CSD), Computer Security Resource Center (CSRC)," August 2003, http://csrc.nist.gov.

[30] "Public Key Cryptography Standards," August 2003, http://www.rsasecurity.com/rsalabs/pkcs/index.html.

Process design and implementation

7.1 Requirements for stable processes

Previous chapters have introduced the process view of information security, shown how it can be decomposed into tactical and strategic activities, and presented the management and design aspects of the strategic-planning cycle. This chapter complements the material covered so far and concentrates on implementation issues. More specifically, this chapter illustrates how to translate policy requirements and requirements arising out of risk analyses into a stable process, capable of adapting quickly to changing business requirements. Because few security officers have the luxury of implementing an approach from scratch, the approach will be one of process improvement.

Process improvement usually occurs in several phases. In early stages, where major changes are foreseen, it is wise to plan these changes in the form of a project. This is often necessary to establish an initial baseline for improvement and should ensure as a minimum that existing procedures are well understood and correctly documented. Once a certain level of stability has been reached, improvement measures are more likely to resemble fine tuning than significant changes and are best viewed as a continuous activity, rather than project-oriented work.

Improving the entire information-security process is likely to be a complex activity. In order to simplify the problem, we break it into a number of smaller problems by decomposing the process into its constituent procedures and improving the individual procedures. For groups of procedures that are strongly interdependent, it may be necessary to minimize these dependencies before any further improvement. To ensure that the most important problems are resolved first, procedures are prioritized based on the number and severity of known issues, and improvement efforts will be directed at those procedures that are most problematic. This approach not only produces results more rapidly, it also tends to liberate resources more quickly. These resources can then be used to identify improvements to other procedures. This is very useful where administration procedures are concerned, as the experience of the administrators themselves is a key input to improving the process.

Before proceeding with a detailed discussion of process-improvement techniques, it is useful to briefly examine why many processes fail to deliver acceptable results, even when the underlying conceptual framework is sound. Figure 7.1 shows the three main areas in which processes must deliver on expectations in order to maintain long-term stability.

Examples of where processes often fail to meet these criteria are discussed next, whereas improvement methods are presented in the following sections.

7.2   Why processes fail to deliver

7.2.1   Productivity issues

One of the most important areas in which processes fail to achieve the desired results is productivity. Common causes for reduced productivity include:

- Inappropriate control objectives;
- Unrealistic service targets;
- Inefficient control mechanisms;

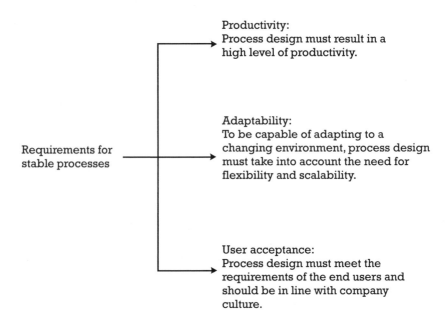

Figure 7.1   Key requirements for stable processes.

> Poorly designed workflow.

Inappropriate control objectives affect productivity in a negative way by diverting resources away from activities that would result in more effective risk mitigation. A control objective is obviously not appropriate if it does not significantly reduce risk or satisfy a regulatory or legal requirement. A set of control objectives can also be inappropriate if it does not provide a reasonably optimal response to mitigating global risk. For this reason, it is essential that the control framework as a whole implement a coherent set of security controls. In other words, it is of little use implementing extremely ambitious controls in one area if these controls can be undermined using weaknesses in other areas.

Where the information-security process delivers a service to others, it is essential that realistic levels of service be agreed with the customer. A particularly good illustration of this is provided by procedures for authorization and access control. Staff expectations that exceed the capacity of the team to deliver this service results in a backlog of requests. Under such conditions, staff may directly contact administrators in an attempt to resolve the situation, which in turn results in administrators spending time on the telephone and causes further service degradation.

Control mechanisms that are not regularly reviewed can quickly become inefficient or obsolete. For instance, requiring a physical signature on paper as authorization to perform some action is no more secure than using a simple mail message if the signature is never checked. Mail messages, on the other hand, are likely to produce a quicker response. If checking signatures proves to be unrealistic from an operational perspective, it may be better to get the risk signed off and implement an electronic solution, which should at least improve response times. This could subsequently be improved by implementing a secure transmission method, such as secure mail, using digital signatures. Of course, neither signed mail messages nor signed documents add any value if the authorizing party does not verify what is being signed.

Poorly designed workflow and inappropriate assignment of responsibilities are a frequent source of problems where the information-security process is concerned. A common mistake is to assign the responsibility for approving requests for security-related changes to members of the senior management team, without allowing for this to be delegated. In most organizations, senior managers perform very few routine operational tasks, and they are not particularly good at processing these requests in a timely manner. This often leads to bottlenecks in the process and can result in critical delays when several approvals are required before a request can be processed.

7.2.2 Adaptability issues

The ability to adapt to change is a second area where many processes experience problems. Issues in this area include:

- Process design that reflects specific and not generic requirements;
- Insufficient use of roles;
- Insufficient emphasis on compensating controls;
- Likely future requirements not built into the design.

Although many control procedures respond to a generic requirement, they often arise in a well-defined context. A typical example would be the requirement for a procedure to control emergency change accounts arising out of an audit of a particular business application. Emergency change accounts are often created by companies to allow developers to carry out changes at unusual hours and should obviously be subject to tight controls. If the resulting procedure is designed to take advantage of features particular to the OS to achieve its goals, it will be difficult to deploy on other systems. Similarly, where procedures are designed to be system specific, they are unlikely to benefit from compensating controls deployed elsewhere in the security architecture.

Procedures that directly reference the organizational structure of the enterprise are less flexible with respect to organizational changes than procedures that use the concept of roles. This is an important limitation for larger organizations where management changes are frequent. In many cases, such changes involve merging or splitting departments, with the consequence that the procedures may refer to positions that no longer exist.

Designing procedures and control measures for individual systems without taking into account architectural considerations greatly reduces the possibility of using compensating controls. As the name suggests, a compensating control is a control that can be used to compensate for a weakness elsewhere. As an example, consider an application that has a known vulnerability that cannot be corrected without extensive redesign. If this application is used only by a small number of users, it may be possible to reduce the risk by placing the server on a protected network segment and strictly limiting visibility of the machine to this user community.

Processes that are designed without any consideration for future requirements are unlikely to provide a strong foundation for growth. Despite this fact, many of the procedures used in modern, distributed environments have been simply carried over from those used in the mainframe era. Procedures for analysis of logging and audit trail data constitute a typical example of this problem, and many organizations still support policies requiring regular analysis of data on all platforms. For most large organizations, such an indiscriminate approach is infeasible due to the sheer volume of data.

7.2.3   Acceptance issues

Successful processes are aligned with the needs of the end user and are designed to fit in with the company culture. Processes that do not take into account the requirements of the participating parties are likely to face opposition and may eventually be rejected. Common process-design issues related to user acceptance include the following:

- Complexity;
- Dependency on specific skill sets;
- Psychological issues.

The issue of complexity is discussed within several different contexts in this book, but the point to be made is always the same: reducing complexity should result in better understanding, and only by understanding a problem can we hope to fix it. It is therefore particularly important that staff members develop a good understanding of the information-security process and the role that they play in this process. Without this level of understanding, they may not be able to recognize unusual events or to react to them appropriately if detected.

In general, process design should aim to simplify as much as possible and to avoid the requirement for specific skill sets. Unfortunately, simplification has its limits, and certain procedures will require staff with specific skill sets. Hence, end users can be helped to select access rights matching their job function by defining roles with meaningful, business-related names, but tasks such as firewall administration remain the domain of experts. In the latter example, merely understanding the syntax and semantics of the control data itself requires a good working knowledge of how communications protocols work. Untrained staff may be able to set up simple rules and report the more obvious problems, but understanding what constitutes normal behavior and managing threats requires expertise.

This last issue is interesting in the sense that capable network engineers tend to prefer project-oriented work to repetitive administration tasks. Indeed, the more repetitive the task, the more difficult it is to motivate skilled staff to perform the required actions correctly (rather than just going through the motions). This problem was also referred to in Chapter 1 using log analysis as the example.

7.3 Process improvement

7.3.1 Methods for process improvement

Process improvement is one of the core objectives of quality management, and a variety of formal methods have been developed for this purpose [1–5]. Many organizations have also published reports on their experiences applying these and other methodologies (for example, see [6–9]). However, formal methods are best employed in a global context as part of the enterprisewide quality-management approach, as opposed to at the department level. Even if it is not mandatory, where organizations have established a process-improvement program, security managers are advised to make use of this approach, rather than carrying out this activity independently. This is an important synergy for both the information-security department and the quality-management department. The information-security department will be able to take advantage of new contacts within business departments and will benefit from the visibility associated with being part of a global initiative. There will also be benefits from the standardization that a global approach can offer. Similarly, the quality-management department benefits from contacts that the information-security team has established and obtains another active participant in the improvement process.

Throughout the following discussion, references to specific methodologies have been avoided, as these are likely to differ considerably from organization to organization. We therefore take a more empirical approach and look at methods for improving productivity, adaptability, and acceptance before presenting an example of how these ideas can be applied to real-life situations. Because changing operational procedures can involve considerable risk, it is necessary to use a structured approach to identifying and carrying out modifications. A simple, but effective approach to achieving this is based on the following steps:

- Understand and document the current process;
- Decompose the process into a set of constituent procedures and supporting mechanisms;
- Prioritize procedures in terms of need for improvement;
- Identify the desired target situation for each procedure;
- Plan implementation as a series of incremental improvements;
- Implement and manage dependencies between procedures.

The first step in improving any process is to understand what is currently in place. Where the current process is fully understood, it is worth verifying that it is also correctly documented, as this documentation will serve as a baseline for future modifications. The process is documented as a number of procedures, each potentially supported by one or more tools. Procedures are then ranked in order of stability based on the number and severity of known issues. This is an important step, as improving processes takes time; it is therefore important to concentrate on those areas causing the biggest problems.

Once procedures have been prioritized, work can begin on identifying improvements. In the cases where there are few interdependencies between procedures, this is best achieved by treating each procedure in isolation. On the contrary, where there are strong interdependencies, it will be easier to examine related groups of procedures at the same time. In both cases, ideas for process improvement should be checked for consistency with other procedures before implementation.

Planning the implementation as a series of incremental improvements limits risk. In the event of unforeseen issues, it will probably be easier to back out of small changes than major ones, which is an important consideration for more critical procedures. This approach also allows those involved with the process to adapt gradually to changes, which is important when resistance to change is likely to be high [10].

Following an analysis of techniques for improving productivity, adaptability, and acceptance, we will illustrate this approach by taking a detailed look at the authorization and access control procedure of The Secure Bank.

7.3.2 Improving productivity

7.3.2.1 Factors affecting productivity

Productivity is a measure of how much output can be achieved from a fixed pool of resources. The greater the productivity, the more output is produced. According to Truby, the main factors influencing productivity are effectiveness, efficiency, and cycle time [11]:

Productivity = f (effectiveness, efficiency, cycle time)

where the notation $P = f(x)$ is simply a shorthand notation for the fact that P depends on x.

Effectiveness is essentially doing the right thing and refers to the extent to which an activity meets it stated objectives. An effective information-security process will therefore mitigate risk in line with management expectations and will neither overprotect assets nor subject them to unnecessary exposure. Efficiency, on the other hand, means doing the thing right. Efficiency measures the cost of producing the output in terms of some input, and a highly efficient process will produce the required output at a very low cost. Finally, the cycle time is a measure of the speed with which the output can be produced. Improving the cycle time reduces the delay between receiving the inputs and producing the outputs. It is important to note that while these factors measure different aspects of a process, they are not totally independent of each other. For example, it makes little sense to talk of a process that is efficient but ineffective.

7.3.2.2 Effectiveness

Improving the effectiveness of a process is effectively synonymous with removing any activity that does not add value. Strictly speaking, this means removing activity that does not contribute to transforming the inputs into the outputs. However, where the information-security process is concerned (see Figure 2.2), this still leaves considerable scope for discussion. For instance, it is pertinent to ask what level of documentation is necessary to mitigate risk in an optimal manner. Similarly, the definition of what constitutes a secure system or a trained staff member is a matter of some debate. As usual, common sense and experience normally prove to be the best tools for deciding what adds value and what doesn't, and the meaning of value in this context will differ from company to company.

Where documentation is concerned, formalized procedures should be used sparingly, as keeping them up to date can require considerable effort. It is therefore important to avoid overdocumenting the process. Administrators, for instance, can reasonably be expected to know the tools with which they are working, and procedures that document routine system administration tasks in detail do not add a lot of value. The correct solution to this issue is to provide adequate training, rather than to redocument material that is usually available in standard textbooks.

It is important to consider all options before implementing a specific solution to mitigate risk. Where procedural controls are onerous and costly, a viable option may be to simply accept the risk or to transfer the risk to a third party. For customer-facing systems, contractual measures often provide an attractive alternative. As an example of such an approach, customers may be willing to accept a lower level of availability of an application if the cost is lower. This is an attractive alternative to a sophisticated technical architecture and associated procedures for ensuring close to 100% availability.

For existing procedures, the first step in improving effectiveness is to check that risk is mitigated in an appropriate manner. In other words, unless a legal or regulatory restriction is at stake, the output of procedures should reflect the level of risk that the management has chosen to accept. Where procedures cannot be shown to reduce information security–related risk, they should be called into question. Organizations that are driven more by policy or best practice than by risk management should be able to improve effectiveness by analyzing procedures in this way. In particular, systematically implementing best-practice solutions is not likely to provide optimal risk mitigation. Best-practice solutions tend to implement very strong security and can easily lead to overengineering. Many organizations might be prepared to implement a less secure solution for a lower cost or increased flexibility.

Improving the effectiveness of a procedure requires a thorough knowledge of what constitutes optimal risk mitigation. This tends to put natural limits on the improvements that can be introduced in this area. Consider, for instance, a procedure performing a backup of data, which requires special treatment of confidential data. For some of the data, it may be possible to limit their value in time. Hence, a confidential report predicting the performance of the world's stock exchanges over the next financial month is of very limited value in 2 months. A procedure that is optimal from the point of view of effectiveness would not expend undue effort in protecting data any longer than is necessary, but analyzing a constantly changing pool of data as a function of time is probably not feasible for most organizations. Even if this were possible, the overhead of keeping track of the status of such data would more than compensate for the potential benefits. Most organizations are therefore expected to classify data once and to maintain that classification.

7.3.2.3 Efficiency

Increasing the efficiency of a process involves reducing the associated cost. According to this definition, a faster process is not necessarily more efficient one. For our purposes, we will classify measures to improve efficiency as organizational, logic related, or tools related.

Organizational measures improve efficiency by changing the way in which procedures affect people. For this reason, organizational measures are likely to have a big impact on acceptance, and this should be taken into consideration as part of the design process. Examples of organizational methods for increasing efficiency include setting realistic objectives, controlling user expectations, prioritizing, reducing dependency on specific skill sets, and ensuring that responsibilities are appropriate.

Setting realistic objectives and agreeing on service levels with users improves efficiency by eliminating unnecessary follow up on the part of end users. As a result of these actions, administrators should be able to dedicate more time to the core process and less time to dealing with dissatisfied users. This in turn results in more satisfied users and breaks the vicious circle described in Section 7.2.1. When defining objectives and establishing service levels, it is worth planning for extreme situations, such as the temporary unavailability of several administrators at the same time. One way to deal with this is to prioritize deliverables and to define a degraded mode of operation, which concentrates on delivering the most important services. The SLA should then explain under what conditions this mode of operation will be invoked and how this will happen.

Prioritizing the procedures that constitute a process helps ensure that available resources are used optimally. Prioritization is therefore an organizational improvement technique, as it is concerned with how people interact with procedures. Resource utilization should not be an issue under normal conditions but becomes important under conditions of high volume or when resources are not available. Similarly, within procedures, it is sometimes possible to prioritize deliverables. For example, under conditions of heavy load, it would usually be appropriate to prioritize requests for access to the production environment over requests for development access.

Reducing the dependencies that a process has on specific skill sets represents an increase in efficiency because unskilled staff members are easier to find than skilled staff members (and they generally cost less). In this case, the benefit would be realized by deploying the skills where they add more value. Similarly, requiring sign off of an action by a senior manager when this is not necessary is inefficient, as the manager concerned would presumably be required to verify that the action had been carried out correctly before approving, and this time could be better used elsewhere. In fact, where the level of sign off is obviously inappropriate, there is also a risk that the manager concerned will not take the task seriously, leading to a lack of control.

Logic-related methods of improving efficiency aim to do so by improving the logical design of procedures. This includes ensuring that the overall design of the process is reasonably optimal in terms of cost and resource utilization. Typically, this will involve enforcing a design in which the scope of individual procedures is well controlled and unnecessary overlaps with other control procedures are minimized. For instance, escalation procedures increase efficiency by ensuring that problems are treated by staff with the appropriate level of authority. Whereas it might take an administrator several hours to convince others of the necessity of shutting down a server, a manager can achieve this in minutes. These methods are also used to improve the design of individual procedures by correcting errors in the logical flow that result in an increased cost.

Finally, efficiency can often be improved by using different tools to obtain the same result or making better use of existing tools. This is mainly achieved by automating manual processes and can be used to implement very significant efficiency gains. This is easy to see where administration procedures are concerned. The creation of a user account and establishment of default access rights can involve a lot of steps on some platforms and can therefore be very time consuming. Using a scripting language to automate these steps and apply companywide standards and naming conventions will often bring about significant productivity gains in this area.

7.3.2.4   Cycle time

Cycle time is a measure of how long it takes to do something. Improving the cycle time of a procedure is therefore equivalent to performing the steps of the procedure more rapidly and represents a productivity gain. Improving cycle times is particularly important in the manufacturing industry, where long order-to-delivery cycle times result in decreased customer satisfaction, higher costs, and high inventory levels [12], but the idea has also been successfully used in other environments [13]. Where information security is concerned, reducing the cycle time is most instrumental in increasing customer satisfaction. This is true not only for routine administration processes, but also for those processes that support the activities of software development and acquisition. In the latter case, a reduced cycle time can result in a faster time to market, which has a direct effect on business opportunities.

If we consider a procedure as a sequential series of tasks, we can improve the cycle time by removing tasks that do not add value, by performing tasks faster, or by reducing the delays between tasks. The first alternative has been discussed under the heading of effectiveness. Speeding up execution can often be achieved using automation. Increasing the number of resources is also an option, of course, but is generally not an appealing option as it increases costs. It may, however, be the only solution for certain time-critical procedures. For many organizations, reducing delays between tasks will offer the greatest opportunity for improvement, and this can often be achieved by improving the underlying workflow.

The likely impact of measures to decrease cycle time should be carefully considered before implementation. If procedures start to resemble conveyer belts, motivation is likely to drop sharply.

7.3.3 **Improving adaptability**

7.3.3.1 Factors affecting adaptability

For the purposes of this book, we define a process's ability to adapt as the ease with which the process can be modified to take account of external changes. The ability to adapt is determined by the flexibility and scalability of the process. Flexibility is the ability to assimilate new functional requirements, and scalability is the ability to cope with increased volume.

$$\text{Adaptability} = f \text{ (flexibility, scalability)}$$

7.3.3.2 Flexibility

Improving the flexibility of a process involves modifying the process in any way that makes it easier to take care of future changes in functionality. One of the easiest ways to increase flexibility is to minimize complexity. This is simply a reflection of the fact that it is easier to understand the impact of changing something simple than that of changing something complex.

In line with this principle, process design should use the principle of modularity. Procedures should have a limited and well-defined scope, and dependencies between procedures should be kept to a minimum. Furthermore, the control flow within procedures should be standardized as much as possible, which involves minimizing the number of exceptional cases that must be dealt with. Where IT systems are concerned, procedural steps that rely on the functionality of particular systems should be replaced by generic steps wherever possible.

7.3.3.3 Scalability

Scalability is a key issue in highly distributed environments, where standard procedures such as authorization and access control, log analysis, and vulnerability management potentially need to be carried out for hundreds, if not thousands, of platforms.

Important techniques for managing scalability include prioritizing deliverables and managing granularity. Both of these techniques achieve scalability at a cost. In the first case, procedures are made more scalable by concentrating on those deliverables that add most value. As an example, the procedure of log analysis can be made scalable by prioritizing logs and proactively inspecting those logs that provide the best return in terms of risk mitigation. Similarly, procedures to detect and repair vulnerabilities can be made more scalable by concentrating on vulnerabilities that are associated with a medium or high level of risk. This is a compromise based on an assessment of the underlying risk—more systems can be managed at the cost of ignoring low risk vulnerabilities.

A similar argument applies when changing the granularity of a control measure to increase scalability. Access-control mechanisms are a classic example in this area. Maintaining granular access rights to a million files for a thousand staff members is clearly infeasible, which is why both people and the resources they would like to access are organized into groups on most systems. However, for many medium and large organizations, this technique may still not be sufficient to exercise real control, and further levels of abstraction may be necessary. The basic idea behind this approach is that although granularity is being sacrificed, the real level of control is increasing due to the increased scalability of the process as a whole.

7.3.4 Improving acceptance

7.3.4.1 Factors affecting acceptance

User acceptance is influenced by a variety of factors, including many of those mentioned earlier. For instance, staff members are not likely to feel motivated to participate in a process that is obviously ineffective and may feel frustrated when processes are inefficient. User acceptance of procedures is likely to be strongly influenced by cultural issues, level of understanding, and psychological factors.

$$Acceptance = f\,(\text{cultural impact, complexity, psychological impact})$$

Each of these factors is considered next.

7.3.4.2 Cultural issues

Cultural issues are known to have a major effect on people's acceptance of change [14–16]. One example of this phenomenon is the number of mergers that fail due to an inability to surmount cultural differences [17–19]. It therefore follows that changes to processes that involve assimilating new cultural values need to be introduced very carefully.

A powerful technique for introducing significant change is to let those involved drive the change process [16]. The basic idea is to provide those involved in the current procedure with the requirements and to provide help in identifying the final solution. Although this may sometimes require a lot of work in terms of explanation and guidance, the final result is much more likely to be a durable one.

That having been said, a certain amount of resistance to change is inevitable and, to some extent, desirable [16]. Resistance is useful because it forces those introducing the change to justify their course of action, not only with respect to other alternatives but also with respect to the existing model. An important point to bear in mind here is that resistance to change operates in both directions. Just as those involved in the current procedure may not welcome the move toward another way of doing things, the team proposing the change may be reluctant to change the proposal to reflect voiced concerns.

Wherever possible, the best approach is to introduce small changes on a regular basis, making sure that staff members are well prepared for each successive change. This allows people to adapt gradually to a new way of doing things and avoids brutal changes [10].

7.3.4.3 Complexity

It is not difficult to understand why complexity is a barrier to acceptance. That which is not understood in life is often mistrusted, and there is no reason that information security should be an exception to that rule. Where process improvement is concerned, complexity is an important issue in two separate areas: the design of the process itself and the way in which the underlying objectives and the design itself are communicated to staff.

Many of the lessons learned in the area of software engineering can be applied to the problem of simplifying process design. Design principles used for reducing the complexity of software, such as partitioning, hierarchy, and modularity [20], are particularly useful in this area. Indeed, measures of complexity that have long been used in software engineering, such as the cyclomatic number, can also be used to measure the complexity of process models [21]. In practice, it is rarely necessary to perform complex calculations in order to measure complexity, and perfectly good results can be obtained by following the spirit of the idea. For example, the number of decision points within a procedure is a good indication of its complexity.

Unfortunately, even where processes are well designed, modern techniques for securing information are not very accessible to the uninitiated, and experts tend to use a lot of specialized vocabulary when describing problems and solutions. Part of the problem where complexity is concerned, therefore, is the way in which information is communicated. Avoiding jargon and keeping documentation short and to the point can help a lot, as can consideration for the form of documents. Simple tools, such as flow charts and checklists, can be very helpful in this area, particularly when they are accompanied by explanations and examples that are familiar to the reader.

7.3.4.4 Psychological factors

The extent to which people associate with the tasks assigned to them is determined by a number of factors, including their ability to perform and the extent to which they consider the task interesting. When an individual's ability to perform a particular task is either substantially below or above the required standard, motivation is likely to be low. In the first case, this lack of motivation will be caused by a continual failure to meet the required standard and in the latter case by the lack of challenge in carrying out the activity.

Actively managing work assignments by ensuring that staff members are assigned tasks that are within their abilities and sufficiently varied can therefore bring about considerable improvements in morale and have a positive impact on productivity. One way to achieve this is to use the appraisal process to identify particular areas of interest and relevant skill sets. Planning assignments can then be approached in a similar way to planning training and education. Rotating staff members between different roles within the team is a useful technique in this regard.

7.4 The Secure Bank: Improving the authorization and access-control procedure

7.4.1 Planning

The initiative to improve the authorization and access-control procedure at The Secure Bank was undertaken as part of the strategic initiative to improve administration procedures. In this sense, administration procedures were already prioritized in terms of need for improvement over the other procedures in the information-security process.

The initial steps of the approach outlined in Section 7.3.1 identified the authorization and access-control procedure as a high priority for improvement. This was based on feedback from stakeholders and administrators and confirmed by an analysis of previous audit recommendations, where issues with authorization and access control were the origin of over 50% of audit recommendations over the previous 3 years.

7.4.2 The current process

In this section, we describe problems surrounding the authorization and access-control procedure initially in place at The Secure Bank and show how the procedure was reengineered to satisfy the bank's requirements for productivity, adaptability, and acceptance.

Figure 7.2 illustrates the documented version of the authorization and access-control procedure as of the start of the process improvement exercise, and Table 7.1 summarizes the major known issues at this time. This table also shows the level of severity associated with each issue based on conversations with stakeholders.

The first action undertaken as part of the improvement process was to document the real version of the procedure. This is illustrated in Figure 7.3 and was used as the baseline for improvement.

The essential differences between the documented procedure and the procedure as applied in reality were as follows:

- Users made requests directly to administrators, who then forwarded these requests for approval to the appropriate line manager.
- Similarly, line managers sent approvals to administrators, who forwarded the messages to application owners (not data owners) for approval.
- The undocumented concept of application owners had developed over time and resolved the problems associated with asking data owners (typically senior management) for approval.

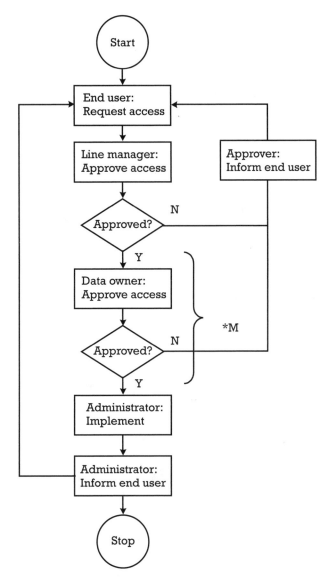

Figure 7.2   Documented authorization and access-control process.

- Application owners responded to the administrators, who executed the request if approved. The administrator then informed the user of the status of the request.

- In case of problems, the administrator helped the user concerned to solve the issue and amended the access rights accordingly.

- Administrators also checked that the number of users defined on the system was covered by the current license and notified the purchasing department in case of problems.

Table 7.1 Known Issues with the Authorization and Access-Control Process

Id	Description of Issue	Severity
AC1	*Incorrect documentation:* The documented version of the procedure was significantly different from the procedure applied in practice.	Medium
AC2	*Customer dissatisfaction:* Internal users of IT systems were dissatisfied with the level of service.	High
AC3	*Insufficient understanding (requesters):* Most staff members had a poor understanding of the access rights associated with the applications they were using.	High
AC4	*Insufficient understanding (approvers):* Managers were not sufficiently aware of the access rights they were approving.	High
AC5	*Backups not defined:* Many approvers did not identify a backup, leading to problems during their absence.	Medium
AC6	*Administrator overload:* Administrators were the central point of contact for all problems and were continually overloaded.	High
AC7	*Lack of quantitative data:* No statistics were available to show the extent of the problem.	Low
AC8	*Low level of automation:* Administrators used little or no scripting, and workflow was completely manual.	Medium
AC9	*Inappropriate responsibilities:* Audit staff members were performing security administration tasks in the mainframe environment.	Medium
AC10	*Inadequate feedback:* Users were not able to verify the status of requests without contacting administrators.	Medium
AC11	*Requirement for specific skill sets:* Providing access required specific skill sets on different platforms.	Medium
AC12	*System-specific procedures:* Minor deviations from the core procedure were necessary to cope with certain system-specific issues.	High
AC13	*Nonvalue-added activity:* Security administrators were carrying out activities that had nothing to do with security, notably checking licenses.	Low

This workflow was valid for most platforms, but variations existed for certain platforms. Two examples will illustrate this. Where the mainframe platform was concerned, audit staff members and not security administrators were responsible for administering access rights. On Windows platforms, access to shared drives was authorized by a project leader or a department head and not an application owner.

A glance at the actual procedure illustrates why many of the known issues involved administrators. In the real procedure, administrators were performing the role of a communications hub, without adding any value.

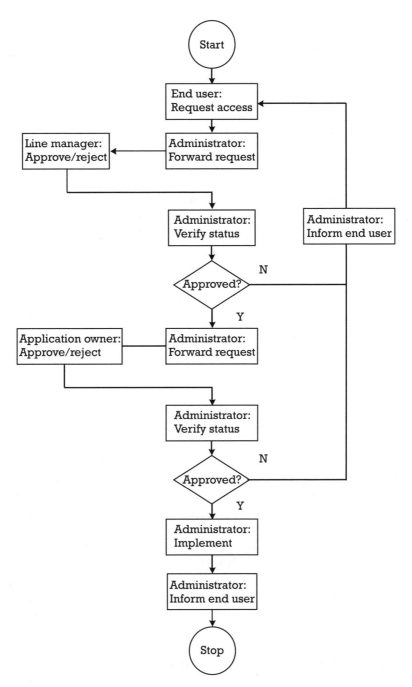

Figure 7.3   Actual authorization and access-control process.

7.4.3   Identifying the target situation

In this first cycle of process improvement, identifying the desired target situation was complicated by the absence of reliable metrics. The only data available describing this procedure was the data collected during the consolidation period concerning the number of requests for access per type of OS (see Section 4.4.7). However, at the start of the exercise, there was not enough data to establish a quantitative baseline for improvement or to predict future trends. Consequently, it was difficult to define quantitative improvement targets, although it was considered important to ensure that this was possible in the future, and the decision was taken to introduce a set of metrics as part of the improvement initiative.

The main productivity requirements were to increase the effectiveness of the procedure and to reduce the cycle time. The number of audit points relating to authorization and access control would be used to monitor improvement in effectiveness, and the target was to decrease the number of outstanding points by 75% in a period of 18 months. The target for cycle-time improvement was to ensure that the backlog in processing requests did not exceed 10% of the average weekly volume at any time during the months of September through May inclusive. This latter target was not imposed on the summer months, as the impact of holidays was known to be high at this time but the risk was low. Experience showed that the majority of access requests in the summer were related to development activities. Prioritization would be used to ensure that business requests were processed in a timely manner.

The only requirements on adaptability were to increase flexibility by removing system-specific parts of the procedure and creating a single procedure for all platforms. Scalability was not an immediate issue, as the business strategy of the bank involved a projected reduction in the number of staff following the reorganization of the branch network.

Acceptability requirements were judged to be the most important of all requirements, largely because the information-security department was in the process of introducing a new approach. The way in which staff in general perceived changes was judged to be a critical factor in deciding whether the approach would be successful. Unfortunately, this was also the area in which it was most difficult to measure improvements. The idea of monitoring the number of problems reported by staff was abandoned, as this would have to be done manually. It was eventually agreed to monitor progress in this area more informally by asking stakeholders and administrators for regular feedback.

7.4.4   Planning incremental improvements

Improvements to the authorization and access-control process were identified in a series of brainstorming sessions involving business representatives, security administrators, and auditors. Most of these discussions centered on the issues documented in Table 7.1, but some new and interesting ideas arose out of the brainstorming process itself. The improvements that were finally agreed on are presented alongside the issues they help resolve in Table 7.2. A new row has been added to this table to cover improvements that are not linked to specific issues. The final column of this table shows the priority associated with the improvement idea.

Table 7.2   Improvement Ideas for the Authorization and Access-Control Procedure

Id	Description of Issue	Improvement Ideas	Priority
AC1	Incorrect documentation	Document actual process.	Done
		Formalize the concept of application owners.	
AC2	Customer dissatisfaction	Simplify by introducing an SLA.	High
		Redefine workflow.	Medium
		Define a degraded mode of operation.	Medium
AC3	Insufficient understanding (requesters)	Improve documentation and understanding.	High
		Introduce Web forms with validity checking.	Medium
AC4	Insufficient understanding (approvers)	Improve documentation and understanding.	High
		Introduce Web forms with validity checking.	Medium
AC5	Backups not defined	Ensure that all approvers have a backup.	High
AC6	Administrator overload	Improve documentation and understanding.	High
		Enforce appropriate workflow.	Medium
		Automate workflow.	Low
AC7	Lack of quantitative data	Implement elementary statistics and reports.	Medium
AC8	Low level of automation	Automate workflow.	Low
		Automate supply of human resources information.	Medium
		Increase scripting.	Medium
		Introduce EUA tool.	Low
AC9	Inappropriate responsibilities	Transfer responsibility to security administrators.	Medium
AC10	Inadequate feedback	Modify workflow to allow users to check status of requests.	Medium
AC11	Requirement for specific skill sets	Deskill the user-administration process using scripting techniques.	Low
AC12	System-specific procedures	Remove system-specific details from the process.	Low
AC13	Nonvalue-added activity	Agree change of responsibility for licensing check.	Medium
NEW		Introduce default profile.	Medium
		Create roles to further simplify administration.	Low
		Introduce centralized telephone number and mailbox.	Medium
		Have managers retrieve status reports rather than sending them.	Medium

The approach to prioritizing improvement ideas was standardized across the whole process-improvement initiative. This involved first classifying ideas as productivity, adaptability, or user-acceptance improvement. Ideas that improved user acceptance would be implemented as a priority, followed by ideas that would improve productivity, and finally ideas that improved adaptability. Within each group, ideas would be further prioritized according to the severity of the issue they resolved. The final result was then adjusted manually to reflect planning constraints and to ensure overall coherence. Although this method may seem to put undue emphasis on user acceptance, stakeholders felt very strongly that obtaining the buy in of staff was the key to success and were therefore prepared to accept more risk in the short term in order to guarantee the long-term objective. This was therefore a risk-based decision.

7.4.5   Implementing improvements

The authorization and access-control procedure was improved in a series of steps spanning a total of 2 years. This includes the implementation of an EUA package, as described in Chapter 8. Once the EAU system was judged to be operationally stable, the procedure was considered to be relatively optimal, and further improvements were made as part of a continual improvement method (i.e., not as project-related work). This section describes the various implementation steps and the benefits they achieved.

7.4.5.1   Step 1—High-priority improvements

The update of the documentation was carried out as part of the analysis activity, and the revised documents were published on the information-security Web site. In agreement with the quality department, the style of the documents was changed to include more graphic content and less text. As a result of the positive feedback from staff, this format eventually developed into a quality standard for the organization.

Following the documentation exercise, work began on producing an SLA. Although it only took 1 month to produce the original proposal, 4 months of time were necessary to agree on this with stakeholders. The SLA was prepared and agreed on with the help of the quality department, the members of whom were keen on promoting the use of such agreements throughout the enterprise. As part of the effort to agree on an SLA, the move to a more efficient workflow, where administrators were not involved in forwarding requests, was agreed on with stakeholders, even though this was not implemented until step 2.

The lengthy approval period was largely due to the proposed guaranteed turnaround time of three working days for requests, which business units initially found unacceptable. This issue was finally resolved by allowing staff to submit urgent requests, which would be executed within one working day. Stakeholders agreed that urgent requests should not account for more than 5% of the total number of requests in any given week and that efforts should be made to reduce this figure with time. The percentage of urgent requests per week was therefore defined as a metric for monitoring the process. The SLA document identified a degraded mode of operation, where the guaranteed turnaround time for urgent requests was unchanged, but other requests would be processed on a best-effort basis (no guaranteed turnaround). A degraded mode of operation would come into effect once resource availability fell below a certain threshold (which was defined on a per-platform basis). The degraded mode of operation would be in effect automatically during the months of June to August inclusive.

In parallel with the effort to develop an SLA for the procedure, the list of application owners was verified and updated, and each application owner was asked to name a deputy. This information was stored in a simple database, which was subsequently made available on the information-security Web site.

The high-priority improvements covered by step 1 were implemented within a period of 6 months.

7.4.5.2   Step 2—Medium-priority improvements

The main effect of the SLA was to reduce the number of calls made to administrators to follow up on requests in progress. This allowed the administrators to dedicate more time to the remaining activities and effectively triggered a positive cycle of improvements. However, the drop in unnecessary calls was not as big as it was expected to be, and it was therefore decided to take immediate steps to enforce the rules that had been agreed on with the business. Administrators were therefore asked to politely refuse to provide detailed status on progress within the agreed turnaround time. To achieve this, a standard reply was agreed on with all administrators, who were asked to reduce time spent on the telephone to an absolute minimum. On the contrary, where requests were not satisfied within the agreed turnaround time, administrators were encouraged to explain the reason to staff and even to hold face-to-face meetings if absolutely necessary. This was difficult in the first few days but began to have a noticeable impact after about a month.

The next big improvement step was to enforce the move toward a sensible workflow by eliminating those steps where administrators were simply forwarding messages between users and approvers. This was achieved in several steps:

- Announcement on the company intranet;
- Use of an adoption period of 1 month;
- Full implementation using preformatted reply messages;
- Transfer of administration tasks from the audit department to the information-security department.

The first step was to announce the new workflow on the company intranet, stressing that stakeholders had agreed to this change. The fact that the list of application owners was now available on the information-security

Web site was a factor that contributed strongly to the success of this transition, as it allowed line managers to identify the appropriate application owner without involving administrators.

During the first month of operation, all requests were treated, irrespective of whether they followed the old or the new workflow. Preformatted messages were used to remind staff of the new workflow whenever the old workflow was used. After an elapsed period of 1 month, requests submitted using the old workflow were refused and a preformatted message was sent to the offending party. In reality, enforcing the new workflow was one of the most difficult tasks to accomplish and much of the time gained as a result of the SLA was used coaching staff through the new procedure.

The last step in this effort involved a transfer of administration activities from the audit department to the information-security department. This was feasible for two reasons. First, the information-security steering group agreed that the administrators within the audit department should be transferred to the information-security department as part of the exercise. Second, the audit department was more than pleased to agree to this, as this procedure had been a major source of difficulties for some time.

As part of the improvement exercise, certain members of the administration team were given the task of improving the efficiency of the core administration activities by using scripting techniques. Those responsible for scripting were specifically instructed to ensure that the "look and feel" of scripts used on different platforms was as uniform as possible and that any system-specific functionality was encapsulated within scripts. These team members were also asked to include the generation of statistics in scripts wherever possible. This scripting initiative not only resulted in a gradual improvement in efficiency, but also reduced the dependencies on specific skill sets.

7.4.5.3 Step 3—Low-priority improvements

The scripting effort was continued throughout step 3 of the improvement initiative and eventually became a part of the continuous-improvement activities. However, further improvements in the area of automation were integrated into the IT security architecture initiative, which included a subproject for the selection and implementation of an EUA system.

Important improvements implemented within the context of this latter project include the implementation of an information feed from the human resources department, an automated workflow system that enabled users to visualize the status of requests, and a standard user interface.

7.5 Continuous improvement

In the future, continuous-improvement activities will concentrate on improving the structure of the access-control data itself. The granularity of the data that administrators have to deal with will be reduced by packaging low-level access rights into commonly required functional groupings. These groupings will then be assigned to business roles. The underlying idea is to reduce the task of administering access rights to one of assigning business roles to users. As this is expected to involve a repackaging of all of the bank's applications, it will be achieved gradually. Prioritization will be used to decide the order in which applications are aligned with this new standard.

The effect of improvement measures will be followed using the following metrics:

- Percentage of urgent requests per week;
- Number of requests processed per platform per week;
- Number of dormant accounts at the end of each calendar month;
- Percentage backlog per week;
- Number of outstanding audit points.

The percentage of urgent requests per week will be used to ensure that this facility is not abused. Once this exceeds the 5% limit agreed with the business, it will be reported to stakeholders, who are then expected to correct the situation. Over time, the percentage of urgent requests should gradually diminish.

The number of requests per platform per week and the percentage backlog per week are indicators of how demand is changing and how well the procedure is coping with this change. By following these metrics it should be possible to anticipate problems and react accordingly (by requesting temporary help, for instance).

A dormant account is an account that is still enabled, but is no longer in active use. The number of dormant accounts and the number of outstanding audit points indicate how effective the procedure is at any given time. Both are expected to decrease as the procedure is improved.

Finally, feedback will be requested at regular intervals from stakeholders in order to ensure that staff members are comfortable with the procedure, both from a usability and a performance point of view.

7.6 Summary

Stable processes must support a reasonable level of productivity and satisfy the expectations of those staff members who work with them. In addition, processes will only remain stable in the face of changing requirements if they are flexible with respect to functional changes and are capable of scaling to meet projected volumes. When attempting to improve processes, it is helpful to decompose the process as a whole into its constituent procedures and supporting controls. The approach is then to prioritize procedures in terms of the issues they present and to improve those procedures most in need of attention.

Methods for improving procedures aim to improve some combination of productivity, adaptability, or acceptance. The major factors influencing productivity are effectiveness, efficiency, and cycle time. Effectiveness is often described as "doing the right thing," whereas efficiency is "doing the thing right." The cycle time of an activity measures how quickly inputs are transformed into outputs. Improving adaptability, on the other hand, involves introducing new flexibility or rendering the procedure more scalable. Finally, acceptance is strongly driven by cultural issues and the ease with which the procedure can be understood. Several techniques have been presented for improving each of these aspects of a procedure.

The example of the authorization and access-control procedure of The Secure Bank was used to illustrate how to apply these ideas in practice. This involved identifying improvement measures and prioritizing them based on criteria agreed with stakeholders. In this example, user acceptance was by far the most important prioritization criterion, but this will vary from organization to organization. The implementation of the main ideas was carried out gradually in order to allow staff the time to become accustomed to the changes and to minimize risk. The entire process took 2 years to complete, but it should be born in mind that this was a complex and highly visible procedure.

References

[1]   "Quality-Based Problem-Solving/Process Improvement," September 2003, http://www.brecker.com/quality.htm.

[2]   "Six Sigma Questions and Answers Q and A," September 2003, http://www.isixsigma.com/library/content/c010204a.asp.

[3]   Malhotra, Y., "Business Process Redesign: An Overview," September 2003, http://www.brint.com/papers/bpr.htm.

[4]   "Business Process Revolution," September 2003, http://www.iec.org/online/tutorials/bus_proc.

[5]   "Business Process Improvement: A Draft Methodology for UNE," September 2003, http://www.une.edu.au/unesis/pdfs/bpi_methodolgy.pdf.

[6]   Caudle, S. L., "Reengineering for Results: Keys to Success from Government Experience, Section 1: Reengineering for Results: Six Critical Success Factors," September 2003, http://www.defenselink.mil/nii/bpr/bprcd/3002.htm.

[7]   Carter, W. L., "The Biggest Mistake Companies Make When Implementing TQM/Process Improvements," September 2003, http://www.firstbiz.com/cartwi01.htm.

[8]   Dolan, T., "Best Practices In Process Improvement," *Quality Progress,* Vol. 36, No. 8, 2003, pp. 23–28.

[9]   "Lessons Learned from High-Performing Organizations in the Federal Government," September 2003, http://www.defenselink.mil/nii/bpr/bprcd/5556.htm.

[10] "Changing Management Culture: Models and Strategies to Make it Happen: Stage 4: Transition," September 2003, http://www.tbs-sct.gc.ca/cmo_mfc/Toolkit2/GCC/cmc08_e.asp.

[11] Truby, C., "Business Process Improvement: A Proactive Way To Improve Margins," *The Quality Management Forum*, Vol. 29, No. 3, 2003, pp. 1, 12–13.

[12] Donovan, M., "Improving Manufacturing Cycle Time," September 2003, http://www.lionhrtpub.com/IM/IMsubs/IM-5-95/cycle.html.

[13] Ligon, G. D., and J. Grayson, "Reducing Cycle Time and Increasing Data Quality for Student Assessments," September 2003, http://www.educationadvisor.com/ocio2001/Reducing%20Cycle%20Time%20and%20Improving%20Data%20Quality.doc.

[14] Sifonis, J., and D. Bisha, "Change, Culture and Social Networks," September 2003, http://business.cisco.com/prod/tree.taf%3Fasset_id=103198&ID=85947&public_view=true&kbns=1.html.

[15] Trader-Leigh, K., "Managing Resistance To Change," September 2003, http://www.asaenet.org/sections/exec/article/1,2261,53937,00.html?headername=Executive+IdeaLink&searchstring=.

[16] de Jager, P., "Resistance To Change: A New View Of An Old Problem," September 2003, http://www.humboldt.edu/~campbell/p403rdg_orgchg2.htm.

[17] Raynaud, M., "Confusions and Acquisitions: Post-Merger Culture Shock and Some Remedies," September 2003, http://www.synergy-associates.com/cultural/Products/Post%20Merger%20Culture%20Shock.pdf.

[18] Karnatz, J., "Merger Culture," September 2003, http://www.insight-mag.com/insight/00/09/art-03.htm.

[19] Tomko, C., "Culture Does Matter When Firms Complete a Merger," September 2003, http://columbus.bizjournals.com/columbus/stories/2002/09/02/focus6.html.

[20] "Three Universal Methods of Reducing Complexity," October 2003, http://www.compapp.dcu.ie/~renaat/ca2/ca214/ca214vii.html.

[21] Latva-Koivisto, A. M., "Finding a Complexity Measure For Business Process Models," October 2003, http://www.hut.fi/~alatvako/Kompleksisuuserikoistyo_2001-02-13.PDF.

Building an IT security architecture

8.1 Evolution of enterprise IT infrastructure

In order to cut costs successfully, while still maintaining revenue, we need to operate more efficiently. One of the tools at our disposal for increasing efficiency is an increase in automation. This has led to several fundamental changes in the IT industry, each associated with a new and different paradigm for adding value to business processes [1].

These changes have been essentially architectural in nature and have resulted in a move from an extreme host-centric architecture (the original mainframe architecture), through client-server and three-tiered architectures to today's highly distributed architectures. The latter are based on technologies such as Java 2 enterprise edition (J2EE), COM+, and CORBA [2].

For many organizations, this evolutionary trend has resulted in a highly heterogeneous IT infrastructure composed of a mixture of host-centric, client-server, and truly distributed systems. Each of these architectures is associated with a certain security model, and over time tools have emerged to support these models. In reality, however, there is little standardization in the way in which these different architectural models implement security functionality, and this is a source of problems when such technologies coexist within the enterprise. Unfortunately, there are still relatively few tools capable of providing a coherent set of security functions across multiple technologies, and, as a result, interfaces between different technologies remain a common source of weaknesses.

These changes in architectural approach have been accompanied by a gradual move towards increasing connectivity, both within and outside the enterprise [3]. In the latter half of the 1990s, this trend was accelerated by the success of the Internet as a preferred medium for marketing and commerce and has lead to a situation in which most medium-and large-sized companies are now critically dependent on their network infrastructure.

Firewalls came about as a result of these two trends, largely in recognition of the fact that complex IT infrastructures are difficult to secure and therefore should not be visible to the outside world. Over the last decade, firewalls have played a major role in network security by enforcing a simple access-control policy at the network perimeter. The underlying assumption of this model is that most people outside the network perimeter of the enterprise should be kept outside, and a relatively small number of people should be allowed to come inside to take advantage of a restricted number of services.

A decade ago, this was a good idea, and time has shown that the concept has worked reasonably well in the intervening period. There is no doubt, however, that the underlying assumption that most people should stay out has changed fundamentally. As a trivial example of this fact, consider the company Web server. This is usually a mouthpiece for the enterprise and is often aimed at the widest audience possible. Unfortunately, we cannot place the Web server outside the firewall, as this would be insecure, and such a Web server would probably not remain intact very long. In fact, many organizations now wish to be more open with respect to the outside world in order to improve business prospects, whether this is by offering access to information, by providing services, or by some other profitable use of existing resources. Equivalently, most companies recognize the need to achieve this openness in a secure fashion—being open may be profitable but being too open will not allow most companies to maintain a competitive edge. The problem is that firewalls are relatively stupid devices on the whole and make their decisions largely on the basis of low-level protocol information, whereas this new way of operating requires a more sophisticated way of granting or rejecting access.

This is gradually leading to a new model of the network perimeter. Rather than being a *hard* perimeter and allowing only a select few to pass, the new model is a highly permeable perimeter, where many can pass but the decision-making process is much more complex [4]. Firewalls still play an important part in this new strategy, as they effectively block a whole range of access methods that remain inappropriate, but they are now reinforced by new technologies geared towards supporting a greater level of access.

8.2   Problems associated with system-focused approaches

As a result of these changes, medium- and large-sized organizations that design and implement security measures on a system-by-system basis are faced with a number of issues when attempting to create a coherent security framework. Examples of such issues include:

> ‣ High degree of complexity;

> ‣ Fragmented monitoring and control systems;

> ‣ Legacy systems with legacy security controls;

> ‣ Poorly defined network perimeter;

> ‣ Inappropriate procedures and working practices;

> ‣ Escalating costs.

The previous section explained how IT infrastructures have evolved into complex environments, often involving several generations of software. In the same timeframe, individual products have become increasingly more sophisticated, offering more functionality and additional deployment flexibility via a wide range of configuration options. The result is usually an IT infrastructure that is complex not only at the architectural level, but also at the product and application level.

Fragmented monitoring and control systems are a direct consequence of the lack of standardization of security-related functionality within commercial products. This has delayed the emergence of tools that are able to operate across several platforms. This is not just a technical problem; it has roots in more fundamental concepts, such as differences in syntax and semantics of commands and nonstandardized nomenclature. As a consequence, security administrators currently use a variety of disparate tools to carry out their day-to-day tasks, which makes it very difficult to see what is happening across different platforms and can easily lead to incoherence.

Legacy systems are problematic for a number of reasons, not the least of which is that the security mechanisms they are equipped with were usually developed to deal with a different set of threats than those currently operating. These problems are compounded by the fact that the documentation for many legacy systems is either lost or hopelessly out of date, and personnel involved in putting these systems into place may no longer be with the enterprise.

The previous section described how the notion of the network perimeter is changing for many organizations, with the consequence that the Internet gateway is usually well protected but dial-in and legacy connections may be insufficiently protected. A coherent approach to network security necessarily involves taking into consideration all connectivity options and ensuring that the level of protection of each such option reflects the associated risks.

One of the biggest issues of all is the impact that this technical evolution has had on administration procedures. This has been discussed in Chapter 7, and in this chapter we will limit ourselves to the observation that any security architecture must go hand in hand with an associated set of operating procedures. These procedures must not only complement the technical approach, they must also be capable of coping with likely future evolution and predicted growth.

Each of the problems described here can be solved to some extent by additional investment—experts can be hired to analyze complex environments or more administrators can reduce the impact of disparate control systems. However, this leads rapidly to unacceptable costs, which is a prime indicator that a different approach is required.

Deploying a security architecture is an efficient way to bring issues such as those discussed in this section under control. This is possible due to a shift in focus away from systems considered in isolation and towards a global approach. Looking at risks and requirements from a global perspective enables security managers to design and implement controls that can be reused across platforms, leading to better risk management through the use of compensating controls, decreased complexity through standardization, and reduced costs.

8.3 A three-phased approach

In the rest of this chapter we will design and implement a security architecture for The Secure Bank. This example is admittedly a little contrived and presents a very ambitious project in order to permit a wider discussion and to illustrate some of the compromises and trade-offs with which a typical organization is likely to be faced. Nevertheless, within these constraints, every effort has been made to keep the example as realistic as possible. At the start of the exercise, The Secure Bank has not performed any kind of risk analysis against its IT infrastructure and has not designed a security architecture. Any security infrastructure that is in place has been deployed to satisfy the requirements of specific business initiatives rather than as an attempt to provide a global solution.

Figure 8.1 provides a slightly more detailed look at how the IT infrastructure of the bank is organized.

This more detailed view of the IT infrastructure of the bank brings out the following new facts:

- Branch offices all have a simple infrastructure consisting of a single server machine and multiple workstations.

- At the headquarters, there is one LAN per floor. Departments are located on the network according to their location in the building. Although Figure 8.1 depicts a single server per LAN, this is just a convention to save space. In reality, the bigger departments have their own departmental server, and the smaller departments share machines wherever possible.

- The production LAN houses all common applications. The company mainframes are colocated on this LAN with approximately 40 midrange servers. A wide range of technologies is present, including many client-server applications and a range of new object-oriented applications, developed using the J2EE and CORBA models.

- The development LAN is used for development and testing and is similar in structure to the production LAN.

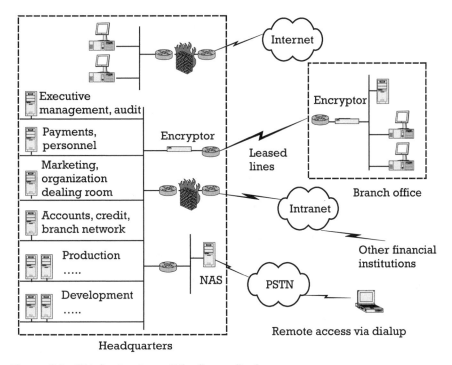

Figure 8.1 IT infrastructure of The Secure Bank.

The key to mastering this complexity is to define and implement security services using a structured approach. Note that structured does not imply complicated or mathematical, and it is extremely important to use formal techniques only to the extent that they facilitate the final goal. The method we use can be subdivided into three distinct phases: a design phase, an implementation phase, and an administration and maintenance phase.

8.4 The design phase

8.4.1 Planning

The design phase comprises the following activities:

- Agreeing basic design principles;
- Modeling the IT infrastructure;
- Performing an architectural risk analysis and deriving security services and procedures;
- Identifying logical components;
- Obtaining signoff for the overall concept.

Most organizations should be able to complete this analysis in a period of 3 to 6 months. The following guidelines are provided with respect to planning:

- Agreeing on design principles should not take longer than 1 month, as these are very high level and usually based on common sense.

- Modeling the infrastructure can take anything from 1 to 3 months, depending on the state of current documentation. For very large organizations having very complex infrastructures, it may be better to take an iterative approach and to refine the analysis in a series of subsequent steps.

- Fast risk analyses should take about three to four hours per analysis.

- Identifying logical components is in some respects the most difficult part, but it should be possible to achieve this within the space of a month.

- Finally, preparing the proposal for the implementation phase should be achievable in 1 to 2 weeks.

Obviously, these are only guidelines, and particular organizations will have to adapt these figures to reflect their experience with similar initiatives.

8.4.2   Agreeing on basic design principles

As IT security is about managing risk, the method for designing and implementing a security architecture will inevitably be risk driven. However, while risk analysis techniques will tell us a lot about what we need to achieve in terms of risk reduction, these techniques will not tell us an awful lot about *how* this can be achieved. It is just as well, therefore, to specify a set of criteria to guide the design process. In order to help organizations select appropriate design criteria, security-design principles have been published by a number of organizations, including the IETF [5], the Organization for Economic Cooperation and Development (OECD) [6], and the NIST [7, 8]. By defining such criteria, we provide ourselves with rules for deciding between different alternatives for reducing risk and are able to take account of other important factors, such as cost and usability.

Returning to our case study, we agree on the following design principles with business and technical managers:

- *The security architecture will be designed to deliver core security services*. Core services are those services that are not specific to a particular application and can therefore be used by several systems. Delivering core security services through a security architecture relieves applications of the burden of implementing these services themselves, which renders application design simpler and allows faster time to market for new systems. This approach also results in a standardized way of delivering the services [9].

- *The security architecture should favor simple solutions whenever possible*. Avoiding unnecessary complexity results in greater transparency and reduces the dependency on highly specific skill sets. It also makes the analysis of incidents easier to carry out once the architecture has been deployed.

- *Security services should be delivered in a scalable fashion.* In particular, the architecture should be able to successfully support the projected infrastructure requirements of the bank for the next 5 years.

- *Wherever possible, publicly accepted standards should be adopted in preference to proprietary solutions.* This principle is adopted by default, as it has already been agreed on with the IT department and applies to all acquisition or development projects and not only to security.

- *Wherever possible, architectural components should be acquired and not built in house.* This principle reflects the fact that expertise of The Secure Bank is in financial services, not in the development of secure software.

- *The security architecture should combine components in such a way that they mutually reinforce each other, thereby achieving defense in depth.* The objective of this design principle is to minimize critical dependencies on individual components and to foresee multiple lines of defense in response to particular threats.

- *Where appropriate, software from multiple vendors should be deployed to reduce the risk associated with vendor-specific vulnerabilities.* Using more than one vendor solution to implement a security service decreases the risk of falling foul to a little-known vulnerability.

- *The implementation of security services should not result in an unacceptable performance bottleneck for business services.* In other words, the business comes first. The key word in this phrase is unacceptable. In reality, should this situation occur, other alternatives would be researched. In an extreme situation, the business would be given the option of signing off the risk. The corresponding service could still, of course, be implemented by specific applications.

8.4.3 Modeling the IT infrastructure

The purpose of the modeling exercise is to reduce the complexity of the problem by emphasizing network and system characteristics that are important from an IT security viewpoint. In order to do this, we construct a high-level model of the infrastructure consisting of the following three components:

1. A decomposition of the IT infrastructure into zones with similar security requirements;

2. A description of what type of system is present in which zone;

3. A matrix summarizing important data flows between zones.

The major advantage of defining zones is that it simplifies the dialogue with management because problems that need to be resolved in one zone need not necessarily affect other security zones. Zones should be chosen to group together systems with similar security requirements. Following this philosophy, an analysis of the internal structure of The Secure Bank indicates the existence of ten security zones (see Figure 8.2). Each zone covers a group of systems or network technologies that are likely to have similar security requirements.

Defining zones 1 and 2 was simple in this case, as both executive management and the internal audit department had internal servers dedicated to their own use. Although the two departments happen to share a common LAN segment, to all extents and purposes, they are operating independently and share little data. When the audit department has data that is of interest to the executive management team, it is released as an audit report. In certain circumstances, both departments have a reasonable requirement to see data belonging to the other party, but this should occur as a result of an organized process, not haphazard access. It therefore makes sense to model this as two separate zones.

Zone 3 groups together departments on the basis of the data they access. All of the departments in zone 3 require extensive access to customer data, albeit for different reasons. The organization department needs to access customer data in order to carry out studies related to internal efficiency and to analyze customer satisfaction reports.

Zone 4 is the production environment and contains all shared resources, including the definitive source of all production data and applications. Production data that is held on departmental servers is taken from the production systems, through the use of either a batch-oriented process or real-time data transfer. As it contains the master copy of all production data, the security of zone 4 is critical to the success of the bank.

On the other hand, zone 5 contains no production data, or it shouldn't at least, as this zone covers the development LAN. Unfortunately, in order to carry out certain types of tests, the development teams have stated the need to access production data. This request cannot be ignored and complicates the process of securing this zone.

Zone 6 encompasses all connectivity infrastructures that are not connected to the Internet, and zone 7 includes all Internet-connected devices. This distinction is made for historical reasons, as the bank has already implemented an Internet connection to an isolated network segment within the enterprise. Personnel working in branch offices do not currently have Internet access.

Zone 8 is the branch office environment. This includes a local server housing data on branch clients and workstations. The server updates the central site and receives updates from the latter via a nightly exchange of formatted files.

Zones 9 and 10 cover all external network infrastructure. Zone 9 includes all networks provided by commercial third parties, and zone 10 covers the Internet.

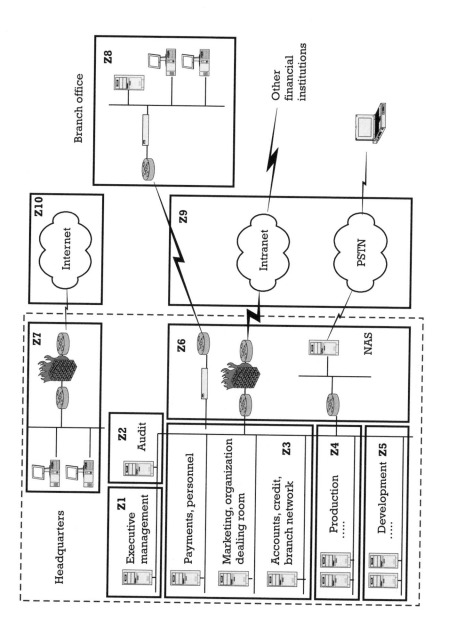

Figure 8.2   The Secure Bank—security zones.

Once we have defined the security zones, we aim to identify the different types of system present in the interior of each zone. The idea is to classify these systems based on their high-level security requirements. This requires judgment, as the goal is not to carry out a detailed risk assessment against these systems (this is the next step). Here, we are trying to further simplify the model of the IT infrastructure by defining a limited number of classes of systems against which we can perform such a risk analysis.

Table 8.1 shows the classes of systems identified within each security zone at The Secure Bank.

Finally, we examine existing flows of data between zones, concentrating on the most important flows. Although these may not be formalized, they do exist and can be helpful in defining network segregation rules and trust relationships during a later phase. The important flows for The Secure Bank are summarized in Table 8.2.

As it does not add a lot of value to describe all of these rules in detail, we will illustrate the process by briefly commenting on some of the more interesting data flows:

Table 8.1 Type of System Present in Each Zone

Zone	Class of System
Z1: Executive management	Department server holding strategic-planning data Standard user workstations
Z2: Audit	Department server holding audit data Standard user workstations
Z3: Customer-related services	Department servers holding customer data Department server with no sensitive data Standard user workstations
Z4: Production systems	Mainframe holding customer data Midrange systems holding customer data Midrange systems with no sensitive data Customer facing transactional systems Infrastructure servers Midrange server holding data warehouse
Z5: Development systems	Mainframe with no sensitive data Midrange servers with no sensitive data Standard user workstations Development workstations
Z6: Intranet infrastructure	NAS Firewall Networking devices
Z7: Internet infrastructure	Company Web server Proxy server Firewall Networking devices Standard user workstations
Z8: Branch office	Department server holding customer data Networking devices Standard user workstations
Z9: Commercial networks	Network infrastructure
Z10: Internet	Network infrastructure

Table 8.2 Important Data Flows Between Zones

| | Destination Zone | | | | | | | | | |
	Z1	Z2	Z3	Z4	Z5	Z6	Z7	Z8	Z9	Z10
Z1	✓									
Z2	✓	✓								
Z3	✓	✓	✓							
Z4	✓	✓	✓	✓	✓	✓				
Z5		✓	✓	✓	✓					
Z6			✓	✓	✓	✓		✓	✓	
Z7	✓	✓	✓	✓	✓		✓			✓
Z8						✓		✓	✓	
Z9						✓		✓	✓	
Z10							✓			✓

(Source Zone labels the rows)

- Flows into zone Z1 are reports to executive management. Apart from mail messages, which link everyone with everyone, very little information flows out of Z1 in electronic form. Communication with middle management usually occurs via weekly meetings.

- Flows into zone Z2 are information flows used to support audit functions.

- Flows from zone Z7 occur via diskette and involve internal users copying downloaded files to the internal network (bypassing the control of the isolated network). While this is currently tolerated and a known problem, the flow of data in the opposite direction is strictly prohibited.

- The flow from zone Z4 to Z5 involves transferring production data to development systems to facilitate testing and represents a major security issue.

The Secure Bank has defined no particular policy requirements related to the segregation of internal networks and currently makes no attempt to control traffic flows within the network perimeter. At this stage, we already have enough information to single out two internal flows worthy of special attention—namely, the latter two flows.

The decomposition of the organizational infrastructure into security zones, together with the classes of system in each zone and the summary of important network flows constitute the model against which we will conduct a risk analysis. In real life, this model would contain more contextual information, such as a description of each class of systems, together with a mapping from the actual architecture to the simplified model. In creating this model, we have considerably simplified the subsequent analysis steps:

- Security zones enable us to discuss specific problems with the appropriate audience.

- By classifying systems within zones, we have reduced the number of systems to be analyzed from approximately 150 servers (including branch offices), a range of networking devices, and 2,000 workstations to 25 types of system.

- Key information flows are useful in deciding whether to implement network access-control measures within the organization and can also help determine how trust relationships are to be established.

By conducting a risk analysis against this model, we will be able to construct a picture of how risks are distributed throughout the infrastructure without getting bogged down in unnecessary detail. This is the objective of the next step.

8.4.4   Risk analysis

In this step of the design phase, a risk analysis is carried out against this simplified architecture, and it is to be expected that this analysis will largely confirm the selected model. However, the design of the security architecture should be seen as an iterative process, and, if necessary, the initial model should be modified to reflect any new information arising out of the risk analysis. It is not usually desirable to start with the risk analysis itself because the infrastructure is too complex. The decision to model the infrastructure first therefore involves a compromise by sacrificing detail in order to obtain useful results in a reasonable timeframe.

The aim of this step is to identify the most important risks with which the IT infrastructure as a whole is confronted. We then classify these risks into two sets: those that can be mitigated using an architectural approach and those that are application specific and are best dealt with locally. Risks in the former category are used to derive required security services at the architectural level, whereas specific risks are checked against current application functionality and dealt with in coordination with the application-support team.

We carry out this analysis as follows:

- Analysis of the risks associated with each class of system identified in the previous step;

- Analysis of the two data flows of interest;

- Identification of required security services at the platform, network, and zone levels;

- Modification to reflect likely future requirements.

FRA techniques are used to perform this analysis (see the Appendix for details). The starting point for such analyses is to ignore any existing security services, as these will be derived by the process. The result is a set of risk analyses that can be summarized in the form of a table, showing how security services are distributed over platforms and networks. Table 8.3 summarizes this information for each defined security zone.

The following comments should be kept in mind when interpreting Table 8.3:

▸ The matrix identifies security services that are required to secure the zone. This information summarizes the risk analyses performed at the platform and network flow levels.

▸ The derived security services are not necessarily implemented within the zone itself. For instance, zones Z1, Z2, Z3, Z4, Z5, and Z8 (rows 1, 2, 3, 4, 5, and 8) require the network access control security service to

Table 8.3 Security Services Required by Each Zone

	System Authentication	System Integrity	System Access Control	System Monitoring	Data Confidentiality and Integrity	Network Authentication	Network Integrity	Network Access Control	Network Monitoring	High Availability
Z1: Executive management	✓	✓	✓	✓	✓			✓		
Z2: Audit	✓	✓	✓	✓	✓			✓		
Z3: Customer services	✓	✓	✓	✓	✓	✓		✓		
Z4: Production systems	✓	✓	✓	✓	✓	✓		✓		✓
Z5: Development systems	✓		✓			✓		✓		
Z6: Intranet connectivity					✓	✓	✓	✓	✓	✓
Z7: Internet connectivity						✓	✓	✓		
Z8: Branch network	✓	✓	✓	✓				✓		
Z9: Commercial networks					✓					
Z10: Internet					✓					

protect them from the outside world, but this service will not be implemented within any of these zones.

▸ Zones Z1, Z2, and Z8 (rows 1, 2, and 8) do not require network authentication because no direct connectivity with the outside world is required. Network access control measures will not allow any connectivity between the external world and these zones.

▸ The risk analysis carried out against platforms in zone Z5 and the network flow from zone Z4 to zone Z5 (see comments following Table 8.2) identified the need to anonymize data used for testing purposes in the development environment. Data anonymization is a more appropriate choice than encryption in this case, as it can be made to be irreversible. Encryption on the other hand is a reversible operation. Data anonymization is an example of a specific service that is not a good candidate for an architectural approach.

▸ The requirements for zone Z10 (row 10 in Table 8.3) anticipate the future strategy of the bank. The data confidentiality and integrity requirement is a result of the bank's desire to offer services over the Internet. In addition, there has been a recent decision to move to an Internet-based payment scheme with an important supplier. Although this hasn't yet happened, it is planned for the near future.

The detailed analyses, together with the summarized data, contain the information required to select logical security components and distribute them between the different zones.

8.4.5   Identifying logical components

Once the risk analysis has been carried out, we have a map of which security services need to be deployed at both the platform and network level and at the level of security zones. We now need to translate this into a series of components that can be implemented using commercially available software or in-house developed solutions. It would be premature to try to relate the services directly to individual products, as we would like to go through a selection process in order to purchase the products that best reflect our requirements. The approach is therefore to identify a set of logical components that not only offer a coherent set of functions, but also group functionality in such a way that commercial products can be used to implement them.

This is the step where a structured approach adds least value. Unfortunately, there is no method for identifying logical components and making the appropriate choice depends on many factors:

▸ The degree to which the model constructed in the previous steps represents reality;

▸ A good working knowledge of currently available security software;

> ‣ A reasonable guess as to how this software is likely to evolve in the medium to long term;

> ‣ A knowledge of how the requirements of the organization are likely to evolve in the medium to long term.

Nevertheless, the design criteria we agreed on with business and technical managers at the beginning of the exercise can be used to guide the process. For example, priority will be given to simple solutions, and commercial software will be preferred over in-house development. With the basic design principles in mind, the following paragraphs describe how The Secure Bank selected suitable components and provide a brief summary of the arguments leading to each decision.

Zones Z1 through Z4 have similar generic requirements, but there are differences that arise out of the detailed risk analysis. We will therefore start with the components that are required by all these zones and then look at individual requirements:

> ‣ For normal users, system authentication will be handled by the NOSSS in the usual manner. This normally means that users have to supply a valid identifier and password. System administrators will be provided with secure access to platforms wherever possible, using either secure shell (SSH) or SSL. The risk analyses performed against UNIX platforms indicated that the root account on many platforms was being shared due to the way current responsibilities are defined. Privilege management software will be deployed to provide selective access to the root account.

> ‣ System integrity will be enforced using a network security scanner and a three-tiered malicious code control framework. The latter involves different antivirus products on the e-mail gateway, internal servers, and the workstation. Using different products is a consequence of the design decision to implement defense in depth. This will provide some degree of protection against product-related vulnerabilities and also result in multiple sources of virus signature information.

> ‣ Access control is already proving to be a problem within the bank, and the decision is made to move toward the use of EUA software. This software will be used to manage access in all zones wherever the OS permits. The mainframe access-control facility will remain in place, but provisioning of access will be done through the EUA software.

> ‣ Log consolidation software will be used to reduce the volume of logging information to a reasonable level and to provide filtering functionality.

> ‣ Access control measures on internal platforms will be used to enforce data confidentiality on internal platforms (as encryption is too onerous). On the contrary, the hard disks of portable computers will be encrypted.

> ‣ Network access control and network authentication will be deployed within zone Z6 and will be configured to protect access to zones Z1 to Z4 according to their detailed requirements.

All of these components provide services to multiple zones, and the server component will therefore be situated in zone Z4. This is in line with the bank's policy of placing all shared resources in the production zone.

In reality, zone Z3 is associated with more stringent requirements, as The Secure Bank has a regulatory responsibility to protect customer data according to very high standards. This will be recognized by deploying additional mechanisms to protect system integrity. This decision is justified by the fact that the NOSSS is being used to protect the confidentiality of the data, and therefore additional effort is expended in securing the NOSSS itself. In recognition of the higher security requirements of zone Z3, host-based security scanners and host intrusion detection systems will be deployed in this zone.

The high-availability requirement of zone Z4 is associated with the customer-facing transaction systems (private-banking information distributed to other banks over the existing intranet connection). This is marked as an architectural requirement because fulfilling this requirement requires other architectural components to be available in a high-availability configuration. In this case, the network connectivity infrastructure will be impacted.

Zone Z5 encompasses only development networks housing anonymized data and therefore has less demanding security requirements. We recognize this fact by taking the design decision to isolate this zone from production-related zones using an internal firewall. To further reduce costs and to better concentrate on the security of production environments, the development teams will be allowed to administer their own environments, subject to the following procedural controls:

> ‣ The security requirements for the development environment will be documented by an IT security standard. The IT security unit will check compliance periodically.

> ‣ Code will be promoted into the production environment according to a strictly controlled procedure. Random source code inspection techniques will be used to detect anomalies.

Zone Z8 is only accessible from the central site over a wide area network, which makes it difficult to secure in the same way as zones Z1 to Z4 are to be secured. Given this constraint, access to the local server will be administered locally according to agreed procedures. System integrity will be enforced by deploying a standard server configuration within each branch office. Compliance with this baseline will be checked by performing random audits using a host-oriented security scanner.

On the network side, we anticipate the inevitable move towards Internet-based financial services (of which the initial home banking project is almost certainly only the first step) and integrate zone 7 into zones Z1 to

Z6. This will provide staff at the central site with access to the Internet from the desktop. Consequently, the expanded zone Z6 will be equipped with firewalls, a Web filter, a NIDS, and a network authentication server.

The network authentication server will be configured to work with handheld tokens that generate a one-time password, and dial-in connections will be encrypted. Despite these measures, dial-in access will be restricted to technical support staff due to the problems associated with controlling confidential data at the client side.

The fact that the bank would like to make much more use of Internet-enabled applications in the future leads to a design decision to gradually implement a layered network at the central site, as shown in Figure 8.3. This design separates groups of platforms on the basis of their connectivity requirements with the outside world. The requirement to provide a high-availability configuration for certain components to support customer-facing systems has been shown on the diagram.

As such, the term *gateway components* groups together all systems that are directly accessible to external parties over the network (essentially routers, firewalls, and the Web server). Infrastructure servers are only accessible once an external connection request has successfully passed the gateway layer. This layer groups servers such as the mail server, domain name service (DNS) server, authentication server, and application server. The latter is only accessible following successful authentication. Finally, the core systems layer covers zones Z1 to Z5 and includes systems that cannot be directly contacted from the outside world. The rationale behind this decision is to provide a region where outsiders can be given limited access to company resources without threatening the core networks.

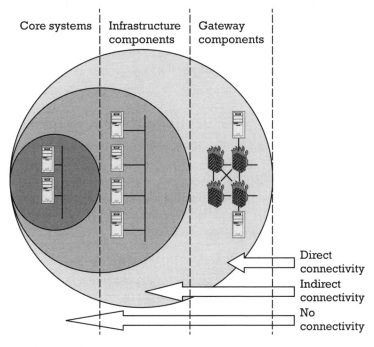

Figure 8.3 Layers of network access.

Discussions with the manager of the branch network led to a decision not to allow Internet access from branch offices, as there is no requirement for such access. However, a cost-benefit analysis showed that considerable cost savings will be achieved by moving the existing leased line connections between the central site and branch offices to the Internet. In order to achieve this, we protect these connections using VPNs and a local firewall. The existing dial-up facilities will be used as a backup solution in case of problems with the Internet. The routers present in the branch offices will be upgraded to support VPN functionality.

8.4.6   Obtaining signoff of the concept

The final step in the design phase is to obtain signoff of the overall concept. Although this has nothing to do with obtaining budget, it is clear that any initiative of this scope will require considerable expenditure, and it is therefore best to preempt discussions related to the viability of the approach by preparing a high-level view of project costs and duration. This involves taking approximate estimates for capital and operational expenditure, based on existing product lines, together with implementation costs of previous projects where available. It also involves prioritizing the implementation of the different components and knowing what can be abandoned if necessary. The purpose of this is to answer rudimentary questions that are likely to be asked during the signoff process. A more complete analysis of costs and timescales will be carried out when preparing the proposal for implementation.

The details of how the design is documented will vary from company to company, but this documentation should contain at least the following:

- The design principles;
- The model of the infrastructure, together with any information needed to interpret it;
- The platform and network risk analyses;
- The component-based architecture.

We will complete this section with a summary of the last element as it applies to The Secure Bank. The final proposed architecture is shown in Figure 8.4 (only security-related components are shown).

The production of the proposed architecture completes the design phase.

8.5   The implementation phase

8.5.1   Planning considerations

At the end of the design phase, a logical architecture has been specified, but no products have been identified. The implementation phase involves the following activities:

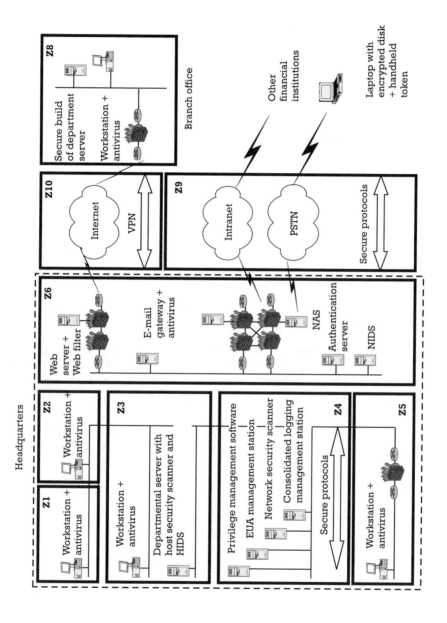

Figure 8.4   Final architecture.

- Identification of priorities and production of a phased deployment plan;
- Preparation of the proposal for the implementation phase;
- Selection of commercial packages;
- Integration and testing;
- Negotiation of SLAs and support contracts;
- Training of administrators and support personnel.

The implementation phase can take up to 2 years to complete, and a big-bang approach is hardly ever appropriate. A better approach is to deploy architectural components in a stepwise manner by dividing the implementation sequence into manageable chunks and defining a separate project for the implementation of each group of components. This approach also facilitates the project-approval phase, as the budget associated with these projects will be smaller. Financial departments will therefore be in a better position to control project-related risk, due to the need to get each project separately approved.

8.5.2   Production of a phased implementation plan

As with any plan, the implementation plan should be regarded as a living document and not something that is defined once and remains unchanged for the duration of the project. Few projects are lucky enough to be totally independent of external events, and the latter are not under the control of the project manager, so plans that do not change are often a sign of ineffective management. The initial implementation plan and individual project plans should be updated throughout the implementation phase to reflect changing conditions, and this often includes a better understanding of the project itself.

A suggested approach for deriving an overall implementation plan and dividing it into manageable projects is to use the following criteria to guide the process:

- Priority of components;
- Impact of introducing a given component on current working practices;
- Projected cost and duration for implementing the component;
- Ease of integration into the existing infrastructure;
- Degree to which components have a mutually beneficial role.

A lot of this will involve making assumptions and using intelligent guesswork and past experience, but it is a good idea to try to identify other companies that have gone through a similar exercise and to seek advice. Documenting the underlying assumptions and thought process will prove invaluable for guiding decisions further down the line.

Components can be prioritized based on the importance of the services they offer. This prioritization should arise straight out of the risk analysis. As this is only one of the factors to be taken into consideration, an approximate ordering is sufficient.

The impact on current working practices is important, as this affects the complexity of the implementation and will have a bearing on the degree to which it will be immediately accepted by the end users. All other things being equal, therefore, components that have a limited impact on current practices are a good candidate for rapid deployment, and those having significant impact are best delayed until the implementation has gathered momentum and chalked up a few successes. Similar arguments apply to the ease with which components can be integrated into the existing IT infrastructure.

Cost and duration estimates are used to ensure that projects have reasonable budget requirements and can be completed within acceptable timescales. This is also a useful technique for controlling project-related risk, as any problems encountered in one project can be addressed as part of the preparation phase for the following project. This is an example of how dividing a big project into several smaller ones can increase transparency and facilitate the tracking process.

Finally, thought should be given to how security components work together, as this might lead to some interesting synergies. For instance, security software that is implemented as an application will usually benefit from a secured OS, so security scanners and other tools used to protect system integrity help provide a strong platform for application-level software.

The overall implementation plan and decomposition into projects for The Secure Bank is shown in Table 8.4 and explained in the following paragraphs.

The initial project is to implement security-scanning software. The reasoning behind this decision is that this software is essential for securing

Table 8.4   The Secure Bank—Implementation Schedule

Project Id	Components Implemented	Timescale
P1	Network security scanner	Months 1–6
	Host security scanners	
	Secure build for branch office servers	
P2	Firewall infrastructure	Months 7–15
	Network authentication server	
	Web filter	
	Secure protocols	
P3	Three-tier malicious code protection	Months 10–16
P4	UNIX privilege management	Months 12–21
	Consolidated logging	
	Secure administrator connections	
P5	Host-intrusion detection	Months 15–24
	Network-intrusion detection	
P6	EUA	Months 12–24

midrange systems, it is relatively nonintrusive and therefore easy to integrate within the existing environment, and it has minimal impact on end users. In addition, the implementation of a network security scanner was identified as a quick win during the consolidation period (see Chapter 4), and the existing implementation will just need to be adapted to meet the requirements identified by project P1. This project will also define and implement the secure build for the branch offices.

Project P2 will be launched following the completion of the first project. This delay is not strictly necessary, but it allows us to concentrate on achieving a smooth initial implementation. This will send an important message to executive management that things are under control. Project P2 implements the network security and will last approximately 9 months. The skill sets required on this project are distinct from those required by project P3, which allows us to overlap the projects. This project does have an impact on end users (the most visible aspect being the handheld tokens) and a lot of emphasis will be placed on ensuring acceptance.

Project P3 will implement antivirus software on the e-mail gateway, on server machines, and on the desktop. The most difficult aspect of this project is unlikely to be the technical work, but it is related to the definition of responsibilities and procedures.

Project P4 is quite complex and will require contributions from staff in many areas. For instance, the consolidated logging project will involve producing an inventory of existing logs, classifying the information they contain, and prioritizing them for the purpose of analysis. This will in turn involve identifying and understanding differences in logging philosophy and content between different platforms. In parallel, the implementation of secure administrator connections will require support from the network security specialists, and this may result in a competition for resources between projects P4 and P2.

Intrusion detection has been delayed because project P2 will involve restructuring the network perimeter to some extent. Project P2 was therefore prioritized both on the basis of risk mitigation and on the basis of a logical constraint. This project implements both host-oriented and network-oriented intrusion-detection software.

Project P6 is probably the most complex project, both in terms of ease of integration and impact on the end user. This project will almost certainly involve changes in roles and responsibilities, workflow, and ways that access-control data is structured and managed. In reality, project P6 will only establish the framework for a new approach to managing access, and this will be gradually implemented and refined over the next few years. Because it involves a fundamental redesign of a core process, project P6 is deemed to be the most difficult project.

8.5.3 Preparing proposals

The final step of the design phase is to prepare the proposal for the first implementation project. Subsequent projects will require similar proposals, but the same principles apply. Proceeding via proposals will be unavoidable for most organizations, as the cost of implementing a security architecture is significant. It will therefore usually be necessary to show that there is a positive return on investment and how this is achieved.

The contents and format of the proposal will obviously vary considerably from organization to organization, but most organizations will require something along the lines of the following example:

> • An executive summary;
> • A description of the objectives;
> • A description of how the objectives will be met;
> • The business case.

Sufficient material has already been presented to support the first three points, but the business case requires estimating the revenue and costs and calculating the return on investment of the exercise.

Where security is concerned, projects do not necessarily generate a revenue stream. Unfortunately, they do always cost money, which presents us with a problem where the business case is concerned. Nevertheless, security-related projects should generate a positive return on investment when taking into account the benefits associated with diminishing risk and any benefits that might arise out of cost avoidance.

Quantitative estimations of risk in the IT security domain are extremely difficult to produce [10, 11], so a useful compromise is to use a qualitative approach where this is acceptable to management. Where this is not accepted, it will be necessary to persuade business managers to come up with figures. Cost avoidance, on the other hand, is often easier to calculate. As an example, if we expect to avoid hiring three new administrators as a result of deploying EUA software, it is relatively simple to turn this into a financial saving.

In preparing the business case, it is important to identify the costs that are associated with administering the architecture once it is in place. In particular, where extra administrators are required, this should be signaled as part of the business case. Failure to do this may result in the deployment of a sophisticated architecture, but nobody to run it on a day-to-day basis!

8.5.4 Selection of commercial packages

If the logical components of the architecture have been derived as described earlier, the selection of commercial packages should not be a difficult exercise, although it is likely to be time consuming. The selection of commercial products occurs as a project activity and is therefore spread over time.

In Section 8.4.5, it was recommended that functionality be grouped in such a way that commercial products can be used to implement components, and this is the key to the issue. In fact, this is more straightforward than it may seem. In recent years, many suppliers have modified their products to include *value-added functionality*, but the core offering has remained quite stable in most cases.

The selection process itself will probably be standardized in most organizations but will probably involve either an invitation to tender or some kind of comparative study carried out in house. In both cases, it is important that the initial risk analysis be supplemented by a detailed set of requirements. As far as security is concerned, these requirements will cover a wide range of issues, such as:

▸ Legal and regulatory requirements;

▸ Policy requirements;

▸ Architectural requirements;

▸ User interface and workflow requirements;

▸ Platform-support requirements;

▸ System-security requirements;

▸ Network-security requirements;

▸ Monitoring and reporting requirements;

▸ Performance and availability requirements;

▸ Requirements on commercial stability of the vendor;

▸ Commercial-support requirements.

Commercial offerings can then be compared on the basis of these requirements.

A few comments are in order here. First, in evaluating commercial software, it is extremely important to examine in detail the security of the software itself. Just because software is implementing security services does not necessarily mean that the software itself is secure! This is particularly important for highly specialized commercial offerings. For example, a software package implementing cryptographic functionality could be reasonably expected to conform to market standards in this domain but might be implemented in such a way that it destabilizes the underlying OS.

Second, it is a good idea to set certain requirements on the commercial situation of the vendor and to have a cursory understanding of the commercial strategy and product roadmap. Basing a core security service of a major financial institution on a product supplied by a vendor that has only been in existence for a year is probably a risky venture, no matter how good the product is. Similarly, very small companies will only be able to supply a limited level of support to large customers, particularly in an international environment.

Finally, where a product will affect end users, they should be consulted when putting together the requirements. People who are familiar with IT are often a poor judge of what end users require, and there is no reason to expect that IT security professionals are particularly gifted in this area.

In order to simplify the process, it is useful to perform this analysis in two stages. The first stage looks at how well commercial solutions measure up to a simplified set of requirements and aims to reduce the number of viable solutions to a short list. The second phase involves a much more detailed analysis using the full set of requirements and will typically involve an active dialogue with the vendors. Once again, visits to sites that have deployed the software provide valuable insight as to what is possible in theory and what is practically achievable.

When contracts are signed, think about aligning payment milestones with other initiatives. This can be very helpful when managing contracts subsequently. It considerably simplifies things if all maintenance contracts are renewed during the same month. This is also useful when negotiating new contractual conditions, as it becomes easier to switch vendors if required.

8.5.5 Testing and integration

Testing and integration cover all activities necessary to put the software into production once it has been selected. In reality, testing often starts with a pilot implementation, and this may well be carried out as part of the software evaluation exercise. It is very important to test acquired security software thoroughly, not only from a functional point of view, also at a more technical level wherever possible. The reason for this is obvious; a vulnerability in a security software package may well open up a much more serious exposure to risk, as an attacker taking advantage of the vulnerability might have control of the associated security service.

Using an independent third party to test the architecture can add value in several ways:

- As such parties will not have been involved in the design process, they are more likely to challenge underlying assumptions and design decisions. This can reveal conceptual problems.
- This may result in a more diverse range of testing methods.
- External companies will be able to leverage experience gained from other environments.

Where external companies are used to test security infrastructure, it is important to agree in advance on the scope of the tests, the methods to be used, and the procedures for managing issues. This is particularly true where more invasive testing techniques, such as penetration testing, are deployed.

A good technique for testing functional requirements is to link acceptance tests back to the requirements document using a requirements traceability matrix (RTM). Essentially, this involves giving each requirement a label and each test scenario a label and using matrix notation to track which test refers to which requirement. This simple technique also provides a clear picture of the level of compliance of suppliers with the original requirements.

Where time permits, more technical tests can be used to probe the stability of the software under stress and to see how it reacts to unusual input or operating conditions. The nature of such tests will be very dependent on the type of software, the language in which it is written, and the operating environment, which makes it hard to create standard test suites for this kind of test. However, a lot of material is available to help construct such a test suite once the type of software and operating environment is known. Examples include the UNIX Security Checklist [12] for UNIX applications and World Wide Web Security FAQ [13] for software running in a Web context. Several vendors also provide security checklists for the products they supply. Examples of vendor-specific checklists include those published by Microsoft [14], Sun [15], and Oracle [16].

Both functional and technical tests should be carried out with current procedures in mind, as it may be necessary to modify certain procedures in order to align them with new functionality. Similarly, carrying out tests in a realistic operating environment provides useful information on how to configure software to best meet the expectations of the administrators and end users. This comment is particularly relevant for aspects relating to performance and workflow, both of which can have a major impact on the degree to which new software is accepted by the user community.

So far we have briefly discussed tests that are carried out prior to putting new software into production, but it is important to remember that new versions, patches, and other changes need to be tested once the system is live. The testing strategy should identify how tests will be carried out for the live product and should also ensure that a testing environment is available to support such tests.

In other words, it is necessary to maintain a certain level of infrastructure and associated procedures to support the testing process once the system is live. Procedures will need to specify how test environments are maintained, including the source and nature of test data and frequency of update. For certain products, such as security scanners, this process will be relatively straightforward, as this type of software is very nonintrusive. Other products, such as cryptographic toolkits, are likely to be embedded in applications and will require more support. It goes without saying that this work should be performed alongside application support and testing teams and that the security department should comply with existing standards and procedures in this domain wherever possible.

8.5.6   SLAs and support contracts

Ideally, SLAs and support contracts should be finalized before new software is released into the production environment. This may be difficult to achieve, however, for organizations that are introducing SLAs at the same time that the architecture is being implemented.

This is the case at The Secure Bank, and we therefore simplify the approach in the following way:

  ▸ SLAs will only be introduced when strictly necessary.

> ‣ Initial agreements will be very simple and will concentrate on essentials. More sophisticated versions will be produced as a series of iterations.

> ‣ Emphasis will be put on the need to be flexible during the first year, and agreements will be updated to reflect experience gained.

In line with the first requirement, the security department will define and agree on two SLAs as part of the implementation of the security architecture. The first SLA is for the network authentication server, and the second is for the EUA deployment. The second of these agreements will replace the existing SLA defined for the authorization and access-control procedure (see Chapter 7). We will also require system administrators to prepare an SLA for updating systems to reflect security requirements revealed by security scanners. In the latter example, the security department is a client of the production department and receives services from system administrators. The production department will therefore take responsibility for the SLA, and agree on it with the security department.

The SLA for the authentication service will establish a minimum number of service levels relevant to the end user. This includes availability of the service, turnaround time for incorporating new users and for deleting old users, out-of-hours support, and conditions for off-site support. The SLA for user administration concentrates on similar issues, but does not allow for out-of-hours support, and off-site support does not make sense in this context. Both SLAs place constraints on the user in order to guarantee the service. These constraints include the necessity to follow the defined procedures and to obtain authorization from the relevant managers before sending the request to the security department.

For all SLAs, very simple metrics will be defined for measuring the level of compliance with the agreed service levels. Metrics will only be used where no significant extra development or additional procedures are necessary to record the data. These metrics will be reported to management as part of the normal reporting cycle and will help the latter request changes where it is evident that these levels are not being met.

Where software support contracts are concerned, The Secure Bank has already implemented an efficient process and uses a standard checklist to help managers ensure that all requirements are covered. This checklist covers the following areas:

> ‣ Responsibilities;

> ‣ Types of support required;

> ‣ Support periods (time of day and day of week);

> ‣ Geographic coverage;

> ‣ Classification of issues, procedures, and response times;

> ‣ Escalation procedures;

> ‣ Dispute-resolution procedures.

The various implementation projects are responsible for agreeing on a support contract within the limitations imposed by the questionnaire or for seeking approval for a nonstandard contract.

8.5.7 Technical training

Within The Secure Bank, the whole issue of training is also dealt with on a project basis, but for historical reasons this is not as organized as the approach to negotiating contracts. At present, there is little standardization, and each project is free to approach the issue as it feels fit.

Knowing this to be the case, we approach the internal quality department with a suggested way forward. The proposal is that the quality department will develop an approach to technical training, and the security department will use the architecture project to test it out and to provide constructive feedback. In addition, the security department will help the quality department to sell the approach internally by taking part in presentations and explaining the advantages. This is a win-win arrangement because the security department doesn't have to tackle the complex task of defining how to provide training to a wide range of profiles within the enterprise, and the quality department is seen to drive an important issue by standardizing the approach at the enterprise level.

The final approach is based on the following considerations:

- Identification of the different profiles requiring technical training;
- Short summary of the requirements of each group (based on interviews);
- Identification of planning constraints;
- Decision to perform in-house training or to outsource;
- Contract negotiation and possibility of using preferred suppliers.

Agreeing on this approach took 6 months, and, as a result, project P1 was not able to benefit from this work. The impact of this was minimal, as one of the criteria for selection of the initial projects was to prefer those projects having a limited impact on end users.

8.6 Administration and maintenance phase

The administration and maintenance phase begins the day that the first component is implemented. In other words, the implementation and administration phases are not sequential; they overlap. One consequence of this fact is that preparation for the administration phase should begin almost simultaneously with the start of the implementation phase. Indeed, many of the requirements according to which products are selected will reflect administration requirements.

The administration and maintenance phase consists of the following activities:

- Routine administration and maintenance activities;
- Managing vulnerabilities;
- Managing incidents;
- Managing risk using risk indicators.

These activities are discussed in the following paragraphs.

8.6.1   Routine administration and maintenance

Day-to-day administration activities must be able to function smoothly in the face of adverse conditions. Well-designed administration procedures will be flexible enough to react to changes quickly. One way to achieve this is to assess the priority of each administration activity and to ensure that this priority is followed when resource contentions occur. Unfortunately, this is not as simple as it first appears, as certain procedures will require specific skill sets. One technique that can be useful in this regard is to allow for a degraded mode of operation by specifying the service level associated with this mode and the conditions that trigger its adoption. This would normally be specified in the SLA for the service in question.

8.6.2   Managing vulnerabilities

Responding to vulnerabilities involves several different activities, the most fundamental of which is keeping track of known problems. Chapter 2 of this book provides information on sites that publish data relating to vulnerabilities and how to deal with them. Tracking vulnerabilities is a critical process, and the average time taken to discover new vulnerabilities is an indicator of the window of risk associated with the site. In general, the longer it takes to discover new vulnerabilities, the more likely it is that a potential attacker will discover weaknesses before they are addressed.

When new vulnerabilities are discovered, a quick analysis should be carried out to see to what extent they affect the organization and to obtain a crude idea of the likely risk. Given the high volume of data relating to vulnerabilities, the estimation of the likely risk will almost certainly be achieved through discussion than via any kind of formal analysis. Once the extent of the exposure and associated risk is understood, mitigating actions can be defined and carried out.

Where tools, such as security scanners, are used to detect vulnerabilities, it is important to cross check the results in order to identify *false positives* before attempting to carry out corrective actions. False positive refers to the detection of a vulnerability that is not really present and is particularly likely to occur in complex environments, where several different types of security software are deployed in parallel. An example of this kind of problem is provided by port scanners, which may falsely report the presence of open ports on the scanned machine if a firewall or virus detection software is being used on the scanning machine [17]. False positives can often be detected by cross checking results using a different utility.

There are several ways to deal with a newly discovered vulnerability:

> Mitigate the risk by modifying security baselines.

> Mitigate the risk by a procedural control.

> Accept the risk.

Modifying security baselines can be as simple as installing a new security patch or downloading and installing pattern files for antivirus software. In the second case, the vendor usually tracks vulnerabilities and releases updated baselines that can be downloaded from a Web site. A more complex example might be the discovery of a new vulnerability related to inappropriate privileges on a standard UNIX program. Solving this particular issue could involve scanning UNIX machines to discover where the program is located, holding discussions with production support staff and external software vendors to identify the impact on current software of using an alternative program, and planning a switchover to this alternative.

Procedural controls should be used sparingly when mitigating specific risks, as these involve human intervention and are in general not scalable. Accepting the risk associated with a given vulnerability is always acceptable as long as there are clear guidelines as to who should make the decision.

8.6.3 Managing incidents

No matter how well the security architecture has been designed, there will always be incidents to resolve. In the context of this discussion, an incident is an unexpected event with a potential negative impact on information or processes. What actually constitutes an incident will therefore vary considerably from site to site. Organizations that have implemented NIDSs will quickly grow accustomed to certain patterns of attack at the network perimeter and will not consider these attacks incidents because they are being handled successfully by the software in place. On the contrary, the successful exploitation of a recently discovered vulnerability resulting in access to a perimeter network would almost certainly constitute a serious incident.

The fact that incidents are an unavoidable fact of life leads inevitably to a requirement for efficient incident-handling procedures. Because incidents represent an unknown threat, such procedures should implement a structured approach for bringing the issue under control. A number of white papers on this subject are available at the Deutsches ForschungsNetz (DFN) CERT site [18].

The incident-response process can be split into several phases (see, for instance, [19]). Although the details may differ from organization to organization, most organizations define a stepwise approach to recovery broadly in line with the following phases:

- Prevention and preparation;
- Identification;
- Containment;
- Eradication;
- Follow up.

As the name suggests, the purpose of prevention and preparation activities is to lay the groundwork for a successful approach to handling incidents once they occur. Prevention activities are aimed at avoiding the occurrence of an incident and include actions such as hardening systems, implementing security mechanisms, and defining proactive administration procedures. Preparation activities, on the other hand, are concerned with defining how to handle an incident once it has occurred. Preparation activities include defining roles and responsibilities for managing incidents and defining and testing the procedures for incident handling.

In addressing the issue of roles and responsibilities, larger organizations should consider establishing a computer security incident response team (CSIRT) [20]. This team will then be responsible for coordinating incident-response activities across the organization, such as ensuring that potential incidents are reported, analyzed, and responded to in an appropriate manner. The detailed responsibilities of the team and the associated authority should be clearly documented by using terms of reference or some similar mechanism. Ideally, the CSIRT should be composed of staff that is representative of the organization as a whole, as this will ease the decision-making process. Finally, almost by definition, successfully managing incidents involves making appropriate decisions under pressure, and, consequently, the team must be capable of handling stressful situations.

The identification phase includes a variety of activities, including recognition of an incident, understanding and measuring its likely impact, collection and analysis of data, and notifying the appropriate personnel. The identification phase should also evaluate and prioritize alternatives for managing the incident. The main output of the identification phase is a recommended plan of action for containment.

Containment activities aim to ensure that the incident in question spreads no further. Examples of containment actions might include taking a server infected with malicious code offline or programming network intrusion detection engines to prevent certain network flows to the outside world. In real-life situations, data collection and analysis continues throughout the containment phase and is used to continually cross check the action plan for containment.

The eradication phase is concerned with eliminating the origin of the incident within the enterprise and restoring normal operations. For the purposes of this discussion, eradication includes the implementation of mechanisms necessary to prevent a recurrence of the incident, although at this stage it may only be possible to define and implement a short-term solution to the underlying problem.

Once containment and eradication have been achieved, normal operations can be resumed. Follow-up activities ensure that the incident is correctly documented and that a long-term solution to the problem is defined and implemented. The follow-up phase should also be used to identify strong and weak points of the current control framework and to improve the latter wherever possible.

8.6.4 Managing risk using risk indicators

One of the key benefits of an established architecture is the security-related information it is capable of supplying. Considered as raw data, this information is of limited use as an aid to decision making (but is of course critically important when analyzing potential incidents). However, many modern tools are capable of aggregating this data and presenting it in an easy-to-use graphic format, and, in this form, the data can be sensibly used to guide decision making.

Risk indicators are metrics that provide a good indication of how risk is evolving in a particular area. Examples of useful risk indicators might include:

- RI1: number of attacks per day detected at the network perimeter;
- RI2: number of active accounts not used in the last 3 months;
- RI3: number of accounts created, modified, and deleted per week;
- RI4: number of viruses detected within the enterprise per week;
- RI5: number of pattern files and security baseline updates applied per week;
- RI6: number of published vulnerabilities affecting the organization per week;
- RI7: number of incidents per month;
- RI8: number of corrective actions carried out per week.

Of these indicators, RI1, RI2, RI4, and RI6 reflect external threats (i.e., threats that are not directly under the control of the information-security department). Risk indicators RI3, RI5, and RI8, on the other hand, reflect the effects of positive actions carried out by the information-security department. Indicator RI7 is influenced by both external threats and by internal preventive actions.

The interesting property of risk indicators is not their absolute value, but how they evolve as a function of time. An important sustained increase in any of these indicators could reasonably be taken to represent an increase in risk in the corresponding area. This enables management to respond to the changing risk profile by implementing additional controls. For example, a sharp increase in the number of viruses detected within the enterprise per week might lead to new restrictions on the transfer of data to and from home computers and an increase in the frequency of pattern file updates. Similarly, a suitable response to an increase in the number of *dormant* accounts would be to request all affected users to confirm their requirements by return of mail and to remove unwanted accounts.

Including risk indicators in reports to executive management therefore provides the latter with the ability to react proactively to changes in the threat environment.

8.7 Summary

This chapter has presented a simple, practical method for designing and implementing core IT security services in the form of an IT security architecture. The reasoning behind this approach is that the architecture will supply standard services to the applications, thus removing the need to implement these services within the applications themselves. From an architectural standpoint, security services will be provided in a standard way, thereby reducing the unnecessary complexity associated with a multitude of proprietary solutions. This will make it easier to understand and manage security incidents.

The basis of the approach is to simplify the existing infrastructure by modeling the important facets from a security perspective and then to perform a risk analysis against this simplified model. By associating particular risks with specific elements of the simplified IT infrastructure, it is possible to identify which security services are required where. This in turn leads to the definition of logical components, which can be implemented using commercial software.

Implementation schedules will reflect a compromise between many factors, including priority of required security services, ease of integration, and impact on the end user. Most organizations will require this plan to be executed as a series of smaller projects, thereby enabling them to examine costs and return on investment at regular intervals. This decreases the project-related risks. Implementation plans need to pay due heed to associated procedures, service levels, and training requirements.

The benefit of a deployed architecture is realized through well-designed administration procedures and proactive risk management. The regular publication of risk indicators is an invaluable aid to higher management when taking risk-related decisions.

References

[1]   Vecchio, D., et al., "Legacy Evolution: Strategies for Reuse, Not Abuse," *Strategy, Trends and Tactics,* Stamford, CT: Gartner Group, 2001.

[2] Sessions, R., *COM+ and the Battle for the Middle Tier,* New York: John Wiley and Sons, 2000.

[3] Velte, T., *Cisco: A Beginner's Guide,* Emeryville, CA: Osborne/McGraw-Hill, 2001.

[4] Sherwood, J., "Opening Up The Enterprise," *Computers & Security,* Vol. 19, No. 8, 2000, pp. 710–719.

[5] Fraser, B., "Site Security Handbook (RFC 2196)," August 2003, http://www. ietf.org/rfc/rfc2196.txt.

[6] "OECD Guidelines For The Security of Information Systems and Networks: Towards a Culture of Security," August 2003, http://www.ftc.gov/bcp/ conline/edcams/infosecurity/popups/OECD_guidelines.pdf.

[7] Swanson, M., and B. Guttman, "Generally Accepted Principles and Practices for Securing Information Technology Systems," August 2003, http://csrc.nist.gov/ publications/nistpubs/800-14/800-14.pdf.

[8] Stoneburner, G., C. Hayden, and A. Feringa, "Engineering Principles for Information Technology Security (A Baseline For Achieving Security)," August 2003, http://csrc.nist.gov/publications/nistpubs/800-27/sp800-27.pdf.

[9] Purser, S., "Some Key Issues in Modern IT Security," *Information Security Bulletin,* Vol. 7, No. 1, 2001, pp. 33–38.

[10] Nosworthy, J. D., "A Practical Risk Analysis Approach: Managing BCM Risk," *Computers and Security,* Vol. 19, No. 7, 2000, pp. 596–614.

[11] Mannion, C., and A. Dang Van Mien, "The Myth of Quantitative Risk Analysis," *Strategy, Trends and Tactics,* Stamford, CT: Gartner Group, 2002.

[12] "AusCERT—UNIX Security Checklist v2.0—The Essentials," August 2003, http://www.auscert.org.au/render.html?it=1968&cid=1920.

[13] Stein, L. D., and J. N. Stewart, "The World Wide Web Security FAQ," August 2003, http://www.w3.org/Security/Faq.

[14] "Microsoft TechNet: Security Tools and Checklists," August 2003, http://www. microsoft.com/technet/treeview/default.asp?url=/technet/security/tools/tools. asp.

[15] "BigAdmin System Administration Portal: Articles, FAQs and How-To's," August 2003, http://www.sun.com/bigadmin/faq/indexSec.html.

[16] "A Security Checklist For Oracle 9i: An Oracle White Paper," August 2003, http://otn.oracle.com/deploy/security/oracle9i/pdf/9i_checklist.pdf.

[17] "Re: [suse-security] Open Ports on Webserver—Why?," August 2003, http://www.netsys.com/suse-linux-security/2002/08/msg00048.html.

[18] Kossakowski, K.,"DFN CERT: Bibliography of Computer Security Incident Handling Documents," August 2003, http://www.cert.dfn.de/eng/pre99 papers/certbib.html.

[19] "U.S. Department of Homeland Security, Federal Computer Incident Response Center: Incident Handling Checklists," August 2003, http://www.fedcirc.gov/ incidentResponse/IHchecklists.html.

[20] "Computer Security Incident Response Team (CSIRT): Frequently Asked Questions (FAQ)," August 2003, http://www.cert.org/csirts/csirt_faq.html.

CHAPTER

9

Contents

Creating a security-minded culture

9.1 Introduction

These days, almost everyone within the organization uses business-related information in one form or another. Consequently, all staff members have a role to play in the information-security process, and any consistent approach to securing information must recognize this. Not only do all staff members have a role to play, many perform a critical role. It is clear, therefore, that the success of the information-security process as a whole depends on staff members being aware of their responsibilities and being capable of carrying out the activities associated with the roles that have been assigned to them.

The need for adequate training in information security has been recognized by the U.S. government for some time. In 1989, the NIST issued special publication SP 500-172, "Computer Security Training Guidelines" [1]. In 1992, the U.S. Office of Personnel Management issued Regulation 5 CFR Part 930 rendering these guidelines mandatory for federal personnel [2]. In addition to reemphasizing that computer security training was mandatory, Appendix III of the 1996 revision of Circular A-130, issued by the Office of Management and Budget in 1996, required NIST to update SP 500-172 [3]. NIST special publication SP 800-16, "Information Technology Security Training Requirements: A Role- and Performance-Based Model," was issued in 1998 in response to this requirement [4].

However, a number of recent surveys in the area of information security indicate that security-awareness training is not viewed as a priority by most organizations. For instance, Ernst and Young's 2003 Global Information Security Survey, which covered 1,400 organizations in 66 countries, states that only 29% of organizations surveyed list employee awareness and training as a top area of information-security spending [5]. Similarly, the Information Security Breaches Survey 2002 [6], sponsored by the Department of Trade and Industry in the United Kingdom, reports that only 28% of U.K. businesses make staff aware of information security–related duties upon hiring or as part of the induction process. Furthermore, according to this study, 13% of U.K. businesses have no procedures at all for educating staff on their responsibilities in this area. The corresponding figures for large businesses are reported as 33% and 4%, respectively. Finally, the Brainbench/ITAA Global Cyber Security Survey 2003 [7] concludes with the statement that plans of action to increase cyber security must assess the security threat posed by people lacking sufficient information-security awareness.

Although security-awareness training is not a priority for many organizations, achieving a situation in which all staff members are aware of their responsibilities in the area of information security and are capable of carrying out their roles correctly clearly represents a major challenge. This is due to a variety of factors:

▸ Staff members may experience difficulties in coping with the rate at which organizations evolve.

▸ Staff members may have difficulties coping with the complexity of modern environments.

▸ Efficiency initiatives force staff members to concentrate on core activities.

▸ Reorganization planners may underestimate the learning curve associated with assuming new responsibilities.

▸ Many staff members may have only a rudimentary knowledge of IT.

One of the most fundamental challenges in creating a coherent security-minded culture is getting people to accept and deal with change. Resistance to change within the workplace is a well-known phenomenon [8–10], but where information security is concerned, this may be aggravated by a lack of understanding of why changes are necessary. In addition, effective security controls can sometimes be rather onerous and involve routine and uninteresting tasks. If staff members are not convinced of the necessity of these tasks, they will probably be bypassed.

Modern business environments are complex. People have to understand more and make decisions faster; they need to interact with more diverse communities both within and outside the enterprise and to communicate effectively with colleagues from different backgrounds, often specializing in other fields. This increasingly demanding working environment requires people to process large amounts of information very quickly, to sort out the relevant information from the irrelevant, and to act accordingly. In the face of such complexity, many staff members may not understand their responsibilities or may not be able to relate their responsibilities to the realities of day-to-day business.

One area of change that is common to most commercial environments is the drive towards increased efficiency. This becomes an issue when performance targets, which measure output in a specific area, do not take sufficient account of responsibilities not directly related to the task at hand. Undertaking initiatives that enable an operational unit to perform a particular task more efficiently might therefore achieve that goal by diverting effort away from security-related activities. Where management is rationalized, for example, the approval of access rights may be inherited by a manager who does not have sufficient knowledge to carry out this task correctly.

Reorganizations are often problematic because they may not allow sufficient time for staff members to assume their new roles correctly. This is particularly true where information security is concerned, as understanding how particular applications implement common security services can take time. This effectively results in a window of risk following the reorganization, and, where managers are concerned, decision making will often be impaired by a limited knowledge of the new area of responsibility.

Finally, as organizations become increasingly dependent on IT, the distinction between information security and IT security is becoming less and less important. In parallel, new technologies are putting more responsibility on the end user to be aware of the consequences of their actions and to make informed decisions as far as security is concerned. Staff less familiar with modern technology will require strong guidance as to what constitutes appropriate and inappropriate behavior in such circumstances.

In many cases, responding to these issues requires fundamentally modifying the company culture, and this will only be possible if staff members at all levels understand and appreciate the need for change. Creating a security-minded culture is therefore a major undertaking. In the rest of this chapter, we will look at four different types of training that can be used to help achieve this goal. However, educating and motivating staff requires more than just training, and the degree to which this is achieved will depend on the ability of the information-security department to establish and maintain a constructive dialogue with all staff members.

9.2 Techniques for introducing cultural change

Launching and maintaining a constructive dialogue with other staff members involves controlling all of the different communications channels over which this dialogue takes place and ensuring that the information exchanged over these channels is consistent and coherent. In particular, it is important to ensure that any important message delivered by a formal channel of communication, such as a presentation or workshop, is reinforced by information that is passed over more informal channels, such as the telephone. For this reason, it is important that more formal training initiatives take sufficient account of the realities of the operational environment and, conversely, that the members of the information-security department try to relate decisions and actions back to basic principles.

In this chapter, we will examine four main techniques for creating a security-minded culture within the enterprise. These techniques are illustrated in Figure 9.1.

Internal marketing and sales encompasses those activities that are designed to promote the information-security department and its services within the enterprise. This communications channel is therefore targeting major groups within the enterprise, rather than individual contacts.

Support and feedback activities, on the other hand, are usually driven by specific user requirements and can be used to strengthen specific relationships. These activities build user confidence and can be used to encourage a collaborative approach to solving problems. High-quality support and feedback, delivered in a timely fashion, demonstrates commitment by the information-security department to solving real-life problems and develops confidence in the approach.

Formal training methods have been divided into two classes, reflecting the distinction between security-awareness training and training designed to improve specific, security-related skills. The IT Security Training Requirements document published by the NIST in 1998 [11–13] makes a similar distinction and defines three successive levels of learning: awareness, training, and education. According to this model, awareness refers to the extent to which an individual is able to recognize IT security concerns and respond appropriately. Training builds on awareness and is aimed at developing those security skills that are required to successfully carry out day-to-day tasks. The education level is more specialized and geared towards information-security specialists.

This distinction between awareness, training, and education is an important one, as it recognizes that although different communities within the

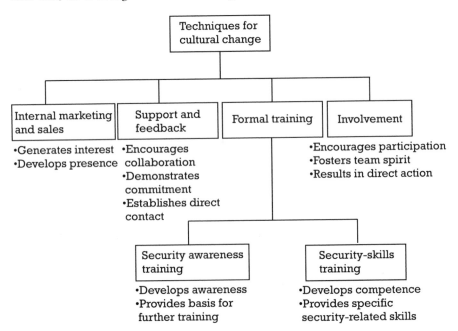

Figure 9.1 Techniques for introducing cultural change.

enterprise have a common need to understand the basics of information security, they have differing requirements when it comes to more detailed knowledge. In other words, the traditional security-awareness program is not sufficient to completely integrate information security into the company culture. This basic awareness needs to be supplemented by more detailed knowledge, which is dependent upon the context in which the individual concerned operates. While recognizing this distinction, the approach we take in this book differs from the NIST approach by concentrating on training methods, rather than on learning.

Security-awareness training is designed to make users aware of fundamental issues and the stance that the organization has taken with respect to these issues, as well as to explain to users their roles and responsibilities. In order to make the best use of the security-awareness program, a distinction will already be made between different user communities at the stage of awareness training. The objective of security-skills training is to teach specific security-related skills to particular target groups, based on their job requirements. Ideally, such training would follow basic security-awareness training, but this is by no means necessary.

Involvement initiatives have no equivalent where NIST learning levels are concerned. The objective of involvement initiatives is to encourage the active involvement of staff within the information-security process. An example of a successful involvement initiative would be the agreement of business managers to appoint a number of information-security liaison points within their departments.

As far as we are concerned, active involvement represents the pinnacle of achievement when trying to adapt the company culture.

9.3 Internal marketing and sales

Few large companies would think of launching an important product without an accompanying marketing initiative and sales campaign. This is because marketing and sales are valuable tools for supporting the process of delivering products and services. It is therefore worthwhile to adopt a similar approach, albeit on a smaller scale, to delivering services within the enterprise.

In this context, marketing involves making staff aware of the services that the information-security department has to offer and learning about which services staff would like to receive. Neither activity is particularly easy. Getting to this stage involves identifying a representative cross section of staff, establishing the current level of understanding, explaining the current approach, and listening to feedback. In order to understand the services available, staff representatives need to develop an understanding of the information-security approach as a whole. Similarly, in order to understand what the real requirements are in a particular area, the information-security manager needs to develop sufficient understanding of that area to appreciate the requirements and to put them in context.

This being the case, it is best to view the internal marketing and sales activity as an iterative process. Indeed, as described in Chapter 4, the first iteration of this process occurs at the start of the consolidation period, when talking to stakeholders for the first time. When interviewing stakeholders or other staff representatives, interviewers should be prepared with the following information:

- The extent to which the area under analysis is understood;
- The extent to which the interviewee is likely to understand the information-security process;
- Any information gleaned through previous interviews or other information sources;
- Any areas for discussion that are likely to be contentious;
- Any areas that might be of mutual interest and may generate synergies;
- Where technical issues are to be discussed, the likely level of understanding of the interviewee.

This information can then be used to plan the meeting in advance. This includes not only defining the agenda, but also thinking about how to steer the conversation to get the best results for both parties. In some cases, it may help to prepare and distribute questionnaires in advance of the meeting. During the meetings themselves, techniques for ensuring mutual understanding of what has been said include:

- Providing regular feedback of what has been said in the form of short summaries;
- Avoiding jargon and explicitly clarifying specialized terminology;
- Using everyday examples to illustrate complex ideas.

Where resources permit, it is well worth building on these initial meetings by arranging for members of the information-security team to spend time in other departments. Indeed, one of the best ways to appreciate practical problems is to have members of the information-security team actually work in other teams for short periods of time. While the practical limitations of this approach are obvious, sending staff out to other departments is an excellent way to build up a network of contacts and demonstrates a willingness to understand operational problems.

To a large extent, the success of the internal marketing and sales drive depends on the ability of the information-security department to listen and adapt to the views expressed by staff members themselves. The feedback from meetings with stakeholders, and staff representatives in general, is used to align the services of the information-security department with the requirements of the business. By aligning offer with demand, there should be less of a need to drive this initiative as time goes on, and the business units themselves will become the drivers.

The overall objectives of the internal marketing and sales exercise are to generate interest in the information-security process and to create a demand for services by making staff members aware of their requirements. In some ways, this exercise can be viewed as the precursor to security-awareness training in that it establishes the "presence" of the information-security department within the enterprise. Note, however, that this is an ongoing activity, and successful departments will be continually on the lookout for changes in demand, which result from changes in the business climate. Conversely, as technology and the threats associated with it evolve, the information-security department will need to influence demand through a process of training and education in order to ensure that business units continue to manage risk appropriately.

9.4 Support and feedback

Internal marketing is geared toward ensuring that the information-security approach is in line with business requirements, and internal sales aims to promote use of the services of the information-security department by business units. Even if in later stages this process may be demand driven, in the beginning it is most likely to be driven by the supplier of services (i.e., the information-security department).

By contrast, requests for support will be driven by business units experiencing problems. This is therefore an ideal opportunity to demonstrate commitment to solving everyday problems. For less mature organizations, the main issue here is likely to be one of volume, and it will be necessary to introduce and agree with stakeholders on clear guidelines for prioritizing issues. Typically, such guidelines will reflect the risk associated with the request for support, although the methods for estimating this risk will be necessarily crude, as requests for support often require rapid action. Prioritization criteria should be as objective as possible, thereby allowing business units to resolve conflicts among themselves. It is also wise to foresee an escalation procedure for the case in which business managers cannot reach an agreement—the information-security department should not be an arbiter for business risk.

As the implementation of the information-security strategy progresses, the volume of requests for support should decline. This is a reflection of the fact that the control framework will be more mature and better aligned with the particular requirements of the organization. For this reason, requests for support become more valuable, as they are symptomatic of problems that are not being handled by the control framework and therefore represent opportunities for learning and improvement.

When this level of maturity has been reached, the issue is no longer one of prioritization, but one of analysis and feedback. More mature organizations should seek to continually improve the process of linking operational problems back to the control framework. The ultimate goal here is to create an approach in which the control framework itself is evolving to reflect operational risk and is no longer merely the reflection of a static policy.

Support and feedback establishes direct contact with operational staff and encourages a collaborative approach to problem solving. By successfully responding to requests for support, the information-security department is capable of changing attitudes and, ultimately, changing people's behavior.

9.5 Security-awareness training

9.5.1 The security-awareness program

For most organizations, security-awareness training will be managed by defining and executing an awareness program. There are many advantages in using this approach:

- ‣ Requirement for a business case in order to obtain funding;
- ‣ Use of a structured approach;
- ‣ Opportunity to involve other departments;
- ‣ Opportunity to leverage management support.

The need to produce a business case forces managers to examine and evaluate the risks associated with a poor level of security awareness and to relate these risks to the cost of the program. Although it is extremely difficult to estimate the impact of particular risks in financial terms (consider risk to reputation, for example), the business case should at least identify the major risks that the program will mitigate and prioritize them.

When considering risks related to awareness, it is important to look at all sources of risk and not just those directly related to a security incident. For instance, poor security awareness might result in the organization failing to meet quality or accreditation standards, which may result in a loss of confidence by customers. Similarly, failure to meet legal or regulatory requirements in this area could result in legal action, financial penalties, or expensive corrective measures. As with most risk analysis exercises, this will involve some degree of professional judgment, and the resulting business case is therefore likely to be open to discussion. However, this discussion provides a first opportunity to make management itself aware of risks and can almost be viewed as part of the security-awareness campaign itself.

A second advantage associated with launching an awareness program is that establishing such programs is usually project driven, which tends to result in a more structured approach. The disadvantage with the project-driven approach is that a successful project might be interpreted as a successful awareness program, whereas the latter is an ongoing activity and not a punctual one. Successful security-awareness programs provide constant guidance and feedback to staff.

Awareness programs provide a good opportunity to involve other stakeholders in the approach. A particularly powerful approach is to encourage stakeholders to participate actively in presentations and the preparation of awareness material. Not only does this reinforce the level of cooperation with the stakeholders themselves, it passes an important message to the target audience—that of openness and collaboration. Where presentations are designed to be interactive or include a period of discussion, the presence of other stakeholders has the additional advantage of providing an alternative perspective on any issues raised.

A well-structured awareness program can provide a focal point for executive-management support. Where presentations are concerned, for example, executive management can recommend or enforce attendance. For important audiences, it is a good idea to have a member of the executive-management team open the presentation with a statement of support for the goals of the exercise. Executive management can also provide input into awareness material, such as a signed statement of objectives for inclusion in posters, personalized mouse pads, and similar material. Last, but not least, executive management can offer support by setting an example to fellow staff members, by recognizing the efforts of those who behave appropriately, and by discouraging inappropriate behavior. It is important that executive management demonstrates a continual commitment to the security-awareness program and does not limit itself to punctual interventions. This is an area in which leading by example can greatly reinforce the important messages of the awareness program.

The security-awareness program can be an extremely powerful tool when used correctly. This program is the major mechanism for ensuring that the company's stance with respect to risk in the information-security area is well understood and that this stance is reflected by the company culture. For this reason, organizations are encouraged to be creative in their approach to designing awareness programs. While face-to-face presentations are likely to remain the preferred method of passing on essential messages, a good campaign will aim to reinforce important points using a variety of supporting techniques. This will be discussed further in Section 9.5.6.

9.5.2 Planning considerations

At The Secure Bank, the need to rapidly conduct an initial security-awareness campaign was identified in the consolidation period. The major objective of this initial campaign was to provide staff with a better appreciation of the risks associated with modern technologies and to provide simple guidelines for dealing with them. The major reason for launching an initial campaign, with a limited scope, was to rapidly respond to a key weakness that had already been identified—namely, that the existing approach to information security was based on concepts that were out of date.

In recognition of the fact that this first initiative was limited in scope, the information-security strategy includes an initiative to provide adequate awareness training for all staff members. This initiative is planned as an initial project including delivery to a pilot group, followed by a series of scheduled courses. The strategic plan foresees an initial project of 6 months, followed by a repeating 6-month program in the first half of every calendar year.

The initial project and pilot phase involved the following steps:

▸ Defining the objectives;

▸ Identifying the audience;

▸ Identifying the message for each audience;

▸ Developing the material;

▸ Defining tracking and follow-up procedures;

▸ Delivering the pilot phase.

The first three activities were considerably simplified by the information gathered from stakeholders during the consolidation period. As a result, it was possible to complete these activities in 2 months. Developing the material and defining tracking and follow-up procedures took a further 2 months.

It was decided to extend the project by a month in order to allow time to test the presentation with three different target groups: executive management, the marketing department, and the IT department. One month was allocated for each group and included the time to give the presentation, collect feedback, and discuss improvement measures.

9.5.3   Defining the objectives

At The Secure Bank, the objectives of the security-awareness program are derived mainly from the business case and reflect the commitment to mitigate risk. In order to ensure that the impact of the security-awareness program could be measured, the high-level business objectives were transformed into a series of more concrete awareness objectives. A set of possible metrics was then identified for tracking each awareness objective. At this stage of the process, possible metrics were proposed, but not analyzed in detail. These metrics were then refined at a later stage to align them with reporting requirements.

The business objectives, awareness objectives, and corresponding candidate metrics identified by The Secure Bank are presented in Table 9.1.

The extent to which the information security–awareness campaign achieved its goals was measured by referring to these objectives. In addition, staff satisfaction with the program was monitored on a continual basis in order to better align the program with staff expectations.

9.5.4   Identifying the audience

A key decision that was made when designing the information security–awareness program at The Secure Bank was to identify the major communities within the organization and to tailor the awareness presentation to

Table 9.1   Objectives of the Security-Awareness Program

Business Objectives	Awareness Objectives	Possible Metrics
1. Reduce risk related to information security by improving risk management.	Ensure all users understand the concept of risk and can apply this to everyday situations.	Percentage of success in follow-up test Number of risk analyses performed
2. Reduce security vulnerabilities due to inappropriate behavior. 3. Reduce the cost of corrective actions associated with unsatisfactory audits.	Ensure all users understand basic security concepts and can apply this to everyday situations. Ensure all users are aware of their responsibilities in the area of information security.	Percentage of success in follow-up test Number of audit points due to insufficient understanding Number of weak passwords detected Number of unattended terminals detected Percentage of staff following clean-desk policy Number of security-related audit points
4. Demonstrate management control of operational information security.	Ensure all users are aware of their responsibilities.	Number of job descriptions referring to information-security responsibilities Number of audit points related to lack of awareness of responsibilities
5. Reduce liability in the event of a legal or regulatory issue.	Ensure all users are aware of legal and regulatory requirements.	Percentage of success in follow-up test Number of audit observations relating to legal and regulatory issues

each audience. The reason for adopting this approach was to make the most of a restricted budget and to ensure that both general and specific messages were passed to the relevant user communities within a reasonable timeframe.

Awareness presentations were therefore divided into two distinct parts. The first part of the awareness presentation would be destined for all staff, whereas the second part would reflect the concerns of particular audiences (see Figure 9.2).

Within The Secure Bank, the different communities were identified as part of the process to identify stakeholders, although some fine tuning was carried out as a result of considerations particular to the awareness campaign. In particular, for the purposes of security-awareness training, it was decided to distinguish between those business staff members who have a customer-facing role and those who do not. Similarly, a distinction was made between IT development staff and IT staff having a production-support role. The geographic location of staff was also an important factor influencing the organization of the awareness program, whereas it had little influence on the identification of stakeholders.

The identified communities were as follows:

▸ Executive management;

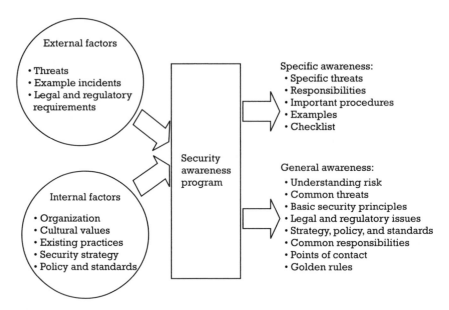

Figure 9.2   The security-awareness program as an information filter.

> Customer-facing business units;

> Other business units;

> Internal audit, legal, and risk management;

> IT development teams;

> IT production staff.

The distinction between customer-facing business units and other business units reflects the fact that most customer data is owned by customer-facing units. In particular, with a few minor exceptions, these units are responsible for creating, modifying, and deleting data related to customers. In addition, special considerations apply to which data can be exchanged with customers and under what conditions. It therefore made sense to limit discussion of these areas to affected staff members.

Internal audit, the legal department, and risk management constitute a natural group, as these departments play an important role in supporting the information-security process. The group-specific part of the awareness presentation planned for this group was therefore oriented towards receiving information with the aim of improving the current process.

IT development staff and IT production staff are considered two separate communities largely due to their differing security requirements. Production staff members play an important role in ensuring that production data is appropriately secured, and this is reflected in many of the day-to-day tasks carried out by this group. Although the issue of development units using production data was recognized at an early stage, it is an anomaly, and ensuring protection of production data is not a responsibility of development staff. Development staff members do, however, have the responsibility of ensuring that code delivered into production environments is secure in the sense that it contains no malicious statements. They are also responsible for agreeing on security measures to be applied to development environments with the information-security department and ensuring that these measures are applied in a satisfactory manner.

Geographic location was noted as a factor to be taken into account during the planning stage of future awareness initiatives. This was a major consideration for business units but had little impact on the other identified communities. The recommendation of the project, which was agreed on with the manager of the branch network, was to carry out site visits where branches were strategically important or employed more than fifty staff members (of which there were only three). Other branches would be required to send a delegate to attend presentations at the organization's headquarters. This delegate would then be responsible for transmitting the information to local staff.

After having identified the different user communities, the executive management, the audit department, the risk-management department, and the legal department were all invited to actively participate in the awareness program by participating in presentations. Executive management agreed to introduce awareness sessions by a small introduction wherever possible, stressing the importance of the initiative from the perspective of higher management. The audit department agreed to participate in all sessions by giving a 15-minute presentation illustrating where risks had materialized in the past. The risk management and legal department declined the invitation due to resource constraints but agreed to intervene on an exceptional basis if a particular requirement arose.

9.5.5 Identifying the message

The information content of the security-awareness program was designed to respond to awareness problems identified during the consolidation period. The most important sources of information used in designing the program were as follows:

- Past audit reports;
- Interviews with stakeholders;
- The initial focused awareness campaign;
- Marketing and sales activity.

Past audit reports provided several clues regarding the level of awareness of staff in general and also revealed several areas of particular concern. Audits carried out over the last year showed that many staff members did not understand basic security concepts and made frequent reference to the fact that responsibilities are poorly defined and not well understood. These reports also indicated that existing procedures are often being bypassed. A rapid analysis of these reports showed that improvement was needed in the areas of access control, document control, and basic physical security. In the case of access control, audits consistently identified the fact that neither users nor approvers had sufficient knowledge of the access rights associated with the systems they used. Document control was an issue because staff members did not understand the current security classification scheme and were therefore not able to follow current guidelines for managing documents. Issues in the area of physical security were mainly related to elementary housekeeping, such as maintaining a clean desk and ensuring that sensitive documents were not left lying in printer trays overnight.

Interviews with stakeholders and direct feedback received from the initial awareness campaign were the main source of information on awareness. Information gathered from these encounters confirmed the points previously raised by audits and identified a number of other areas where awareness training would add value. Meetings with stakeholders were a particularly efficient way of identifying areas of concern specific to a particular community.

The design of the security-awareness program reflects the issues that were identified during the information-gathering phase. The common part of the program is summarized in Table 9.2, which identifies security-awareness topics to be addressed with all staff members.

The information presented in Table 9.3 illustrates the approach to providing specific awareness training. For specific awareness sessions, both the subjects to be addressed and the detailed content were chosen to reflect issues important to the audience in question.

In the case of executive management, the specific part of the awareness program included a presentation of data describing the global economic impact of past security incidents. This data was taken mainly from surveys published on the Internet (for examples of such surveys see [5–7] and [14, 15]). The treatment of risk management concentrated on the need to rely less on policy as a decision-making tool and to ensure that business managers played an active role in taking decisions related to information security. This was followed by a summary of the major risks with which the organization was faced, which prompted a discussion on how the organization should position itself with respect to certain specific risks.

The section on crisis management was used to underline the need for a structured plan of action in the event of a serious security incident. In particular, there was a need to prepare an approach for dealing with the media and controlling the flow of information in such circumstances.

9.5.6   Developing the material

At The Secure Bank, the principal tool for delivering the security-awareness campaign was a series of presentations. Presentations were divided into two parts, reflecting the design decision to include a set of common topics and a set of topics specific to the audience. With the exception of the section on internal incidents, which was prepared by the audit department, the information content of the core presentation was prepared by the information-

Table 9.2 Awareness Topics Relevant to All Audiences

Subject	Description
Understanding risk	Risk = threat + probability + impact
	Risk versus opportunity
	Methods for handling risks
Common threats	Examples from the media
	Internal examples (presented by the audit department)
	Internal versus external threats
Basic security principles	Confidentiality, integrity, and availability
	"Need to know" and "need to do"
	Importance of a coherent solution—relating logical security to physical security
	Defensive behavior
	Handling problems
Legal and regulatory issues	Important legal requirements
	Important regulatory requirements
Strategy, policy, and standards	Current weaknesses
	Overview of strategy
	How to use policy and standards effectively
	How to obtain a policy waiver
Common responsibilities	Good housekeeping and clean desk
	Desktop security rules
	Rules for classifying and storing data
	Rules for managing accounts
	Rules for home working
	Recognizing and reporting issues
Important procedures	Account management and access control
	Virus control
	Remote access
Points of contact	Key contact points
	Escalation procedures
Golden rules	Summary of everything in this table

Table 9.3 Awareness Topics Specific to Executive Management

Subject	Description
Economic impact	Global economic impact of security incidents (examples)
Management support	Importance of management support
Attitude to risk	Risk as a consequence of business opportunities
	Move towards more active risk management
Major risks	Most important known information-security risks
Crisis management	Incident handling
	Managing critical incidents
Examples	Examples from the media illustrating the need for action by executive management

security department. The final presentation was prepared with the help of an external consultant specializing in the design and delivery of presentations.

In addition to face-to-face presentations, several techniques for reinforcing the central ideas on a day-to-day basis were considered:

- Pamphlets and brochures;
- Newsletters;
- Articles posted on the company intranet;
- Training videos;
- Live demonstrations;
- Breakfast discussion groups;
- Internal security classes and workgroups;
- Customized login screens;
- Memory aids.

Of these different techniques, the use of the intranet, training videos, live demonstrations, breakfast discussion groups, and memory aids were used. Pamphlets, brochures, and newsletters were not adopted, as these did not fit in well with the established culture, which was to publish information on the company intranet. Internal security classes and workgroups were considered, but it was finally decided to concentrate on establishing discussion groups. Finally, customized login screens were not adopted, as certain screens had already been customized for other purposes.

Training videos were constructed by contacting broadcasting companies and requesting the use of news clippings and other material that had been previously broadcast. Training videos were followed by a discussion of the material presented.

Live demonstrations of existing exploits were organized on a punctual basis and were used mainly to convince skeptical staff of the need for vigilance. Demonstrations were designed to show staff the importance of some particular behavior (such as opening the attachments of unsolicited mail messages), but were also used to show the power of modern hacking software. In carrying out these demonstrations, every effort was made to avoid sensationalism and to portray an accurate picture of how vulnerabilities are exploited in practice. As a matter of policy, all demonstrations were carried out in strictly controlled environments, and only vulnerabilities that were completely under control were used.

Breakfast discussion groups were funded by the information-security department and typically ran until 10 A.M. This approach was agreed on with stakeholders and was extremely popular due to the convivial atmosphere and interesting discussion topics. A deliberate attempt was made to ensure that breakfast sessions were attended by staff members from several different areas in order to broaden the scope of the discussion. The theme of the discussion was posted on the company intranet a week in advance and was usually chosen to be provocative.

A variety of memory aids were considered to help reinforce the main messages of the awareness program, including credit card–sized plastic cards, key chains, and T-shirts, but posters and mouse pads were finally selected as the most appropriate solution in this area. Posters were used throughout the organization to remind users of the "golden rules," which summarized the common part of the awareness presentations. Initially, there was little support among stakeholders for the idea of using mouse pads in addition to posters. However, after considerable discussion, the fact that mouse pads are always situated next to the workstation convinced stakeholders that this was an ideal way of reminding users of rules relating to desktop security.

9.5.7 Defining tracking and follow-up procedures

Tracking and follow-up procedures were designed to provide feedback on two separate aspects of the program:

- Staff appreciation of the program itself;
- The extent to which the program was meeting business goals.

Staff appreciation was monitored in two different ways. Attendees were asked to complete evaluation forms (anonymously) at the end of each session. More informally, a member of the information-security department was present at all presentations in order to take note of questions, issues, and problems. This person was asked to follow up with attendees on an informal basis and to continually look for improvement ideas.

Business objectives were followed by using a series of metrics derived from the candidate metrics identified in Table 9.1. Business managers were also asked to provide feedback by evaluating the operational impact after a period of 3 months. After discussion with stakeholders, the idea of using a test to measure how well certain ideas had been transmitted to the target audience was rejected due to logistic difficulties. The idea of keeping statistics on the number of unattended and unprotected terminals was rejected for similar reasons. On the positive side, executive management suggested that the number of proposals including an assessment of information security–related risk would be a good indicator of the improvement of risk management, and this was adopted.

Metrics were reported to senior management as part of the normal reporting process and, together with the statistics identified in Section 4.4.7, these metrics eventually developed into key risk indicators.

9.5.8 Delivering the pilot phase

The project to establish the security-awareness program concluded with a pilot phase. The purpose of the pilot phase was to provide a proof of concept and to identify planning and logistic constraints before the real exercise took place.

The following issues arose during the pilot phase:

▸ Many staff members were not available due to late notification.

▸ Executive management had problems meeting their commitment.

▸ The core presentation was judged to be too long.

▸ Insufficient time was allocated for discussion.

The first point provided valuable input into future campaigns and was mainly due to the fact that the pilot phase coincided with the beginning of the holiday period. This was particularly true for the last group, where sessions were planned for the month of July. As a result of these problems, planning for future awareness campaigns began 3 months before the start of the initiative.

Of the three awareness sessions planned for the pilot phase, the executive-management team had to cancel two appointments at the last moment. Although this was partly attributable to the fact that this was only a pilot exercise and not the real thing, it was clear that an executive manager would not be available to open all sessions. For this reason, it was decided that the head of the department concerned would replace executive management in the event of a last-minute problem.

Feedback from the first three sessions indicated unanimously that the core presentation, which lasted two hours, was too long. A significant number of attendees also suggested that more discussion on certain topics would be appreciated. The presentation was redesigned to take account of these comments, and it was decided to introduce a coffee break between the core presentation and the specific topics.

9.6   Security skills training

9.6.1   General remarks

The essential difference between security-awareness training and security-skills training is one of scope. Security-awareness training aims to provide staff with a basic knowledge of the whole information-security process but does not analyze any particular area in depth. Security-skills training, on the other hand, is more focused. The major objective of security-skills training is to help staff achieve a certain level of competence in a specific area related to information security. In a perfect world, staff would always undergo security-awareness training before participating in more specialized training, but this is not always possible, and operational constraints may dictate other priorities.

Where security awareness is concerned, staff members are expected to attend a single security-awareness presentation, and this may be followed by other initiatives designed to reinforce the key messages of the program. Tracking the progress of security-awareness training may be time consuming, but it is not particularly difficult, as all staff members follow variations of the same program. Security-skills training is much more complex, as different departments will require different skills.

Organizing and tracking security-skills training therefore requires a different approach. The content of security-skills training should be agreed on beforehand with stakeholders. This is likely to be a complex process, requiring a thorough understanding of the activities being carried out together with a knowledge of specific applications and how they implement security functionality. In addition, the content of security-skills training should reflect the risk posture adopted by the department head, so as not to confuse staff. Following agreement on the content, training methods need to be identified, and these methods should be chosen to reflect the character and needs of the target audience. For instance, whereas IT staff could reasonably be expected to react well to CBT methods, business lines may prefer classroom-style learning, which provides more opportunities to ask questions and develop a dialogue. Tracking the progress and effectiveness of security-skills training will therefore involve following up on a range of different activities aimed at different audiences.

Given these constraints, it is recommended that the management of security-skills training be decentralized, thus allowing department heads to plan and monitor training for their own staff. This is a particularly effective way of doing things for organizations that link training to the performance-appraisal process. Managers can then include information-security training in yearly training plans by defining and tracking training objectives alongside performance objectives. Whichever approach to management and follow up is taken, it is important to ensure that training is not carried out in a haphazard way. Security skills often build on each other, and getting the most out of training for both staff and the organization involves long-term planning.

Taking a long-term view on training has benefits for management and staff alike. From a management perspective, training requirements can be aligned with career paths, enabling staff to be trained before moving into positions of increased authority. Investing time and effort into providing a well-structured training program is also a way for management to demonstrate commitment to their staff and is likely to result in increased motivation. Staff members benefit from this approach in a number of ways. More junior staff members are forced to think about career progression at an early stage and to actively participate in shaping their own future. Mature staff members will benefit from a coherent set of training objectives and regular feedback. Finally, regular progress monitoring will help both management and staff members establish a constructive dialogue, leading to better mutual understanding and more appropriate training.

9.6.2 The information-security team

Training the information-security team presents particular challenges, as information security is the core competence of team members. In order to make appropriate decisions, team members will need to develop an understanding of the different areas of information security to a depth that goes far beyond awareness, while still developing an expertise in a particular domain.

From the perspective of the organization, almost every branch of IT is influenced by security considerations in one way or another, as are a number of nontechnical disciplines. Large and medium-sized organizations, which are typically organized into specialized functional departments and are likely to deploy a wide range of technologies, place heavy demands on the information-security department in terms of its ability to supply the necessary skills.

The challenge facing the information-security manager is therefore twofold. First, the right skill sets need to be available to the organization at all times; second, members of the information-security team should benefit from a structured development plan that will allow them to fulfill their career objectives. A successful training plan therefore begins with a knowledge of both areas. The most likely outcome of this exercise is a mismatch between the supply of skill sets and the demand. The extent to which this gap can be closed will determine the extent to which the team can fulfill the requirements of the organization.

It is useful to look at the organization's requirements for skill sets in terms of how these skill sets are usually acquired. This will then result in a number of groups of commonly encountered skills, which can be used as a basis for training staff. To take a rather technical example, it is quite unusual to find individuals that are experts in both networking and database technologies (probably due to the enormous effort required to master both fields). It therefore makes sense to consider skills related to networking and skills related to databases as two separate classes of skills.

That having been said, a certain amount of cross training between different areas of specialization in the team is desirable. This approach encourages experts in one area to develop a reasonable understanding of other specialist areas, which in turn results in better communications within the team. One useful technique for achieving this is to ask team members to summarize what they have learned in external courses in such a way that other specialists can benefit from this information. This forces specialists to think about the requirements of their colleagues and also develops their presentation skills.

When discussing current skills and career objectives, managers should encourage team members to think about their career from a long-term perspective and help them make sensible choices. For many organizations this is done as part of the appraisal process. Irrespective of the way in which it is achieved, ensuring that staff members plan and manage their own future in an organized way is a critical management activity. Managers who do this well will help their team members to realize their own goals, and by aligning these goals with the goals of the organization, they will ensure that the team as a whole realizes the objectives laid down by higher management. Viewed in this way, establishing and managing a coherent training plan is an integral part of the team-building exercise.

Ideally, individual training plans should have a long-term and a short-term component. The long-term component will reflect important career choices, such as the desire to take on management responsibility or to develop technical expertise. Even if younger staff members cannot make this choice immediately, it is a good idea to have them think about such issues as these as early as possible. When creating long-term plans, it may prove useful to identify and track one or more *threads*, such as management training, technical training, and business training.

The short-term component of the training plan should satisfy clear requirements and should be measurable. The training objectives should also relate to the learning process. Hence, identifying and understanding important trends in information security is an example of a training objective, which might be defined as a result of a requirement to carry out an analysis of strategy in a particular area. Attending a security conference is not an objective in itself, but constitutes one way of achieving this objective. Figure 9.3 presents an example of a structured training plan, presented in graphic form. Horizontal bars represent training activity in a particular area, which will typically involve some combination of self study, CBT, classroom training, and application of what has been learned to everyday problems. Training objectives are illustrated by solid triangles. In this example, training objectives are directly related to the ability to perform a particular role within the team.

As a final word on this topic, information security is an area where background reading can be of enormous value. This is largely because it is necessary to have a solid understanding of a system before one can attempt to secure it. In many cases, it is worth making attendance of external courses dependent on acquiring a basic awareness of the subject in question. This

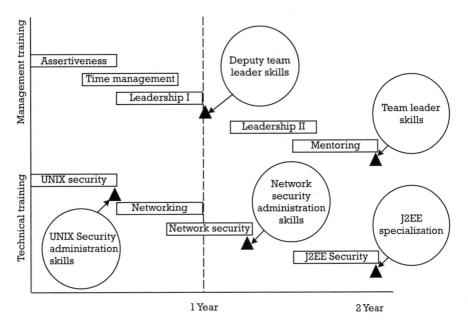

Figure 9.3 Example of a structured training plan.

might involve requiring staff to take CBT courses and provide evidence of background reading as a prerequisite to the attendance of external courses. This encourages staff to regard training as a responsibility that is shared between the staff member and the organization, which it clearly is. For more motivated team members, organizations might consider funding formal certification schemes, such as CISSP [16].

9.6.3 Other staff

Establishing a structured information-security training program for members of other departments should be viewed as an activity that is shared between the information-security manager and the manager of the department concerned. Ideally, the information-security plan will be a coherent part of a more general training plan, thus enabling the trainee to relate security principles and guidelines back to their day-to-day activities. Indeed, the more integrated the security-related training is with other training material, the more trainees are likely to view security as part of their daily tasks. The extent to which this is achievable will depend to a large extent on how well individual departments are organized.

Achieving this involves a number of key steps:

- Understanding the responsibilities of the department;
- Understanding roles and responsibilities of department members;
- Matching security skills to roles;
- Designing the training program;
- Monitoring and improvement.

Of these steps, the first two should be under the control of the information-security manager, whereas the last three should be managed by the head of the department concerned.

Understanding the responsibilities of the department is a process that begins when the first interviews with stakeholders are carried out. The goal here is to understand how these responsibilities are distributed among department staff so that a number of training profiles for the department can be developed. Where they exist, formal job descriptions or terms of reference can be a lot of help here, but it is always a good idea to verify with staff that the job description still reflects reality. Similarly, comparing individual roles and responsibilities with the responsibilities of the department is a good way of verifying overall coherence. Where job descriptions do not exist, this information will have to be collected by interviewing staff. Nevertheless, where resources permit, this is effort well spent, as it helps establish a dialogue, increases understanding, and can also bring interesting control issues to the surface.

The output of this preliminary analysis is an agreed set of roles and associated responsibilities within the department. Identifying the corresponding training profiles involves mapping responsibilities to the security skills required to carry them out. There is not necessarily a one-to-one relation-ship between functional roles and training profiles, but it is likely that most departments will derive at least two different profiles, corresponding to the different requirements of managerial and operational staff.

The design of the training program is the responsibility of the depart-ment manager, but training related to information security should be dis-cussed with the information-security manager. A good training program will ensure that the information security–related component is both rele-vant and in proportion to other needs of the individual in question. It will also ensure that the training methods are adapted to the trainee's particular needs.

One of the most difficult aspects of organizing security training for staff in other departments is evaluating the effect that such training has on day-to-day activities. As far as information-security training is concerned, there-fore, an important part of the design of the training program is related to monitoring and improvement. Having departments agree to collect metrics is an ideal approach, but this is likely to be extremely difficult for all but the most mature enterprises. A useful compromise is to ask managers to provide a short written feedback summarizing the effect (if any) that training has had on behavior. This can then be used to discuss improvements in the program.

9.7 Involvement initiatives

Getting staff actively involved in the information-security process is the pin-nacle of success as far as the creation of a security-minded culture is con-cerned. In general, the more staff willingly involve themselves in security-related activities, the greater the chances of success for the program as a whole. The key to getting people more involved is to create projects and activities that have a clear benefit for those participating. This often requires investing time and resources in the short term to solve problems in other areas, some of which may only have an indirect impact on the information-security process. However, if initiatives are chosen well, the long-term benefits will far exceed the initial costs.

Examples of involvement initiatives taken from The Secure Bank include:

- Creating security expertise within development teams;
- Aligning audit requirements with the approach to information security;
- Exploiting synergies in the area of quality management.

In preparing for the Internet home-banking project, development teams experienced considerable problems in the area of network security. These problems were partly related to a misunderstanding of concepts and partly related to implementation concerns. The information-security department reacted to this situation by organizing a series of workshops on network security and cryptography. Once the conceptual issues had been resolved, developers were encouraged to test evaluation versions of common products with the help and support of information-security staff. This eventually led to the selection of a preferred product. This cooperation became stronger in the period leading up to the implementation project and eventually resulted in a core of expertise within the development teams. Toward the end of the project, the development teams were proactively managing implementation issues. In addition, this experience was being used to prepare for new projects requiring network security and eventually led to a standard approach driven almost entirely by the development community.

Where the audit department was concerned, the problem was not so much one of involvement, but one of approach. The way in which the problem of overambitious targets was handled was described in Chapter 4 and involved an appeal to stakeholders to be more active in managing risk. The audit department accepted this decision with good grace but had difficulties adapting to this new approach. The information-security department therefore suggested a biweekly meeting to discuss contentious points before they were released in formal audit reports. Over time, a standard approach to dealing with issues naturally arose out of these meetings, which involved the audit department preparing the case for certain observations using its internal methodology and information security commenting on the appropriateness of the observations from the point of view of risk and applicability.

The last example is in the area of quality management. The quality department had been trying for some time to introduce a formal quality system and was interested in acquiring formal certification for a number of core processes in the long term. An obvious synergy therefore was to use the information-security department as a pilot phase. The resulting cooperation was beneficial to both parties, both in terms of direct support and internal communications.

Involvement initiatives often succeed or fail due to the commitment of one or two key individuals. It is highly recommended that the contribution of such individuals be recognized by the organization. The way in which this is done will vary from company to company and might involve awards or prizes or both. Recognition is an important feedback mechanism to staff and a good incentive for others to take an active role.

9.8 Summary

Although information security is the responsibility of everyone within the enterprise, statistics show that awareness training is not currently a priority for many commercial organizations. Mature organizations will recognize the need for awareness and participation in the information-security approach and will launch a series of initiatives to educate and involve staff.

Creating a security-minded culture involves using all communications channels in a consistent manner. One of the major challenges of managing this process is ensuring that information exchanged by different means and with different user communities is coherent. This chapter has looked at four techniques for introducing cultural change in some detail.

Internal marketing and sales activities are used to promote the information-security approach in the same way that a commercial product would be promoted on the open market. This type of activity is used to establish the presence of the information-security department within the organization and generates interest in the services it is offering.

Support and feedback activities reinforce individual relationships by encouraging collaboration and demonstrating the commitment of the information-security department to participate in operational activities. Where the volume of operational incidents is high, clear rules for prioritizing issues should be agreed on beforehand. These should be accompanied by procedures for escalation.

Security-awareness training is an ongoing activity—not a punctual one. The business objectives of the awareness program should be to reduce risk in the area of information security, and this should be reflected by the corresponding awareness objectives. The awareness program is developed as a series of steps, including the identification of important audiences and the definition of key messages for each audience. While the primary delivery method is likely to be face-to-face presentations, a number of techniques exist for reinforcing this message. These include use of multimedia, workshops, discussion groups, and memory aids. The extent to which the awareness program is successful can be measured using simple metrics.

Security-skills training provides expertise in a particular area and supplements awareness training. Wherever possible, security-skills training should be part of a structured training plan, which in turn should be aligned with the career path of the individual concerned. Where the information-security team itself is concerned, training plans should achieve a compromise between the needs of the organization and the needs of the individual. Security-skills training is not limited to attending courses, but involves a mixture of self learning, classroom teaching, and practical experience. Training plans should be monitored on a regular basis, and this should include monitoring the impact on day-to-day operations.

Involvement initiatives encourage participation, foster team spirit, and result in direct action. Successful involvement activities have a direct impact on operational risk and therefore represent the height of achievement in this area.

References

[1]   Todd, M. A., and C. Guitian, "Computer Security Training Guidelines," NIST, special publication [SP] 500-172, 1989.

[2]   "Office of Personnel Management: 5 CFR Part 930: RIN 3205-AD43," September 2003, http://csrc.nist.gov/secplcy/opm_plcy.txt.

[3] "Appendix III to OMB Circular No. A-130: Security of Federal Automated Information Resources," September 2003, http://www.whitehouse.gov/omb/circulars/a130/a130appendix_iii.html.

[4] Wilson, M., et al., "Information Technology Security Training Requirements: A Role- and Performance-Based Model: Part 1—Document," September 2003, http://csrc.nist.gov/publications/nistpubs/800-16/800-16.pdf.

[5] "Global Information Security Survey 2003," September 2003, http://www.ey.com/global/download.nsf/International/TSRS_-_Global_Information_Security_Survey_2003/$file/TSRS_-_Global_Information_Security_Survey_2003.pdf.

[6] "Information Security Breaches Survey 2002," September 2003, http://www.pwcglobal.com/Extweb/ncsurvres.nsf/docid/845A49566045759E80256B9D003A4773.

[7] "Brainbench/ITAA Global Cyber Security Survey 2003," September 2003, http://www.itaa.org/infosec/docs/BrainbenchITAAGlobalCyberSecuritySurvey.pdf.

[8] Foote, D., "The Futility of Resistance (To Change)," September 2003, http://www.computerworld.com/managementtopics/management/story/0,10801,56246,00.html.

[9] "26+ Reasons Why Employees Resist Changes," September 2003, http://www.andersonconsulting.com/org/resist.htm.

[10] Vizjak, Dr. A., "Change Management Course, Part 6: Impact of Internal Resistance on Organizational Change," September 2003, http://www.ku-eichstaett.de/Fakultaeten/WWF/Lehrstuehle/OP/Downloads/skripten/Sections/content/6%20Impact%20of%20resistance%20on%20change.pdf.

[11] Wilson, M., et al., "Information Technology Security Training Requirements: A Role- and Performance-Based Model: Part 1—Document," September 2003, http://csrc.nist.gov/publications/nistpubs/800-16/800-16.pdf.

[12] Wilson, M., et al., "Information Technology Security Training Requirements: A Role- and Performance-Based Model: Part 2—Appendix A–D," September 2003, http://csrc.nist.gov/publications/nistpubs/800-16/AppendixA-D.pdf.

[13] Wilson, M., et al., "Information Technology Security Training Requirements: A Role- and Performance-Based Model: Part 3—Appendix E," September 2003, http://csrc.nist.gov/publications/nistpubs/800-16/Appendix_E.pdf.

[14] "2002 CSI/FBI Computer Crime and Security Survey," *Computer Security Issues and Trends*, Vol. 8, No. 1, 2002, pp. 1–22.

[15] "2002 Australian Computer Crime and Security Survey," September 2003, http://www.auscert.org.au/Information/Auscert_info/2002cs.pdf.

[16] Harris, S., CISSP, MCSE, CCNA, *All-In-One CISSP Certification: Exam Guide*, Berkeley, CA: McGraw-Hill/Osborne, 2002, pp. 1–17.

Appendix: Fast risk analysis

A.1 Introduction

In Chapter 2 of this book, we made several references to FRA techniques without providing further information on how these techniques are applied or the type of result they yield. This short annex aims to fill this gap by presenting a simple method for carrying out such analyses and by illustrating the method with an example taken from the case study.

It should be pointed out that the method described was developed by the author and has no particular merit other than that it is extremely simple to use and has been successfully used over a period of several years in a variety of contexts. Readers are therefore encouraged to consider what follows as a starting point for developing an approach to risk analysis that reflects their own requirements.

In line with the comments we made in Chapter 2, this approach is not quantitative and is geared toward helping business managers understand risks and potential mitigation actions in semiquantitative terms. This being the case, the approach is most effectively used as a way of increasing awareness of risk and as an aid to decision making.

A.2 The method

The risk-analysis method we describe in this section is carried out against an identified target system. The scope of this system must be clearly defined, particularly where the network is concerned. In other words, the boundary between "inside" and "outside" should be crystal clear. Failure to do this is likely to result in confusion and a blurred analysis.

The aim of the exercise is to identify the most significant risks associated with this system, to propose security services or procedures to reduce these risks to acceptable levels, and to identify the residual risk. This residual risk is the risk that must be accepted by the business, and this is one area in which a formal sign off adds a lot of value.

The method will give better results when carried out as a group exercise. Ideally, groups will consist of interested parties from the business, technical experts, and a representative of the security department. The role of the latter is to lead the exercise by suggesting risk scenarios, managing the ensuing discussion, and ensuring that the outcome of each discussion is recorded and agreed on by all parties. It should be made clear to all parties that there will be a time limit imposed on the exercise, as this will help the group stay focused on important risks. Three hours should be more than sufficient in most cases.

The analysis is carried out in three steps:

1. Identification of threat scenarios;
2. Description of the most significant risks;
3. Description of mitigating controls and residual risk.

The first step of the analysis is to identify the most important threats associated with the target system, without giving too much thought to the probability of occurrence or the likely impact of the threat. The critical point in identifying and evaluating threat scenarios is the following:

> In identifying and discussing threat scenarios, it is important to ignore any security services or mechanisms already in place, as taking account of these services complicates the discussion and the services that are relevant will be derived anyway.

Taking this approach ensures that we do not make unwarranted assumptions about the existing security mechanisms and simplifies the discussion. It also renders the analysis independent of the current context, which means that it remains valid when the security architecture is changed.

Once the most significant threat scenarios have been (concisely) described, a description of the probability of occurrence and likely impact is provided for each scenario. Both the probability of occurrence and the likely impact are described as high, medium, or low. This is the most difficult part of the exercise, as it involves judgment. In particular, assigning a probability to the scenario involves judging the prevalence of the type of attack in question, whereas assigning a likely impact involves knowledge of the attacks themselves. For most organizations, even this is quite a difficult exercise, and aiming for more granular measures is unlikely to bring any real benefit. This is summarized in a table with the following columns:

•   An identifier for the risk scenario;
•   A description of the scenario;
•   Probability of occurrence (high, medium, low);
•   Impact (high, medium, low) and description.

The third and last step involves identifying security services for mitigating the risk and evaluating the residual risk. This part of the exercise will almost certainly be led by the representative of the security department, and the evaluation of the residual risk will depend on how well the latter can describe the effect of these services to the rest of the group. The results of this step are summarized in a second table with the following columns:

•   The identifier for the risk scenario;

> ‣ A description of the mitigating services;
>
> ‣ An evaluation of the residual risk (high, medium, low);
>
> ‣ Any comments.

Purists will argue that the second table should also characterize risks in terms of probability and impact. This helps when understanding and discussing the risk, but business managers will probably be more comfortable signing off on one value rather than two. The important point is that the resulting tables provide a fair and true picture of the conclusions of the group. We are trying to achieve a reasonable understanding of the risk, not mathematical precision.

A.3 A worked example

The risk-analysis table for the introduction of the Web server at The Secure Bank is shown in Table A.1, and the results are shown in Table A.2.

A.4 Comments

The following comments should be kept in mind when interpreting the analysis of Section A.3:

> ‣ Risks R1 to R5 cover attacks conducted from the outside. The attacker is assumed to have no special access rights or privileges. For these risks, the presence of individuals with sufficient motivation to attack the site is beyond doubt. The probability is therefore related to technical difficulty. In the absence of specific security services, the probability of a successful attack is therefore high.
>
> ‣ Risks R6, R7, and R8 cover attacks conducted by internal staff who have some degree of authorized access to the Web server. For these risks, the degree of technical expertise necessary to carry out the attack is less, as access has already been granted (although the author of such an attack would presumably want to cover his or her tracks). The probability of attack is therefore related more to motivation than to technical difficulty.
>
> ‣ Risks R9 to R13 cover attacks conducted from the internal network. The attacker is assumed to have no special access rights or privileges over and above that he or she is situated within the network perimeter. Nevertheless, the motivations of the internal attacker are assumed to be different than those of external parties due to controls carried out as part of the recruitment process. As in the previous cases, the probability of an attack is related more to motivation than to technical difficulty in this example.
>
> ‣ Risks R15 and R16 cover events that are not under the control of the bank.

Table A.1   Risk-Analysis Table

Id	Description	Probability	Impact
R1	*External attack leading to unauthorized modification of data content:* This is an attack carried out from the Internet that leads to a modification of published data. This attack includes notably the hacking of Web pages.	*High:* Available statistics indicate high level of activity in this area	*High:* Damage to reputation Probable loss of customers Long-term sustained damage to the image of the bank
R2	*External attack leading to unauthorized modification of Web server configuration:* This is an attack carried out from the Internet and leading to some form of reconfiguration of the Web server software.	*High:* Available statistics indicate high level of activity in this area	*High:* Possible change in behavior of the Web server If visible, will result in damage to reputation May facilitate attack on data
R3	*External attack leading to unauthorized modification of system configuration:* This is an attack carried out from the Internet that leads to some for.m of reconfiguration of the OS.	*High:* Available statistics indicate high level of activity in this area	*High:* Loss of control of OS configuration Facilitates attack on Web server configuration and data May be used as a basis for penetrating the internal network
R4	*External attack leading to compromise of user workstations by implementing malicious mobile code:* This is an attack carried out from the Internet involving the installation of malicious mobile code components on the server. These components are then downloaded by clients and result in local damage to the client.	*Medium:* Attack judged to be difficult to carry out	*High:* Damage to reputation Probable loss of customers Possible legal action against the bank
R5	*External attack resulting in denial of service:* This is an attack carried out from the Internet that leads to denial of service.	*High:* Available statistics indicate high level of activity in this area	*Medium:* Limited impact on reputation Limited impact on home-banking clients
R6	*Publication of material violating privacy laws:* This is insufficient control of how information is segregated on the Web server, leading to the leakage of private information from the home banking system to the public Web pages.	*Low:* Due to current awareness levels of privacy issues	*High:* Damage to reputation Probable loss of customers Possible legal action against the bank

Table A.1 (continued)

Id	Description	Probability	Impact
R7	*Publication of offensive data content by a disgruntled staff member:* This happens when a disgruntled staff member with sufficient access rights to publish material on the Web server abuses these rights by publishing offensive data.	*Low:* Web publishing is restricted to a small number of staff Efficient staff counseling procedures and escalation mechanisms	*High:* Damage to reputation Probable loss of customers Possible legal action against the bank Long-term sustained damage to the image of the bank
R8	*Insertion of malicious code statements in a server script by a disgruntled staff member:* This happens when a disgruntled staff member with sufficient access rights to publish material on the Web server abuses these rights by publishing malicious code.	*Low:* Web publishing is restricted to a small number of staff Efficient staff counseling procedures and escalation mechanisms	*High:* Damage to reputation Probable loss of customers Possible legal action against the bank
R9	*Internal attack leading to unauthorized modification of data content:* This is an attack carried out from the internal network by a user with no special privileges. The attack leads to a modification of published data. This attack includes notably the hacking of Web pages.	*Low:* Thorough selection procedures for internal staff Limited use of external service providers	*High:* Damage to reputation Probable loss of customers Long-term sustained damage to the image of the bank
R10	*Internal attack leading to unauthorized modification of Web server configuration:* This is an attack carried out from the internal network by a user with no special privileges. The attack leads to some form of reconfiguration of the Web server software.	*Low:* Thorough selection procedures for internal staff Limited use of external service providers	*High:* Possible change in behavior of Web server If visible, will result in damage to reputation May facilitate attack on data
R11	*Internal attack leading to unauthorized modification of system configuration:* This is an attack carried out from the internal network by a user with no special privileges. The attack leads to some form of reconfiguration of the OS.	*Low:* Thorough selection procedures for internal staff Limited use of external service providers	*High:* Loss of control of OS configuration. Facilitates attack on Web server configuration and data May be used as a basis for penetrating the internal network

Table A.1 (continued)

Id	Description	Probability	Impact
R12	*Internal attack leading to compromise of user workstations by implementing malicious mobile code:* This is an attack carried out from the internal network by a user with no special privileges. The attack involves the installation of malicious mobile code components on the server. These components are then downloaded by clients and result in local damage to the client.	*Low:* Thorough selection procedures for internal staff Limited use of external service providers	*High:* Damage to reputation Probable loss of customers Possible legal action against the bank
R13	*Internal attack resulting in denial of service:* This is an attack carried out from the Internet that leads to denial of service.	*Low:* Thorough selection procedures for internal staff Limited use of external service providers	*Medium:* Limited impact on reputation Limited impact on home-banking clients
R14	*Spoofing of the site by a third party:* This is when a third party sets up a spoofed site in order to lure clients into risky financial investments. The site uses similar logos and design characteristics.	*Low:* Attack judged to be difficult to carry out	*Medium:* Newer clients may trust the site and engage in risky investments Established clients are expected to check first with their contact point
R15	*Unavailability of service due to fire, flood, or other environmental causes:* This covers all natural disasters.	Low	*Medium:* Limited impact on reputation Limited impact on home-banking clients

Table A.2   Results of Risk Analysis

Id	Mitigating Service	Residual Risk	Comments
R1	*Firewall services:* A limitation of protocols and services through router directives, packet filtering, and proxy services. *Network intrusion detection:* NIDS on Web perimeter segment.	*Low*	Network authentication service will be required once home banking is implemented
R2	*Firewall services:* Limitation of protocols and services through router directives, packet filtering and proxy services. *Network intrusion detection:* NIDS on Web perimeter segment. *Defensive configuration of Web server:* The configuration of the Web server is verified by a host-oriented scanning tool on a periodic basis.	*Low*	Host-oriented security scanner must be capable of recognizing and analyzing Web server software

Table A.2 (continued)

Id	Mitigating Service	Residual Risk	Comments
R3	*Firewall services:* Limitation of protocols and services through router directives, packet filtering, and proxy services. *Network intrusion detection:* NIDS on Web perimeter segment. *Defensive configuration of OS:* The configuration of the OS is verified by a network scanning tool.	*Low*	
R4	*Firewall services:* Limitation of protocols and services through router directives, packet filtering, and proxy services. *Network intrusion detection:* NIDS on Web perimeter segment. *Defensive configuration of Web server:* Cryptographic checksums are kept for mobile code components. The configuration of the Web server is verified by a host-oriented scanning tool on a periodic basis.	*Low*	Home banking will require additional protection, and downloaded code should be signed
R5	*Firewall services:* Limitation of protocols and services through router directives, packet filtering and proxy services. *Network intrusion detection:* NIDS on Web perimeter segment. *Backup server:* A backup server that can be brought on-line in less than 30 minutes will be maintained at a remote site.	*Low*	Requires fail-over procedures capable of retrieving data
R6	*Procedural controls on published material:* Data to be published on the Web server will be inspected by a business representative before publication.	*Low*	Security staff will be notified in case of problems
R7	*Procedural controls on published material:* Data to be published on the Web server will be inspected by a business representative before publication.	*Low*	Security staff will be notified in case of problems
R8	*Risk accepted:* Existing random code inspection procedures are judged to be sufficient.	*Low*	
R9	*Network segregation:* Network segregation techniques will be used to limit the visibility of the Web server from the internal networks.	*Low*	Implemented as packet-filtering rules on internal router and internal interface of firewall
R10	*Network segregation:* Network segregation techniques will be used to limit the visibility of the Web server from the internal networks.	*Low*	Implemented as packet-filtering rules on internal router and internal interface of firewall
R11	*Network segregation:* Network segregation techniques will be used to limit the visibility of the Web server from the internal networks.	*Low*	Implemented as packet-filtering rules on internal router and internal interface of firewall

Table A.2 (continued)

Id	Mitigating Service	Residual Risk	Comments
R12	*Network segregation:* Network segregation techniques will be used to limit the visibility of the Web server from the internal networks.	*Low*	Implemented as packet-filtering rules on internal router and internal interface of firewall
R13	*Network segregation:* Network segregation techniques will be used to limit the visibility of the Web server from the internal networks.	*Low*	Implemented as packet-filtering rules on internal router and internal interface of firewall
R14	*Procedures for alerting customers:* Procedures will be developed for alerting customers of security issues beyond the control of the bank. The corporate communications department will be involved in this exercise.	*Low*	Information will also be provided on the Web site itself
R15	*Backup server:* A backup server that can be brought on-line in less than 30 minutes will be maintained at a remote site.	*Low*	

About the author

Steve Purser graduated from Bristol University in 1981 with a degree in chemistry, and from the University of East Anglia in 1985 with a doctorate in chemical physics.

From 1985 until 1993, he worked for a major software house as a consultant and project manager. In 1993, he joined CETREL Luxembourg as a project manager. Later that year, he took over the role of head of security and quality. From 1997 to 1999, he held the position of head of IT security at the Banque Générale du Luxembourg, where he was responsible for all aspects of IT security.

Steve Purser is currently the director of ICSD Cross Border Security Design and Administration at Clearstream Services.

Index

A

Acceptable behavior, 138
Acceptance
    complexity and, 167
    cultural issues, 166–67
    factors affecting, 166
    improving, 166–68
    issues, 158–59
    psychological factors, 167–68
    requirements, 172
Access control, 13–14
    actual process, 171
    documented process, 169
    improvement ideas, 173
    improving, 168–76
    known issues, 170
    network, 68–71
    problems, 168
    system, 56–58
Access management tools, 56–58
    functionality, 56
    uses, 56
Adaptability
    flexibility and, 165
    improving, 165–66
    issues, 157–58
    requirements, 172
    scalability and, 165–66
Administration and maintenance phase, 208–13
    beginning of, 208
    incidents management, 210–12
    risk management, 212–13
    routine administration/maintenance, 209
    vulnerability management, 209–10
Agent software, 57
American National Standards Institute
    (ANSI), 145
Antivirus software, 54–55
    concept, 55

design, 55
Application layer security, 50
Application-level firewalls, 69
Appropriate security, 109
Audience
    awareness topics, 229
    security-awareness program, 224–27
Audits, 40–41
    logs, 59
    preparation, 41
Authentication, 51
    defined, 51
    network, 62–65
    protocols, 62–63
    servers, 63–65
Authentication devices, 79–80
    asynchronous, 80
    biometric, 79
    defined, 79
    handheld, 79–80
    smart cards, 79
    tokens, 79
Authorization
    actual process, 171
    documented process, 169
    improvement ideas, 173
    improving, 168–76
    known issues, 170
    problems, 168
    servers, 63–65
Awareness
    education and, 9–11
    end users, 10–11
    lack of, 9
    management, 9–10
    topics, 229
    training and, 38–40
Awareness campaign, 40
    hands-on demonstrations, 39

Reengineering Yourself and Your Company: From Engineer to Manager to Leader, Howard Eisner

The Requirements Engineering Handbook, Ralph R. Young

Running the Successful Hi-Tech Project Office, Eduardo Miranda

Successful Marketing Strategy for High-Tech Firms, Second Edition, Eric Viardot

Successful Proposal Strategies for Small Businesses: Using Knowledge Management to Win Government, Private Sector, and International Contracts, Third Edition, Robert S. Frey

Systems Approach to Engineering Design, Peter H. Sydenham

Systems Engineering Principles and Practice, H. Robert Westerman

Systems Reliability and Failure Prevention, Herbert Hecht

Team Development for High-Tech Project Managers, James Williams

For further information on these and other Artech House titles, including previously considered out-of-print books now available through our In-Print-Forever® (IPF®) program, contact:

Artech House
685 Canton Street
Norwood, MA 02062
Phone: 781-769-9750
Fax: 781-769-6334
e-mail: artech@artechhouse.com

Artech House
46 Gillingham Street
London SW1V 1AH UK
Phone: +44 (0)20 7596-8750
Fax: +44 (0)20 7630-0166
e-mail: artech-uk@artechhouse.com

Find us on the World Wide Web at:
www.artechhouse.com